11+ Maths

Study and Practice Book

Rebecca Brant

Name _____

Schofield & Sims

Contents

Introduction 5

Number and place value 6
- [ ] Place value 6
- [ ] Ordering and comparing numbers 7
- [ ] Rounding 9
- [ ] Estimating 10
- [ ] Negative numbers 11
- [ ] Factors 12
- [ ] Multiples 14
- [ ] Divisibility rules 15
- [ ] Prime numbers and prime factors 17
- [ ] Square and cube numbers 19
- [ ] Roman numerals 20
- [ ] Number and place value practice pages 21

Calculations, algebra and number sequences 25
- [ ] Addition 25
- [ ] Subtraction 28
- [ ] Multiplying and dividing by 10, 100 and 1000 30
- [ ] Multiplication 31
- [ ] Division and remainders 33
- [ ] Order of operations 36
- [ ] Word problems 38
- [ ] Function machines 39
- [ ] Algebra 40
- [ ] Number sequences 41
- [ ] Finding the nth term 42
- [ ] Calculations, algebra and number sequences practice pages 44

Fractions, decimals and percentages 48
- [ ] Fractions of shapes 48
- [ ] Fractions of quantities 49
- [ ] Equivalent fractions 51
- [ ] Improper fractions and mixed numbers 52
- [ ] Simplifying fractions 53
- [ ] Ordering fractions 54
- [ ] Adding and subtracting fractions 56
- [ ] Multiplying and dividing fractions 58

Contents

- [ ] Fraction sequences 59
- [ ] Decimal fractions 60
- [ ] Ordering decimals 61
- [ ] Rounding decimals 62
- [ ] Adding and subtracting decimals 63
- [ ] Multiplying and dividing decimals 64
- [ ] Percentages 66
- [ ] Converting between fractions, decimals and percentages 68
- [ ] Word problems 69
- [ ] Ratio and proportion 70
- [ ] Fractions, decimals and percentages practice pages 72

Measurement 76

- [ ] Length, mass and capacity 76
- [ ] Imperial measures 79
- [ ] Reading scales 80
- [ ] Scale 82
- [ ] Time 83
- [ ] Time zones 86
- [ ] Days, weeks, months and years 87
- [ ] Speed 89
- [ ] Money 91
- [ ] Temperature 93
- [ ] Perimeter and area 94
- [ ] Volume and surface area 99
- [ ] Measurement practice pages 100

Geometry 106

- [ ] Parallel and perpendicular lines 106
- [ ] Angles 107
- [ ] Directions of turn 110
- [ ] Properties of 2D shapes 111
- [ ] Regular shapes 113
- [ ] Circles 114
- [ ] Symmetry 115
- [ ] Rotational symmetry 116
- [ ] Properties of 3D shapes 117
- [ ] Nets of 3D shapes 120
- [ ] Rotations of 3D shapes 121

Contents

- Coordinates 122
- Reflections 124
- Translations 126
- Geometry practice pages 127

Statistics 133

- Tables 133
- Pictograms 134
- Tally charts and frequency tables 135
- Bar charts 136
- Line graphs 137
- Pie charts 138
- Venn diagrams 140
- Mean, mode, median and range 141
- Probability 143
- Statistics practice pages 144

Parents' notes 150

Practice test 151

Answers 158

Index and Glossary 182

Introduction

This book will help you to prepare for the maths part of your 11+ exam. It will help you improve your maths knowledge and practice a range of maths skills, focusing on key areas, such as fractions and the properties of shapes. You are likely to have covered most of the topics already in school. However, there are some topics, such as algebra, which you may not have learnt about yet.

The topics are grouped into six sections:

- number and place value
- calculations, algebra and number sequences
- fractions, decimals and percentages
- measurement
- geometry
- statistics.

You might not be tested on all these topics in your 11+ exam, but it is important to revise them in case they do come up.

If you are sitting an 11+ exam set by CEM, you might find that a part of your exam is described as numerical reasoning. Numerical reasoning questions can be straightforward mathematical calculations or word problems that you will need to use logic to solve, both of which you will be familiar with from your maths lessons. The examples and explanations in this book provide complete practice in the skills you need for a numerical reasoning exam.

How to use this book

Before you start using this book, write your name in the box on the first page. Then decide how to begin. If you want a complete course in maths, work right through the book. If you want to find out about a particular topic, use the Contents page or the Index to find the pages you need. Whichever way you choose to use the book, don't try to cover too much at once – it is better to work in short bursts.

When you are ready to begin, find some rough paper. You may find this useful for your workings out. As you make a start, look out for the symbols below, which mark different parts of the text. Find out about words in grey by turning to the Glossary on pages 182 to 184.

Activities

These are the questions that you should complete after you have revised each topic. There are spaces provided for you to write your answers, but you will need a separate piece of paper to do any calculations. After you have worked through all the questions, turn to pages 158 to 181 to check your answers. If you got any of the answers wrong, read the topic again, and then have another go at the questions. When you are sure that you understand a topic, tick the box beside it on the Contents page.

Tip

This text gives you helpful tips on how to tackle a particular question type.

Important

This text gives you useful information, rules and techniques you should remember.

At the end of the book, there is a timed Practice test. You should attempt this once you are sure that you understand all the question types.

Place value

The position of each digit in a number tells you its value.

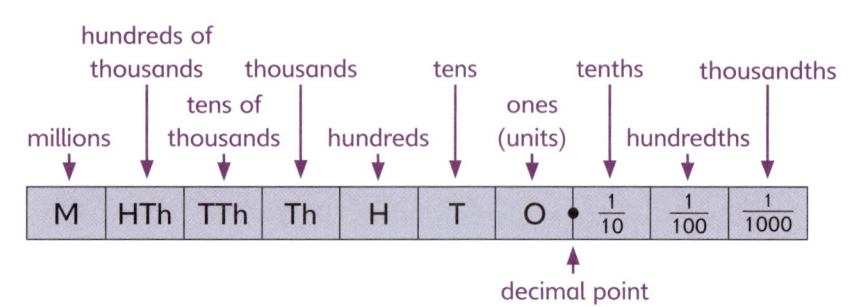

millions	hundreds of thousands	tens of thousands	thousands	hundreds	tens	ones (units)		tenths	hundredths	thousandths
M	HTh	TTh	Th	H	T	O	.	$\frac{1}{10}$	$\frac{1}{100}$	$\frac{1}{1000}$

↑ decimal point

TIP Each digit in a number has ten times the value of the digit to its right. For example, 1 hundred is equal to 10 tens.

Any digit in the M column is worth millions, in the HTh column is worth hundreds of thousands, in the TTh column is worth tens of thousands, and so on.

The number 3 471 928 is made up of 3 millions (3 000 000), 4 hundred thousands (400 000), 7 tens of thousands (70 000), 1 thousand (1000), 9 hundreds (900), 2 tens (20) and 8 ones (8).

M	HTh	TTh	Th	H	T	O
3	4	7	1	9	2	8

The easiest way to read a long number is by grouping digits in threes according to which column they are in. Each group of three digits consists of the same types of values:

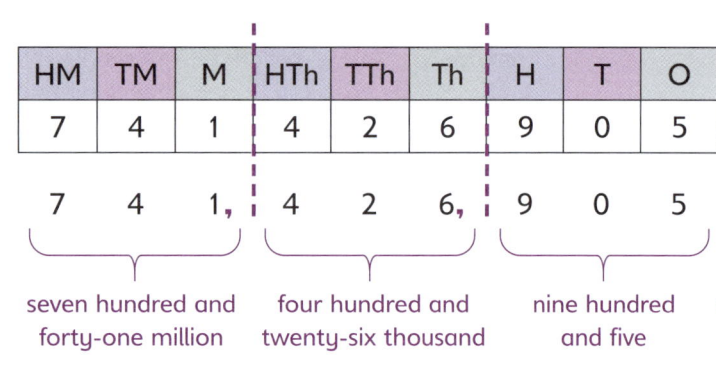

HM	TM	M	HTh	TTh	Th	H	T	O
7	4	1	4	2	6	9	0	5

7 4 1, 4 2 6, 9 0 5

seven hundred and forty-one million | four hundred and twenty-six thousand | nine hundred and five

The ones: ones, (one) thousand, (one) million.
The tens: tens, tens of thousands, tens of millions.
The hundreds: hundreds, hundreds of thousands, hundreds of millions.

741, 426, 905

seven hundred and forty-one million, four hundred and twenty-six thousand, nine hundred and five

The trick is to count back three digits from the decimal point and put in a comma, then count back another three digits and put in another comma. Then read each group of numbers separately.

When there are decimals in the number, they are just read as digits.

O	.	$\frac{1}{10}$	$\frac{1}{100}$	$\frac{1}{1000}$
4	.	5	8	3

This is read as four point five eight three.

! When writing a number in words, the commas go in the same places as when you write it in figures.

✎ Write these numbers in words.

1. 78 913 _____

2. 1.825 _____

Write these words as numbers.

3. eighteen point three four two _____

4. one hundred and thirty-eight million, forty-seven thousand, five hundred and ninety-nine _____

What is the value of the underlined digit?

5. 27<u>5</u>7 _____   **6.** 1<u>3</u>2 638 _____

6   Schofield & Sims

Ordering and comparing numbers

When ordering and comparing large whole numbers, first look to see how many digits each number has. If a number has more digits, it will be larger.

> Which number is larger, 3 674 915 or 546 710?
>
> The first number has seven digits, while the second number only has six. Therefore, 3 674 915 is larger.
>
> **Answer: 3 674 915**

> ❗ This method only works for whole numbers. For comparing decimals, turn to page 61.

If the numbers have the same number of digits, you need to look at the value of the digits starting with the largest value (the one furthest to the left).

> Which number is smaller, 278 093 or 276 935?
>
> They both have six digits, so that does not help.
>
> They both begin with a 2, worth 200 000, so that does not help.
>
> The second digit in both numbers is 7, worth 70 000, so that doesn't help either.
>
> The third digit is 8 in the first number, worth 8000, and 6 in the second number, worth 6000. This means that the second number is smaller because 6000 is smaller than 8000.
>
> **Answer: 276 935**

You can use this method to order large whole numbers in both ascending and descending order.

> Write these numbers in descending order.
>
> 9 456 893   567 168   84 792   2 742 062   84 737

Start with the largest number. The two longest numbers are 9 456 893 and 2 742 062. The first begins with a 9 (worth 9 000 000), so it is larger than the second, which begins with a 2 (worth 2 000 000).

The next longest number is 567 168, so that will come next in the order.

The final two are the same length. They both begin 847, but the tens are 9 (worth 90) and 3 (worth 30), making 84 792 larger than 84 737.

Answer: 9 456 893   2 742 062   567 168   84 792   84 737

✏️ Now answer the following questions.

1. Which number is smaller, 89 903 or 89 894? _____

2. Write these numbers in descending order.

    234 895   562 876   23 869   56 290   652 122

    _____

11+ Maths Study and Practice Book

Ordering and comparing numbers

You may be asked to use the greater than and less than signs > and <. The wider end of the arrow always faces towards the larger number, so 278 093 > 276 935.

> Write these numbers in ascending order using < or > signs.
>
> 406 714   5 140 428   897 234   34 912

The smallest number is 34 912 as it is the shortest number. It has only five digits. The largest number is 5 140 428 as it is the longest number. It has seven digits. The other two numbers are the same length. They both have six digits. The first digit of 406 714 is worth 400 000 and the first digit of 897 234 is worth 800 000, so 897 234 is the larger of the two numbers.

Answer: 34 912 < 406 714 < 897 234 < 5 140 428

You may also be asked to insert the correct signs within a set of numbers.

> Use < or > to make this number sentence correct.
>
> 3 567 284 _____ 678 362 _____ 8 284 024 _____ 2 483 921

3 567 284 is larger than 678 362, which is smaller than 8 284 024, which is larger than 2 483 921.

Answer: 3 567 284 __>__ 678 362 __<__ 8 284 024 __>__ 2 483 921

You may also see the signs ≤ and ≥. They mean 'the same or less than' and 'the same or greater than'. The same rule applies that the wider end of the arrows faces the larger number. You use these when you are not sure exactly what the value of something is.

> A container can hold 6 litres of liquid. How much liquid is in the container?

We cannot be sure as we are not told the exact amount. However, we know the maximum is 6 litres and it could be that or anything less. Therefore, the answer would be ≤ 6 litres.

Answer: ≤ 6 litres

✏️ Now answer the following questions.

3. True or false, 157 934 > 175 423? _____

4. Use < or > to make this number sentence correct.

    6 837 942 _____ 6 837 892 _____ 6 738 813 _____ 6 952 824

5. Write these numbers in ascending order using < or > signs.

    5 789 267   2 683 683   67 362   412 789   348 235

    _____

6. Ron ran at least 5km to his friend's house. How far did he run? _____

Rounding

When rounding a number, look at the digit in the column to the right of the number you are rounding to. If you are rounding to the nearest 10, look at the digit in the ones column. If you are rounding to the nearest 100, look at the digit in the tens column.

The value of the digit in that column will tell you whether you need to round the number up or down. If the digit is less than 5, round down. If the digit is 5 or more, round up.

Round 567 to the nearest 100.

You are rounding to the nearest 100, so look at the digit in the tens column. It is a 6, so round up to the next hundred. The next hundred after 567 is 600.

H	T	O
5	6	7

Answer: 600

If you are asked to **approximate** numbers, this means you need to round them. You might approximate numbers when doing a calculation to make it easier.

Approximate 143 + 129.

143 can be rounded down to 140. 129 is rounded up to 130.

140 + 130 = 270, so the answer to 143 + 129 is approximately 270.

Answer: 270

With decimals, rather than being asked to round, you may be asked to write a number to a certain number of **decimal places** (sometimes written as d.p.).

Write 2.34 to 1 decimal place.

This means that there should only be one digit after the decimal point, so you need to round the number to the nearest $\frac{1}{10}$. You need to look at the digit to its right, in the $\frac{1}{100}$ column. As it is a 4, the $\frac{1}{10}$ needs to be rounded down, which means the 3 will stay the same.

Answer: 2.3

Now answer the following questions.

1. Round 12 781 to the nearest 1000. _____

2. Approximate 4.76 to 1 decimal place. _____

3. Round 236 810 to the nearest 100 000. _____

4. Approximate 13.812 to 2 decimal places. _____

5. Round 385.429 to the nearest hundredth. _____

6. Round 52.572 to the nearest tenth. _____

11+ Maths Study and Practice Book

Estimating

When you estimate, you use what you know to make a really good guess.

> Estimate the number on the number line.

To make a good estimate, narrow down what the possible answers could be. The easiest way to do this is to find out where half-way is.

You now know that your estimate should be higher than 50 as the arrow is further along the line than half-way.

Now mark in another half-way line.

You now know that your estimate should be higher than 50 but lower than 75. It is also closer to 75 than 50.

half-way between 50 and 100 = 75

You could add in another half-way line.

You now know that your estimate should be higher than 62.5 but lower than 75. It is also quite close to 62.5.

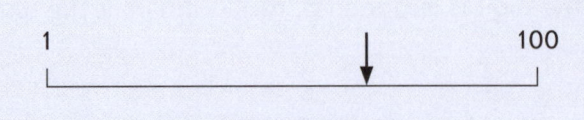

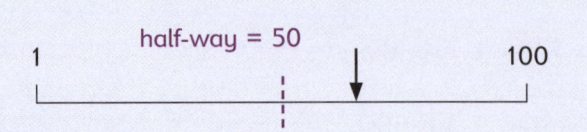

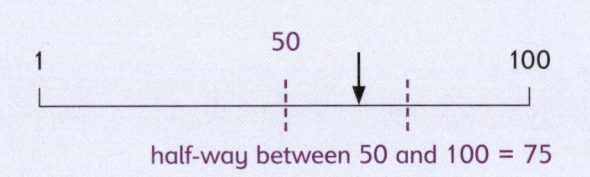

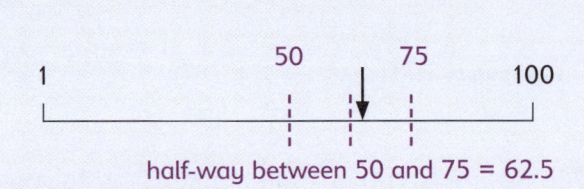

half-way between 50 and 75 = 62.5

You can now make a good estimate of what number the arrow is pointing to.

Answer: Any number between **63** and **68** would be correct.

You may also be asked to estimate calculations. This means you need to round the numbers first, which makes the calculation easier.

Sally had 416 books and Rajesh had 582. Use rounding to estimate how many books they had altogether.

Sally's 416 can be rounded to 420 and Rajesh's 582 can be rounded to 580. 420 + 580 = 1000

Answer: 1000 books

✏️ Estimate the numbers on the number line.

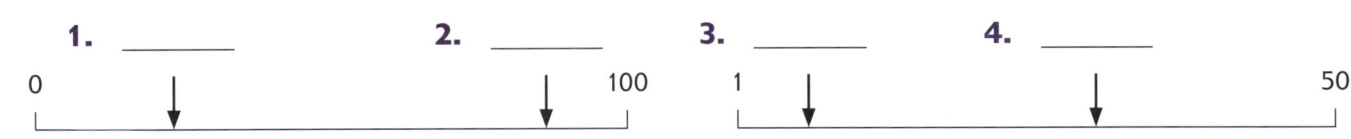

1. _____   2. _____   3. _____   4. _____

5. Jackson found 273 shells and Aubrey found 145. Use rounding to estimate how many shells they found altogether. _____

6. Daisy had 792 pennies. After buying a book she had 177 pennies left. Use rounding to estimate how many pennies she used to buy the book. _____

Negative numbers

Negative numbers are numbers that are less than zero. They work in the opposite way to positive numbers. Positive numbers move to the right along the number line from 0, whereas negative numbers move to the left from 0.

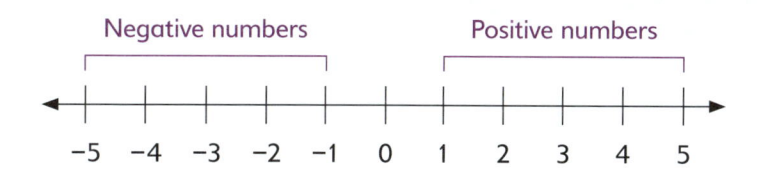

Negative numbers begin with a minus sign. Just as with positive numbers, when you add, you move to the right along the number line and when you subtract, you move to the left.

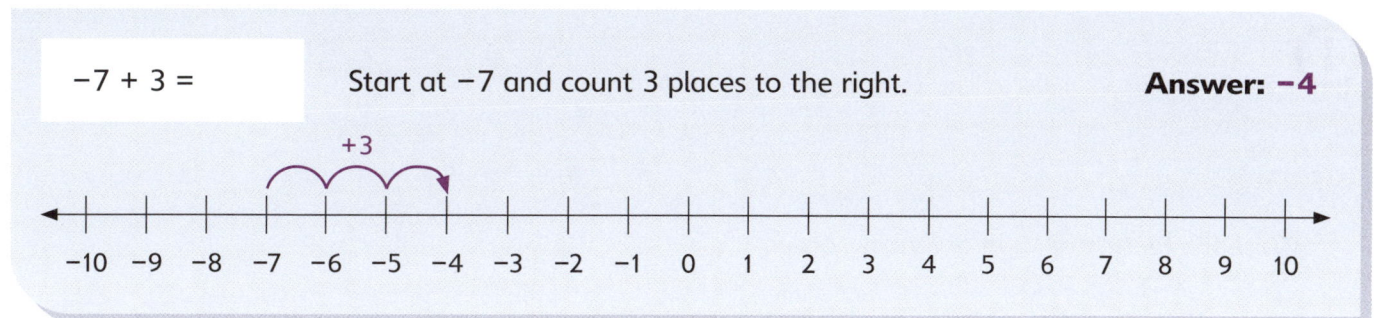

−7 + 3 =   Start at −7 and count 3 places to the right.   **Answer: −4**

Negative numbers are often used when referring to temperatures below zero and to debt.

The temperature was 5°C. It dropped by 7°C. What is the new temperature?

Start at 5 and count down 7 places.

5°C − 7°C = −2°C

Answer: −2°C

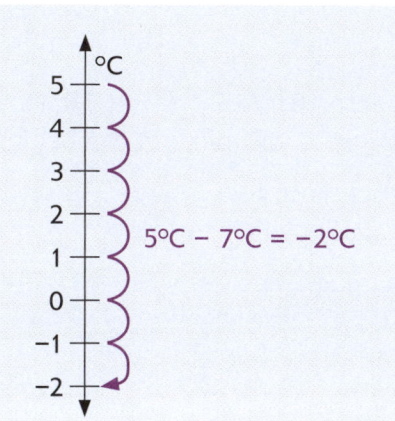

TIP Remember to count the number 0 when you are moving along the number line or thermometer.

You will also come across negative numbers in calculations and number sequences.

Write the missing numbers in this number sequence.

−7,   −3,   ____,   5,   9,   ____

Work out the difference between two adjacent numbers. Here, the difference is 4, so you need to add 4 each time. The missing numbers are therefore 1 and 13.

Answer: −7,   −3,   __1__,   5,   9,   __13__

Now answer the following questions.

1. 4 − 9 = _____
2. −2 − 9 = _____
3. Overnight, the temperature dropped 10°C from 6°C. What was the new temperature? _____
4. Mark had £24 in the bank. He spent £32 on books. What was his new bank balance? _____

Write the missing numbers in these number sequences.

5. 4,   1,   −2,   _____,   _____
6. −11,   _____,   _____,   1,   5,   9

Factors

The **factors** of a number are all the whole numbers that it can be divided by without a **remainder** (an amount left over). You can check these by doing the **inverse** operation, which is multiplication.

For example, the factors of 6 are 1, 2, 3 and 6 because 6 can be divided exactly by all these numbers: $6 ÷ 1 = 6$, $6 ÷ 2 = 3$, $6 ÷ 3 = 2$, $6 ÷ 6 = 1$. You can check your answer by multiplying factor pairs: $1 × 6 = 6$ and $2 × 3 = 6$.

In order to find all of the factors of a number, you can follow a set process, starting with 1 because 1 is a factor of all numbers.

> ❗ The factors of a number will never be larger than the number itself.

Write the factors of 18 in ascending order.

Start with 1. What is multiplied by 1 to make 18? $1 × 18 = 18$. You have found the first two factors of 18: 1 and 18. Set them out as if they are on an invisible number line with 1 at the beginning and 18 at the end.

1   18

After 1 comes 2. Does 2 go into 18? Yes. $2 × 9 = 18$. Now you have found two more factors: 2 and 9. Add these to the number line. 2 will join 1 at the beginning and 9 will join 18 at the end.

See how the number line is split into two groups? By setting it out like this, you can discount all the numbers between the ones you have written.

Now you can see that no numbers between 9 and 18 are factors of 18.

1, 2   9, 18

After 2 comes 3. Does 3 go into 18? Yes, $3 × 6 = 18$. Now you have found two more factors: 3 and 6. Add these to the number line.

1, 2, 3,   6, 9, 18

After 3 comes 4. Does 4 go into 18? No, so we move onto 5. Does 5 go into 18? No. After 5 comes 6, but we already have 6 written on our number line. This means that the two ends of the number line have met, so we have found all the factors.

See how the pairs of factors can be linked like a rainbow? No numbers between 6 and 9 or 9 and 18 are factors of 18 because they wouldn't have a pair that they could be linked to in the first half of the number line.

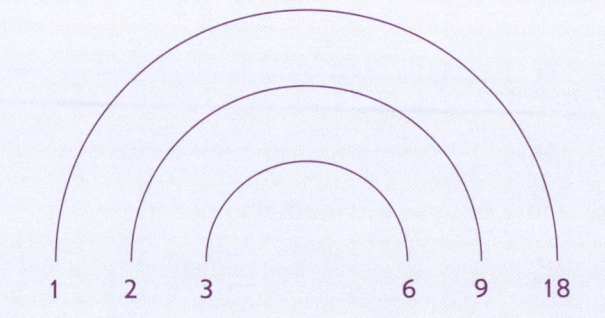

1   2   3   6   9   18

Answer: 1, 2, 3, 6, 9, 18

Factors

When you work out the factors of a **square number**, you only need to write down the **square root** once. The square root will also be the final number in the centre of the number line.

A square number is the number you get when you multiply a number by itself. For example, 4 × 4 = 16, so 16 is a square number. The square root is the opposite. It is the number that is multiplied by itself to make a square number, so the square root of 16 is 4 because 4 × 4 is 16. Square numbers will be covered on page 19. Here are all the factors of 16, including the square root:

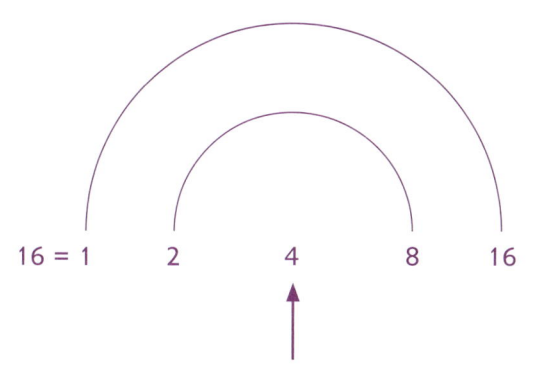

16 = 1   2   4   8   16

The square root will sit on its own in the centre of the 'rainbow'.

> Factors always come in pairs, except for square numbers when the square root will be on its own in the centre.

You may be asked to find the **highest common factor** (or **HCF**) of a pair or group of numbers. This is the highest factor that the numbers have in common.

> Find the HCF of 18 and 24.
>
> First, find all of the factors of 18 and 24. Then circle the highest factor that they have in common.
>
> The factors of 18 are: 1,   2,   3,   (6,)   9,   18
>
> The factors of 24 are: 1,   2,   3,   4,   (6,)   8,   12,   24
>
> The highest factor that 18 and 24 both have in common is 6, so the HCF is 6.
>
> **Answer: 6**

Write the factors of these numbers in ascending order.

1. 12 _____
2. 36 _____
3. 54 _____
4. 80 _____

TIP Remember to write the factors at either end of an invisible number line and gradually work towards the centre.

Find the HCF of these pairs of numbers.

5. 15 and 21 _____
6. 28 and 42 _____

Multiples

Multiples are all the numbers in a multiplication table.

For example, the multiples of 5 are 5, 10, 15, 20, 25, 30, 35, 40, and so on.

They can go on indefinitely. 5 689 745 is a multiple of 5 because 5 × 1 137 949 = 5 689 745.

Multiples can be divided by a number without a remainder. For example, 18 is a multiple of 6 because 6 × 3 = 18 and 18 ÷ 6 = 3. 23 is not a multiple of 6 because 23 cannot be divided by 6 exactly.

Understanding divisibility rules will help you to determine whether numbers are multiples of another number. You will learn about divisibility rules on pages 15 and 16.

The **lowest common multiple** (**LCM**) of two or more numbers is the smallest number that is a multiple of each of them.

Find the LCM of 3 and 4.

The first few multiples of 3 are: 3, 6, 9, (12,) 15, 18, 21, 24

The first few multiples of 4 are: 4, 8, (12,) 16, 20, 24

The lowest multiple that 3 and 4 both have in common is 12, so the LCM is 12.

Answer: 12

Now answer the following questions.

1. Circle the multiples of 7.

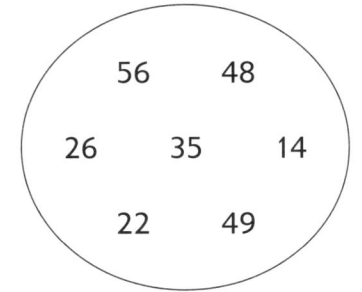

56   48
26   35   14
22   49

2. Circle the multiples of 12.

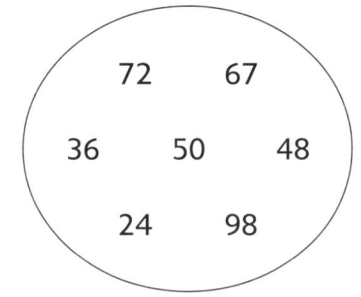

72   67
36   50   48
24   98

3. Circle the multiples of 9.

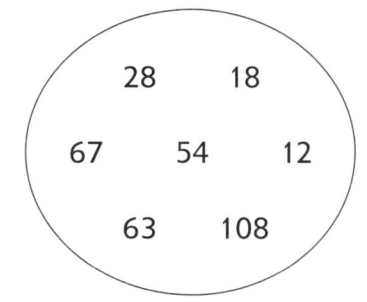

28   18
67   54   12
63   108

Find the LCM of these pairs of numbers.

4. 3 and 8 _____

5. 12 and 4 _____

6. 8 and 4 _____

TIP To find the LCM, start counting up in the larger number until you get to a number that is also a multiple of the smaller number.

7. Circle the number that is **not** a multiple of 6.

132   222   108   414   536

Divisibility rules

It is very important that you know your multiplication tables up to 12 × 12.

However, many numbers have sneaky features in their times tables that can help you to work out whether larger numbers can be divided exactly by them.

Divisibility rules are rules you can apply to any number to see which numbers it can be divided by exactly. Knowing divisibility rules will save you a lot of time when you are asked whether a number has certain factors.

A number is **divisible** by:

2	if	it is even.	574 is divisible by 2 because it is even. 683 is not because it is odd.
3	if	the digits add up to 3, 6 or 9.	36 is divisible by 3 because 3 + 6 = 9. 97 is not because 9 + 7 = 16 and 1 + 6 = 7.
4	if	the digits in the tens and ones columns can be divided by 4 **or** it can be halved and halved again to leave a whole number.	324 is divisible by 4 because 24 is a multiple of 4. 947 is not because 47 is not a multiple of 4. 576 is divisible by 4 because half of 576 is 288 and half of 288 is 144. 486 is not because half of 486 is 243, but 243 cannot be halved because it is odd.
5	if	it ends in a 5 or a 0.	175 is divisible by 5 because it ends in 5. 134 is not because it does not end in a 5 or a 0.
6	if	the digits add up to 3, 6 or 9 **and** the original number is even.	456 is divisible by 6 because it is even and 4 + 5 + 6 = 15 and 1 + 5 is 6. 225 is not because it is an odd number.
7	if	you can double the ones digit and take it away from the number created by the remaining digits and get a number that is divisible by 7 (including 0).	378 is divisible by 7 because 8 × 2 = 16 and 37 − 16 = 21, which is divisible by 7. 484 is not because 4 × 2 = 8 and 48 − 8 = 40, which is not divisible by 7.
8	if	if the hundreds, tens and ones can be divided by 8 **or** if you can halve, halve and halve it again (halve 3 times) to get a whole number.	24 800 is divisible by 8 because 800 can be divided by 8. 168 is divisible by 8 because half of 168 = 84, half of 84 = 42 and half of 42 = 21. 244 is not because half of 244 = 122 and half of 122 = 61, which cannot be halved to form a whole number.
9	if	the digits add up to 9.	72 is divisible by 9 because 7 + 2 = 9. 99 is also divisible by 9 because 9 + 9 = 18 and 1 + 8 = 9. 134 is not because 1 + 3 + 4 = 8.
10	if	it ends in a 0.	40 and 170 are divisible by 10 because they end in a zero. 346 is not because it does not end in a 0.

Divisibility rules

You can also use divisibility rules to solve problems involving remainders.

> Which number has a remainder of 1 when divided by 9?
>
> 346   722   453   352
>
> The easiest way to work this out is to think of the remainder as an extra number that isn't needed. If you take the remainder away from each number, you will be left with the number that is divisible by 9, which you can then identify using divisibility rules.
>
> So 346 − 1 = 345, 722 − 1 = 721, 453 − 1 = 452, 352 − 1 = 351
>
> Now use divisibility rules to work out the answer. Only 351 has digits which add up to 9 (3 + 5 + 1 = 9) and is therefore divisible by 9, so 352 must be the number that has a remainder of 1 when divided by 9.
>
> **Answer: 352**

Now answer the following questions.

1. Circle the numbers that are divisible by 6.   456   345   574   132   621

2. Circle the numbers that are divisible by both 5 and 3.   135   432   785   345   995

3. Circle the number that has the factors 2, 4 and 7.   765   1120   790   372   1234

4. Complete the table. Put a tick in the box if the number in the first column is divisible by the number in the top row.

	2	3	4	5	6	7	8	9	10
624									
1530									
2205									
572									

5. Circle the number that has a remainder of 7 when divided by 10.

   568   317   269   713

6. Circle the number that has a remainder of 4 when divided by 9.

   345   760   260   194

Prime numbers and prime factors

Prime numbers are numbers that can only be divided by themselves and 1.

To decide whether a number is a prime number, first use divisibility rules to see if it is divisible by anything. Even numbers larger than 2 are not prime because they can be divided by 2. If it is not even, check to see if it can be divided by 3 or 5 using the divisibility rules.

If it is not divisible by 2, 3 or 5, do a quick calculation to see if it can be divided by 7. You may also want to do a quick division calculation for 11 if the number is larger than 144 (you should know your multiplication tables up to $12 \times 12 = 144$).

> ! The only even prime number is 2 as it can only be divided by itself and 1. 1 is **not** a prime number because it only has one factor.

You do not need to work out if a number is divisible by 4, 6, 8, 10 or 12 as all multiples of these numbers are even and will be divisible by 2.

You do not need to work out if a number is divisible by 9 as all multiples of 9 are divisible by 3.

> **TIP** Numbers that are **not** prime numbers are called **composite numbers**. These are numbers that can be divided by numbers other than themselves and 1. 1 is a special number. It is neither prime nor composite.

> Which of these numbers is a prime number?
> 54   153   19
>
> 54 is even. Therefore, it is not a prime number because it can be divided by 2. You don't need to work out what other numbers it can be divided by as you now know it's not prime.
>
> The digits in 153 add up to 9. This means that it's not prime because it can be divided by 3. 19 does not fit any divisibility rules and is therefore a prime number.
>
> **Answer: 19**

> **TIP** It is a good idea to memorise the first few prime numbers because they are often used in number sequences: 2, 3, 5, 7, 11, 13, 17, 19, 23, 29

For each of the numbers below, write if it is prime. If you don't think the number is prime, give one number that it is divisible by and explain why. For example: It is divisible by 5 because it ends in a 5.

1. 31 _____
2. 46 _____
3. 117 _____
4. 235 _____
5. 211 _____
6. Jamal is thinking of a number. It is larger than 35 but smaller than 40. It is a prime number. What is the number Jamal is thinking of? _____

Prime numbers and prime factors

Prime factors, as the name suggests, are a combination of prime numbers and factors.

They are the prime numbers that can be multiplied together to create a number. You will normally be asked to write a number as 'the **product** of its prime factors'.

When you are working out the prime factors of a number, it helps to draw a factor tree.

Write 18 as a product of its prime factors.

Pick a pair of factors for the number. It can be any pair at all (except 1 and the number itself).

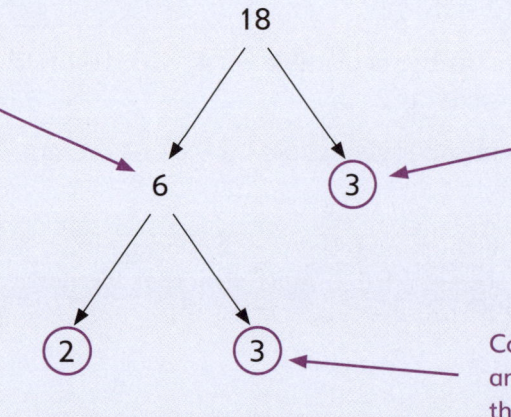

If either of the numbers is a prime number, put a circle around it. You have finished with that number.

Continue finding pairs of factors for any composite numbers, circling them if they are prime numbers.

Answer: $2 \times 3 \times 3$

TIP Check your answer by working out the multiplication: $2 \times 3 = 6$, $6 \times 3 = 18$.

Write 32 as a product of its prime factors.

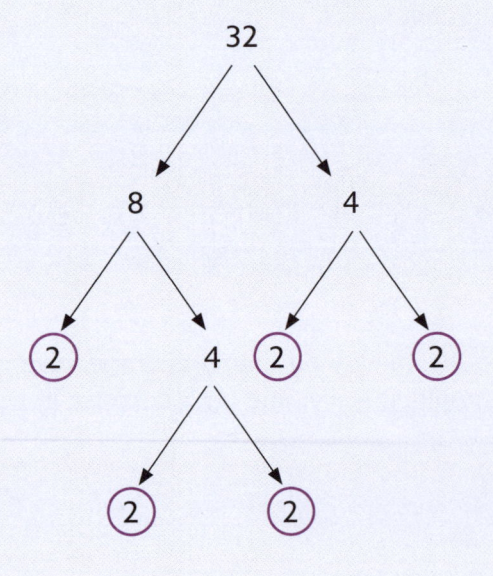

You can see how the prime factors you have found make 32 by multiplying them back together.

$2 \times 2 = 4$ $8 \times 2 = 16$

$4 \times 2 = 8$ $16 \times 2 = 32$

Answer: $2 \times 2 \times 2 \times 2 \times 2$

TIP As all the prime factors of 32 are the same, they could be written as 2^5 (or 2 to the **power** of 5), in the same way as 2×2 can be written as 2^2 and $2 \times 2 \times 2$ can be written as 2^3. We will look at powers on page 19.

Write each number as a product of its prime factors.

7. 24 _____   10. 27 _____

8. 49 _____   11. 56 _____

9. 45 _____   12. 38 _____

Square and cube numbers

Square numbers

When a number is multiplied by itself, the answer is known as a square number. They are called this because they can make a square pattern.

The sign for a squared number is a small 2, which shows that the number has been used twice. For example, $6 \times 6 = 6^2$. It is also known as an **index** or a power. For example, 4^2 would be 4 to the power of 2. When you write 4^2, you are writing 4×4 in index form.

$1 \times 1 = 1$ $2 \times 2 = 4$ $3 \times 3 = 9$

> You should know the first 12 square numbers off by heart. They are often used in number sequences:
> 1, 4, 9, 16, 25, 36, 49, 64, 81, 100, 121, 144

Square root

The opposite of a square number is a square root. This is the original number that was multiplied by itself to make the square number. The sign for a square root is $\sqrt{}$. For example, $\sqrt{64} = 8$ because 8×8 is 64.

Now answer the following questions.

1. $6^2 - 3^2 =$ _____
2. Which two square numbers add up to 74? _____
3. Which number squared gives a product of 196? _____
4. What is the square root of 81? _____
5. $\sqrt{144} - \sqrt{100} =$ _____
6. Write 8×8 in index form. _____

Cube numbers

Cube numbers are numbers that are multiplied by themselves three times. They are called this because they can make a cube pattern. As with the square root, the **cube root** is the original number that was multiplied by itself three times to make the cube number. The symbol for a cube root is $\sqrt[3]{}$.

The sign for a cube number is a small 3 because the number is used three times. For example, $3 \times 3 \times 3 = 3^3$.

> You should know the first five cube numbers off by heart. Like square numbers, they will often appear in sequences and number patterns: 1, 8, 27, 64, 125

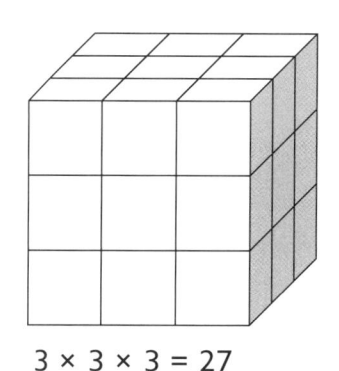

$3 \times 3 \times 3 = 27$

Now answer the following questions.

7. $4^3 =$ _____
8. $2^3 + 5^3 =$ _____
9. $3^3 - 1^3 =$ _____
10. $7^3 =$ _____
11. Which number cubed gives a product of 216? _____
12. Write $5 \times 5 \times 5$ in index form. _____

Roman numerals

Roman numerals are the numbers that were used by the Romans. They did not have a separate symbol for each number as we do, but instead used a system of seven letters.

Roman numeral	I	V	X	L	C	D	M
Number	1	5	10	50	100	500	1000

Notice how all the numbers begin with a 1 or a 5.

Roman numerals can be put together to make any number using addition or subtraction. However, there are a few rules you need to remember.

Rule 1: If a bigger value comes before a smaller value, you need to add. VI = 6 as 5 + 1 = 6

If the values are the same, you also need to add. XX = 20 as 10 + 10 = 20

If a smaller value comes before a bigger value, you need to subtract. IX = 9 as 10 − 1 = 9

Rule 2: Numerals can be repeated a maximum of three times. For example, you can have III (3), but 4 will not be IIII. Instead, you need to move on to the next letter and use a subtraction, so IV (5 − 1, or 1 before 5) = 4.

Only I, X, C and M can be repeated. V, L and D (the numbers beginning with a 5) cannot be repeated.

Rule 3: You can only put a letter before another letter in order to do a subtraction if that letter is no more than 10 times smaller. For example, IV (4) is fine, as I (1) is only 5 times smaller than V (5). However, you cannot have IL (49), as I (1) is more than 10 times smaller than L (50). Instead, you need to think about the individual value of the digits.

To make the 40 you can't use XXXX, as that goes against rule 2. You therefore need to move on to the next letter and do a subtraction. The letters XL would be 40 because they show 10 before 50 (50 − 10). You then need to think about how you would make 9. You can't have VIIII, as that would go against rule 2, so you need to move on to the next letter and do a subtraction. The number 9 would then be written as IX (10 − 1). The number 49 is therefore XLIX.

There are only six combinations of numerals that can be subtracted:

IV = 4 (5 − 1)   XC = 90 (100 − 10)
IX = 9 (10 − 1)   CD = 400 (500 − 100)
XL = 40 (50 − 10)   CM = 900 (1000 − 100)

❗ You cannot subtract two numbers. Only subtract when you cannot add.

Rule 4: You need to use a horizontal bar above the numerals to write numbers larger than 3999. This works by multiplying that number by 1000.

$\overline{IV}$ = 4000 (IV = 4, 4 × 1000 = 4000)
$\overline{V}$XI = 5011 (V = 5, 5 × 1000 = 5000.   XI = 11, so 5000 + 11 = 5011)

✏️ Write these Roman numerals as numbers.   Write these numbers as Roman numerals.

1. CDXXVII _____   4. 581   _____

2. MCCCXCVI _____   5. 2832 _____

3. $\overline{VI}$CXXVIII _____   6. 9466 _____

Number and place value practice page 1

Now test your skills with these practice pages. If you get stuck, go back to pages 6 to 20 for some reminders.

Place value

Write these numbers in words.

1. 645 103 _____

2. 1 362 086 _____

Write these words as numbers.

3. forty-two thousand, eight hundred and seventy-two _____

4. two million, three hundred and fifty-eight thousand, six hundred and four _____

What is the value of the underlined digit?

5. 5<u>6</u>7 025 _____
6. 7<u>42</u>8 401 _____

Ordering and comparing numbers

Use < or > to make these number sentences correct.

7. 367 158 _____ 367 518
8. 8 174 479 _____ 8 147 479

9. Write these numbers in descending order.

    452 782   458 235   45 278   56 263   4 672 456

    _____

10. Circle the largest number.   4 728 578   4 782 567   4 728 758   4 782 657

11. Use < or > to make this number sentence correct.

    2 145 673 _____ 214 657 _____ 412 756 _____ 2 415 673 _____ 4 215 637

12. Ben was able to measure the length of a bench by stretching out
    a single 4m tape measure. How long was the bench? _____

Rounding

Round these numbers to the nearest 1000.

13. 54 798 _____
14. 123 439 _____

Round these numbers to the nearest 10 000.

15. 537 934 _____
16. 973 672 _____

Approximate the answers to these calculations.

17. 456 + 321 = _____
18. 2034 × 49 = _____

11+ Maths Study and Practice Book

Number and place value practice page 2

Estimating

Estimate the numbers on the number lines.

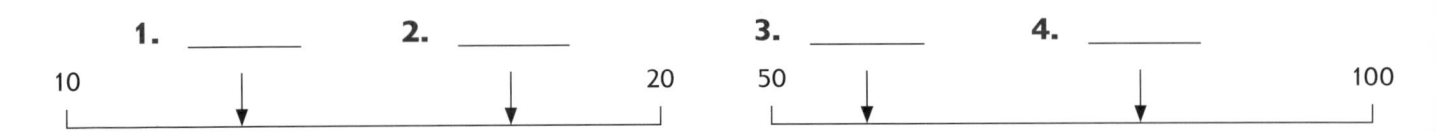

1. _____   2. _____   3. _____   4. _____

10 ———————————————— 20   50 ———————————————— 100

5. Maeve had 57 pairs of blue shoes, 72 pairs of green shoes, 41 pairs of black shoes and 112 pairs of pink shoes in her shop. Approximately how many pairs of shoes did she have altogether? _____

6. Sonal counted the pennies in some jars. She had 1372 in one, 789 in another and 1221 in another. Use rounding to estimate the total number of pennies. _____

Negative numbers

7. 3 − 9 = _____

8. 12 − 36 = _____

9. 26 − 100 = _____

10. −6 + 9 = _____

11. −27 + 19 = _____

12. At 16:00 the temperature in London was 2°C. By midnight it had dropped by 7°C. What was the temperature at midnight? _____

Factors

Write the factors of these numbers in ascending order.

13. 24 _____

14. 72 _____

15. 49 _____

16. 84 _____

Find the HCF of these pairs of numbers.

17. 12 and 28 _____

18. 15 and 27 _____

19. 24 and 72 _____

20. 18 and 108 _____

Number and place value practice page 3

Multiples

1. Circle the multiples of 11.

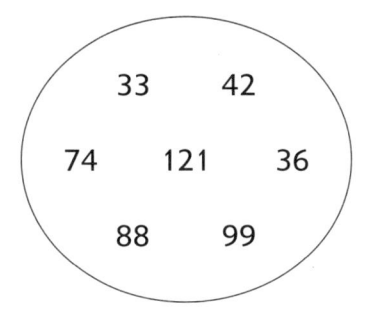

   33 42
   74 121 36
   88 99

2. Circle the multiples of 25.

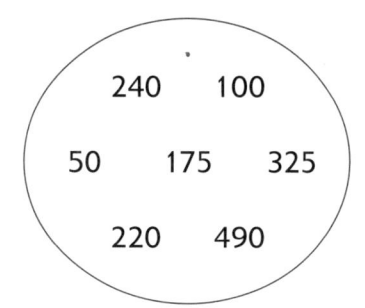

   240 100
   50 175 325
   220 490

Find the LCM of these pairs of numbers.

3. 6 and 9 _____

4. 3 and 14 _____

5. Circle the number that is **not** a multiple of 7.

   49   35   84   54   77

6. Circle the number that is **not** a multiple of 40.

   240   480   360   160   300

Divisibility rules

Are these statements true or false?

7. 1056 is divisible by 8. _____

8. 2631 is divisible by 9. _____

9. 6345 is divisible by both 5 and 6. _____

Use this set of numbers for questions 10 to 13.

234   135   240   124   392   105   252

10. Which of the numbers above are divisible by both 6 and 9? _____

11. Which of the numbers above is divisible by both 8 and 3? _____

12. Which of the numbers above is divisible by both 5 and 7? _____

13. Which of the numbers above is divisible by 3, 4 and 9? _____

Number and place value practice page 4

Prime numbers and prime factors

1. List the first six prime numbers. _____

2. Circle the number that is **not** a prime number.

    19   63   53   29   71   89

3. Circle the number that is a prime number.

    69   77   57   67   85   111

What is the next prime number after each of these numbers?

4. 34 _____   5. 56 _____   6. 72 _____

Write these numbers as a product of their prime factors.

7. 24 _____   10. 16 _____

8. 56 _____   11. 58 _____

9. 74 _____   12. 120 _____

Square and cube numbers

13. $5^2 =$ _____   16. $\sqrt{81} =$ _____

14. $11^2 =$ _____   17. $3^3 =$ _____

15. $3^2 + 8^2 =$ _____   18. $5^3 =$ _____

Roman numerals

Write these Roman numerals as numbers.

19. CCLXVII   _____

20. DCCLXI   _____

21. $\overline{\text{XII}}$CCCXLV   _____

Write these numbers as Roman numerals.

22. 59 _____

23. 193 _____

24. 567 _____

Addition

There are many methods for adding numbers. The trick is to choose the best method for each calculation. This means using the method that you find easiest, quickest and most accurate.

For some problems, a mental calculation will be the best method.

Number bonds

Knowing your **number bonds** is very important. If you know by heart the numbers that go together to make 1 to 10 and multiples of 10, it will make addition calculations much easier.

Samara received £17 for her birthday from her sister and £13 from her brother. How much money did she receive altogether?

You should recognise that 7 + 3 = 10 and therefore 17 + 13 = 30.

Answer: £30

> ! Look out for these words and phrases in questions – they all mean 'add': **altogether**, **plus**, **sum**, **total**, **in all**, **increase**.

You can also use your knowledge of number bonds when adding groups of numbers together.

18 + 13 + 12 + 17 =

You can add these numbers in any order. Choose pairs that are easier to add. 18 + 12 = 30 and 13 + 17 = 30. Then 30 + 30 = 60.

18 + 13 + 12 + 17
18 + 12 = 30   13 + 17 = 30

Answer: 60

Adding 8, 9, 18, 19, and so on

Both 8 and 9 are very close to 10, so, rather than trying to add 9, you could add 10 then subtract 1. For 8, add 10 and subtract 2.

For 19, add 20 and subtract 1, and so on.

29 + 38 =

Round both numbers up to the nearest ten and add them together.
30 + 40 = 70
Subtract the extra ones that you added on when rounding.
70 − 1 − 2 = 67

Answer: 67

Addition

Adding through 10, 100

It can sometimes be easier to add together numbers by adding up to the nearest 10 or 100.

187 + 46 =

Using your knowledge of number bonds, you should know that 187 + 13 = 200. Having used 13 of the 46, you are left with 33 (46 − 13 = 33).

200 + 33 = 233, so 187 + 46 = 233

Answer: 233

Doubles and near doubles

You should be able to double all numbers mentally. You should know the doubles of numbers up to 20 off by heart. Beyond this, you should be able to work them out quickly by doubling the tens, doubling the ones and then adding them together.

If a calculation is close to a double, you can use this knowledge to quickly work out the answer.

25 + 26 =

Double 25 = 50, therefore 25 + 26 = 51

Answer: 51

Partitioning

You can often **partition** a number in your head, especially if you have the numbers written down in front of you. If you partition something, you divide it into parts. When you partition a number for an addition calculation, you separate its hundreds, tens and ones so that you can add it more easily.

231 + 146 =

Partition each number into its hundreds, tens and ones. Then add the hundreds together, the tens together and the ones together.

200 + 100 = 300, 30 + 40 = 70 and 1 + 6 = 7

Finally, add the hundreds, tens and ones back together.

300 + 70 + 7 = 377

Answer: 377

Addition

Written calculations

For other addition problems, you will need to carry out a written calculation as the numbers may be too big for you to work out quickly, easily and accurately in your head. In these cases, it is usually quicker and easier to do a vertical addition calculation.

There are 2756 books on one library shelf and 3021 on another. How many books are there altogether?

You might be able to work this out mentally, but it will be a lot quicker, easier and more accurate to do a vertical addition calculation.

```
    2 7 5 6
  + 3 0 2 1
    5 7 7 7
```

$2 + 3 = 5$
$6 + 1 = 7$
$7 + 0 = 7$
$5 + 2 = 7$

> ❗ You must always start your addition from the right-hand side of the number.

Answer: 5777 books

In vertical addition calculations, it is important to keep the digits in the correct place value columns and to think carefully about any digits you have to carry over. Remember to add on the digits you have carried over.

```
    4 2 6 7
  + 2 8 9 5
    7 1 6 2
    1 1 1
```

$4 + 2 = 6$. Add on the carried $1 = 7$. Put the 7 in the thousands column.

$7 + 5 = 12$. Put the 2 in the ones column and carry the 1.

$2 + 8 = 10$. Add on the carried $1 = 11$. Put the 1 in the hundreds column and carry the 1.

$6 + 9 = 15$. Add on the carried $1 = 16$. Put the 6 in the tens column and carry the 1.

✎ For each of the following questions, decide whether to do a mental calculation or a written one. If you need to do a written calculation, do it on a separate piece of paper.

1. 26 + 27 = _____

2. 56 + 29 = _____

3. 379 + 256 = _____

4. 17 383 + 1436 = _____

5. 48 734 + 6543 + 235 = _____

6. Danny had £3768 in his bank account and sold his car for £5178. How much money did he have altogether? _____

Subtraction

Just as with addition, there are many different methods for subtracting numbers. Once again, the most important thing is to use the easiest, quickest and most accurate method for each calculation.

For some calculations, a mental method may be best.

Number bonds

Knowing number bonds not only helps with addition, but also subtraction. If you know that 35 + 65 = 100, then you also know that 100 − 65 = 35.

> **!** Look out for these words and phrases in questions – they all mean 'subtract': **deduct**, **minus**, **less**, **left**, **how many more/ fewer**, **find the difference**.

Subtracting 8, 9, 18, 19, and so on

As 8 and 9 are close to 10, you can subtract 10 and then adjust by adding on 2 or 1. For 19, you can subtract 20 and add 1, and so on.

John had 37 shirts. He gave 19 of them to a charity shop. How many did he have left?

37 − 20 = 17 and 17 + 1 = 18, so 37 − 19 = 18

Answer: 18 shirts

Partitioning

With subtraction, only partition the second number in the calculation. The first number must stay intact.

367 − 216 =

367 − 200 = 167, 167 − 10 = 157 and 157 − 6 = 151
So 367 − 216 = 151

Answer: 151

Counting on

Sometimes, it may actually be easier to count on rather than take away.

3000 − 2998 =

Rather than write out a vertical subtraction calculation that will involve lots of borrowing (or exchanging) from neighbouring columns, it is much easier to count on from 2998 to 3000.

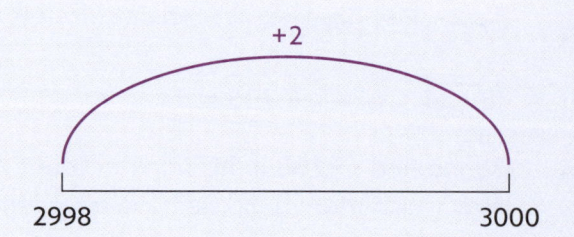

Answer: 2

Subtraction

Written calculation

Generally, problems involving larger numbers will require you to carry out a written calculation, using vertical subtraction. You need to subtract the digits in each column one at a time.

```
    3 8 9
  - 1 2 3
    2 6 6
```

$3 - 1 = 2$ → $2 6 6$ ← $9 - 3 = 6$

$8 - 2 = 6$

> **!** Always start your subtraction from the right-hand side of the number. Make sure that you write the digits in the correct place value columns.

With vertical subtraction, you may need to borrow from the next-door column in order to be able to carry out the calculation.

245 − 138 =

> **!** You can only ever borrow from the next-door column to the left. You cannot borrow from a column that is not directly next door.

You cannot do 5 − 8, so you need to borrow 1 from the tens column and give it to the ones column. This does not change the value of the entire number. Instead of 245 being made up of 200 + 40 + 5 it is now made up of 200 + 30 + 15.

You can now do the ones subtraction. 15 − 8 = 7. Then 3 − 3 = 0 and 2 − 1 = 1.

```
    ³
  2 4ˑ¹5
 − 1 3 8
  1 0 7
```

Answer: 107

Sometimes, it may be necessary to borrow from more than one column before you can do the calculation.

3202 − 1469 =

You cannot do 2 − 9, so you must borrow from the tens column. There is nothing in the tens column, so you need to borrow from the hundreds and give to the tens. This will make the tens column worth 10, which will mean you can give one to the ones. After you have done this, the ones will be worth 12, the tens will be worth 9 and the hundreds will be worth 1.

```
   ² ¹¹ ⁹
  3 2 ¹0 ¹2
 − 1 4 6 9
  1 7 3 3
```

Now you will not be able to carry out the hundreds subtraction as you cannot do 1 − 4. Instead, you will have to borrow from the thousands column to make the hundreds 11. Rather than the number reading 3000 + 200 + 0 + 2, it now says 2000 + 1100 + 90 + 12.

Answer: 1733

For each of the following questions, decide whether to do a mental calculation or a written one. If you need to do a written calculation, do it on a separate piece of paper.

1. 56 − 18 = _____
2. 376 − 223 = _____
3. 4000 − 3994 = _____
4. 5723 − 2908 = _____
5. 9001 − 4782 = _____
6. 6386 − 2853 − 564 = _____
7. Hasan wanted to buy trainers costing £54. He found £7 in his piggy bank and got £19 for his birthday. How much more money did he need? _____

Multiplying and dividing by 10, 100 and 1000

You may have been taught that when you multiply a number by 10 you add on a 0 and when you divide by 10 you take off a 0. This can be helpful but it's important to know why zeros can appear and disappear.

The value of each place value column gets 10× bigger as you move to the left. This means that when you multiply by 10 you are actually moving the digits one place to the left to show that their value has increased 10 times.

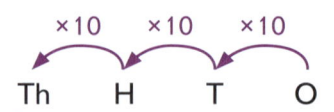

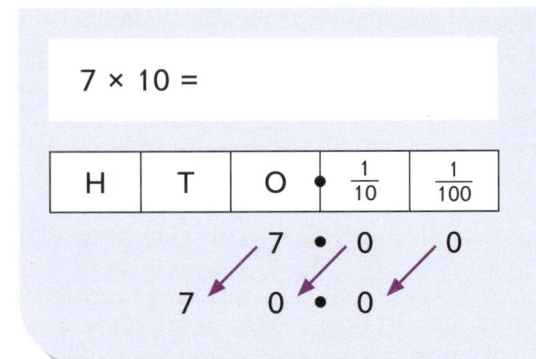

7 × 10 =

The 7 will move one place to the left, from the ones column to the tens column.

As the 7 moves, so will the digits to the right of it. There will be a 0 in the $\frac{1}{10}$ column so that will move into the ones column. Each digit moves one place to the left.

Answer: 70

The number of zeros determines how many places the digit you are multiplying has to move: **× 10 (1 zero)** means 1 place to the left, **× 100 (2 zeros)** means 2 places to the left, **× 1000 (3 zeros)** means 3 places to the left, and so on.

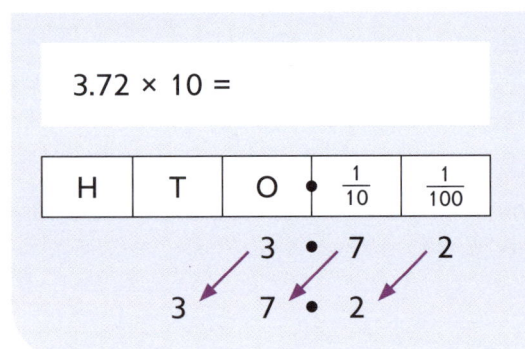

3.72 × 10 =

When you multiply decimals, you can't just add a zero to the end. You have to move all the digits to the left, including the **decimal fractions**.

Each digit moves one place to the left.

Answer: 37.2

When dividing, you need to do the opposite and move digits to the right.

67 ÷ 10 =

Each digit moves one place to the right.

Answer: 6.7

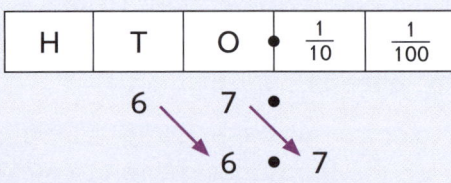

Now answer the following questions.

1. 4.5 × 100 = _____

2. 0.6 × 1000 = _____

3. 1.2 ÷ 100 = _____

4. 74.2 × _____ = 7420

5. Brooklyn shares £142 equally between 10 friends. How much does each friend get? _____

6. A jug can hold 1.2l of liquid. How much liquid could 1000 jugs hold in total? _____

Multiplication

As with addition and subtraction, there are many methods that can be used for multiplication and division calculations. Find the method that is easiest, quickest and most accurate for each individual question. Sometimes, a mental calculation will be best.

> Aisha has £26. She needs four times that to buy the game she wants. How much does her game cost?
>
> An easy way to multiply by 4 is to double (×2) and double (×2) again. Double 26 = 52 and double 52 = 104.
>
> **Answer: £104**

Multiplying whole numbers that are multiples of 10 can be made easier by initially ignoring any zeros that may be on the end then putting the zeros back on.

> 120 × 60 =
>
> Think of it as 12 × 6 = 72. You ignored two zeros when doing the calculation, so you have to put two zeros back on your answer.
>
> ⓘ You can only do this with whole numbers. To multiply decimals by multiples of 10, use the methods described on page 30.
>
> **Answer: 7200**

You should know your times tables up to 12. However, calculations often involve larger numbers and times tables larger than 12 that you haven't learnt. In these cases, you will need to do written calculations.

Multiplying by a known times table (1 to 12)

Multiplying by a number for which you know the times tables is relatively simple as long as you set it out correctly and multiply the numbers in the correct order. You must make sure you multiply each digit in turn.

```
    2 7              2 7                 2 7
  ×   9            ×   9               ×   9
  -----            -----               -----
                       3               2 4 3
                     6                     6
```

First work out 7 × 9 = 63.

Put the 3 in the ones column and carry the 6.

It is up to you where you write the 6 (above or below the number).

Now work out 2 × 9 = 18.

You must then add on the carried 6. 18 + 6 = 24. The 4 will go in the tens column and, as there are no more calculations to do, you can place the 2 in the hundreds column.

Answer: 243

> ⓘ Always start your multiplication with the digit in the furthest right-hand column.

Multiplication

Multiplying by a larger number

To multiply by a larger number, you can use some of the techniques you've used in other calculations.

$27 \times 18 =$

TIP When multiplying by 11 or 12, you do not need to partition the number because you know the 11× and 12× tables. Simply multiply each column by 11 or 12.

```
    2 7
  ×  1 8
  -------
    2 7 0   (×10)
          (×8)
  -------
```

Partition the number and do two separate calculations. First, 27 × 10 = 270.

```
    2 7
  ×  1 8
  -------
    2 7 0   (×10)
    2 1₅6   (×8)
  -------
```

Next, multiply 27 × 8. As before, you can partition: 8 × 7 = 56. Put the 6 in the ones column and carry the 5. Then 8 × 2 = 16. Add on the carried 5 = 21. Put the 1 in the tens column and the 2 in the hundreds column.

```
    2 7
  ×  1 8
  -------
    2 7 0   (×10)
  + 2 1₅6   (×8)
  -------
    4 8 6
```

Now add together the two calculations.
270 + 216 = 486

Answer: 486

If you are multiplying by a number that is larger than 20, the first calculation will be slightly trickier.

$45 \times 37 =$

```
    4 5
  ×  3 7
  -------
  1 3₁5 0   (×30)
          (×7)
  -------
```

Again, partition the number. To multiply by 30, put a zero in the ones column to multiply by 10 and then multiply by 3. 3 × 5 = 15, so put the 5 in the tens column and carry the 1.

3 × 4 = 12, add on the carried 1 = 13. Put the 3 in the hundreds and the 1 in the thousands column, so 45 × 3 = 135. Therefore, 45 × 30 = 1350.

```
    4 5
  ×  3 7
  -------
  1 3 5 0   (×30)
    3 1₃5   (×7)
  -------
```

Next, do 45 × 7.

7 × 5 = 35, so put the 5 in the ones column and carry the 3.

7 × 4 = 28. Add on the carried 3 = 31. Put the 1 in the tens column and the 3 in the hundreds column.

45 × 7 = 315

```
    4 5
  ×  3 7
  -------
  1 3 5 0   (×30)
  + 3 1 5   (×7)
  -------
  1 6 6 5
```

Finally, add together the two calculations.
1350 + 315 = 1665

Answer: 1665

For each of the following questions, decide whether to do a mental calculation or a written one. If you need to do a written calculation, do it on a separate piece of paper.

1. 9 × 8 = _____

2. 32 × 16 = _____

3. Taylor has 12 boxes, each containing 11 torches. How many torches does Taylor have? _____

4. Beatrix saves £25 every week for 30 weeks. How much money does she save? _____

5. Laptops cost £298. A shop sells 19 in one day. How much money does the shop make? _____

6. Alia makes 42 cupcakes every day for 31 days. How many cupcakes does Alia make? _____

Division and remainders

As well as knowing your times tables up to 12, you also need to know the associated division facts. There will be many division calculations that you will be able to do mentally using this knowledge.

Naadiya shared 25 sweets between 5 friends. How many sweets did each friend get?

If you know your times tables, this is a simple mental division.
$25 \div 5 = 5$

Answer: 5 sweets

> ❗ Look out for these words and phrases in questions – they all mean 'to divide': **share**, **split**, **how many each?**

You can also use division facts to work with larger numbers.

$360 \div 9 =$

If $36 \div 9 = 4$, then $360 \div 9 = 40$.

Answer: 40

If there are zeros on the end of both the numbers in the division calculation, these can be cancelled out. For example, $480 \div 80 = 6$, just like $48 \div 8 = 6$. You must cancel the same number of zeros on both sides.

$900 \div 30 =$

As there is only one zero to cancel on the 30 you can only cancel one zero on the 900, so it would be 9̶0̶0̶ ÷ 3̶0̶, which is $90 \div 3 = 30$ ($9 \div 3 = 3$, therefore $90 \div 3 = 30$). So, $900 \div 30 = 30$.

Answer: 30

When calculations involve larger numbers, you will need to do written calculations. 'Bus stop division' is the most obvious choice for carrying out written division calculations.

The parts of a division calculation have specific names.

If you are dividing by a number whose multiplication facts you know, it is relatively straightforward.

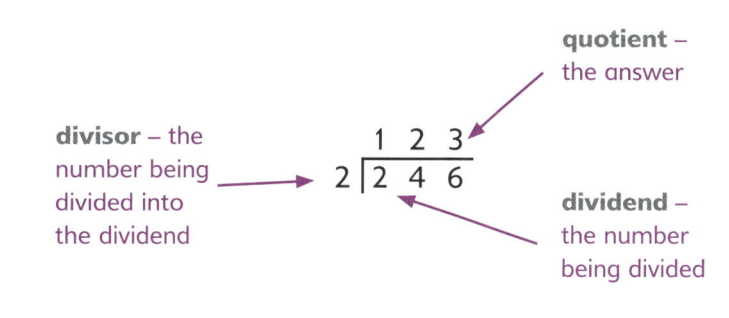

quotient – the answer

divisor – the number being divided into the dividend

$$2\overline{)246}$$ with 123 above

dividend – the number being divided

$567 \div 7 =$

$$7\overline{)5\,{}^56\,7}$$ with $0\,8\,1$ above

7 does go into 7. It goes in once, so a 1 is written above. It goes in exactly, so there is nothing left over to carry.

7 does not go into 5, so a 0 is written above the 5. The 5 is then carried to sit next to the 6.

7 does go into 56. It goes in 8 times, so an 8 is written above. It goes in exactly, so there is nothing to carry.

> ❗ Division is the only written calculation where you start calculating with the highest value number (the furthest left) rather than the smallest value number.

Answer: 81

11+ Maths Study and Practice Book

Division and remainders

If you are dividing by a larger number, it may be that you can still use the method on page 33.

384 ÷ 16 =

```
      0 2 4
1 6 ) 3 ³8 ⁶4
```

16 × 4 = 64, so 16 goes into 64 exactly 4 times and 4 is written above.

16 does not go into 3, so a 0 is written above the 3. The 3 is then carried to sit next to the 8.

16 × 2 = 32, so 16 goes into 38 twice with 6 left over. This can be carried to sit next to the 4.

Answer: 24

Sometimes, though, you may have to work in smaller steps.

798 ÷ 19 =

As you don't know your 19× table, go with what you know. 19 × 2 = 38, so 19 × 20 = 380. Start by subtracting that. Keep subtracting until you reach 0.

```
1 9 ) 7 9 8
    − 3 8 0    19 × 20
      4 1 8
    − 3 8 0    19 × 20
         3 8
       − 3 8    19 × 2
           0
```

The repeated subtraction of groups of 19 shows that 19 goes into 798 exactly 42 times.

Answer: 42

✎ For each of the following questions, decide whether to do a mental calculation or a written one. If you need to do a written calculation, do it on a separate piece of paper.

1. 48 ÷ 8 = _____
2. 215 ÷ 5 = _____
3. 350 ÷ 7 = _____

4. Meena bought 125 rose bushes to plant in her 5 flower beds. If she had the same number of rose bushes in each bed, how many rose bushes did she have in each bed? _____

5. Levi had been collecting stickers for 7 years. His collection totalled 868. If he had collected the same number of stickers each year, how many did he collect in one year? _____

6. Joey emptied his penny jar. He had 360 pennies. How many sweets costing 15p could he buy? _____

Remainders

When dividing, the divisor does not always go into the dividend exactly. There may be a remainder.

15 ÷ 2 =

2 goes into 15 seven times to make 14 and 1 remaining. Write the remainder next to a small 'r.', which means 'remainder'.

Answer: 7 r.1

❗ A remainder can be written in three ways: as a remainder (as shown), as a fraction or as a decimal.

Division and remainders

Remainders as fractions

To convert a remainder into a fraction, simply write the remainder above the divisor (the remainder becomes the **numerator** and the divisor becomes the **denominator**). The numerator is the top number in a fraction and the denominator is the bottom number. For example:

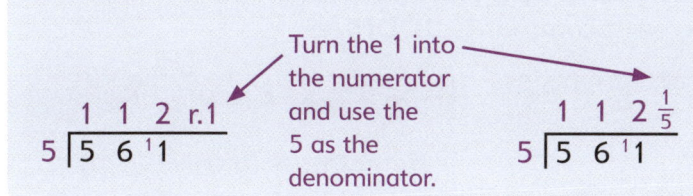

$$\begin{array}{r} 1\ 1\ 2\ \text{r.}1 \\ 5\overline{\smash{)}5\ 6\ ^11} \end{array}$$

Turn the 1 into the numerator and use the 5 as the denominator.

$$\begin{array}{r} 1\ 1\ 2\frac{1}{5} \\ 5\overline{\smash{)}5\ 6\ ^11} \end{array}$$

! The divisor initially becomes the denominator. However, it may be that the fraction can then be simplified. We will look at simplifying fractions on page 53.

Remainders as decimals

To convert a remainder into a decimal, rather than writing the remainder after the quotient, you add a decimal point after the dividend and keep dividing. For example:

Rather than writing the 1 as a remainder, it is carried over and put next to the 0 in the $\frac{1}{10}$ column to make 10.

5 goes into 10 twice, so a 2 is written above.

$$\begin{array}{r} 1\ 1\ 2.2 \\ 5\overline{\smash{)}5\ 6\ ^11.^10} \end{array}$$

Add a decimal point and a 0 in the $\frac{1}{10}$ column.

When solving word problems with remainders, you may need to round the answer up or down.

109 children went on a school trip to the theatre. Each minibus held 10 children. How many minibuses were needed to transport all the children?

10 minibuses will not be enough for 109 children, so the answer needs to be rounded up.

$$\begin{array}{r} 1\ 0\ \text{r.}9 \\ 10\overline{\smash{)}1\ ^10\ 9} \end{array}$$

Answer: 11 minibuses

✏️ Now answer the following questions. For questions 7 to 9, write each remainder as a number, a fraction and a decimal.

7. 98 ÷ 5 = _____

8. 145 ÷ 2 = _____

9. 237 ÷ 10 = _____

10. Al packs eggs into boxes of 6. How many boxes could Al fill with 458 eggs? _____

11. Maddie needs 297 bags of sweets for a festival. There are 7 bags in a box. How many boxes does she need? _____

12. A school buys 1000 balloons. The head teacher divides them between the 12 classes. How many balloons will be left over? _____

Order of operations

You will sometimes come across calculations where there is more than one operation to be carried out.

Operations are the individual parts of calculations, such as $+$, $-$, $\div$, $\times$, ^{2}, ^{3}, $\sqrt{}$ and $\sqrt[3]{}$.

It is not as simple as reading the calculation from left to right and calculating as you go. If you did that, your answer would be incorrect.

You need to know the correct order in which to do the various operations. This process has a number of different names that you should be familiar with. The most common is **BODMAS**.

BODMAS	**BIDMAS**	**PEMDAS**
Brackets	**B**rackets	**P**arentheses (brackets)
Order (powers and roots)	**I**ndices (powers and roots)	**E**xponents (powers and roots)
Division	**D**ivision	**M**ultiplication
Multiplication	**M**ultiplication	**D**ivision
Addition	**A**ddition	**A**ddition
Subtraction	**S**ubtraction	**S**ubtraction

Brackets/Parentheses

The brackets (also known as parentheses) need to be worked out first.

$2 + (3 \times 5) = 2 + 15 = 17$ correct

$2 + (3 \times 5) = 5 \times 5 = 25$ incorrect

! If you see a number followed by a bracket without a sign between them, you need to multiply everything in the brackets by the number outside the brackets. You will still follow the usual order of operations. For example, 3 (2 + 1) means 3 × (2 + 1), so 3 × 3, which is 9. Write the × sign in if it helps you remember to multiply the brackets.

Order/Indices/Exponents

These are the next operations that must be carried out if they are present in a calculation.

The **order** shows how many times a number is used in a calculation. For example, 4^2 means you need to use the 4 twice (4 × 4). It is also known as a power. 4^2 is 4 to the power of 2. Any number can be a power. For example, 10^6, or 10 to the power of 6, means you use 10 six times.
$10 \times 10 \times 10 \times 10 \times 10 \times 10 = 1\,000\,000$.

The most common powers are squared and cubed numbers, for example, 5^2 and 2^3.

The opposite of powers is roots. A root is the original number that was multiplied by itself, so the square root of 36 is 6 as 6^2 (or 6 × 6) is 36. The cube root of 27 is 3 as 3^3 (or 3 × 3 × 3) is 27.

$10 \times 3^2 = 10 \times 9 = 90$ correct

$10 \times 3^2 = 30^2 = 900$ incorrect

Order of operations

Division and multiplication

Division and multiplication have equal weighting. Once any brackets or powers and roots have been calculated, you then have to work out any multiplication or division calculations. As they are equally weighted, you work out whichever comes first in the calculation.

$30 \div 5 \times 3 = 6 \times 3 = 18$ correct

$30 \div 5 \times 3 = 30 \div 15 = 2$ incorrect

Addition and subtraction

As with division and multiplication, addition and subtraction have equal weighting, so you need to do whichever of the calculations comes first.

$15 - 7 + 4 = 8 + 4 = 12$ correct

$15 - 7 + 4 = 15 - 11 = 4$ incorrect

You may be asked to do several operations in the correct order.

$12 + (3 \times 2) - 4^2 =$

Think back to your acronym. First, you must tackle the brackets. $3 \times 2 = 6$, so the calculation now reads:

$12 + 6 - 4^2 =$

You must work out 4^2 next. $4^2 = 16$, so the calculation now reads:

$12 + 6 - 16 =$

As addition and subtraction are equally weighted, you work out the calculations in order from left to right. $12 + 6 = 18$, $18 - 16 = 2$

Answer: 2

TIP Write the individual calculations above each part of the question to help you.

Now answer the following questions.

1. $7 + (3 \times 6) + 2^2 =$ _____

2. $6 \times 4 + 9 \div 3 =$ _____

3. $(4 + 4)^2 \div 2 =$ _____

4. $8 \div 2 + 15 \times 3 =$ _____

5. $18 - 3 \times 4 =$ _____

6. $2^3 \times 7 - 6 + 3 =$ _____

Word problems

When you come across a word problem you need to think about **RUCSAC**:

Read the problem and make sure you understand it.

Underline key words and numbers.

Choose the correct operation(s).

Solve the problem by working out the calculation.

Answer the question (remember the question ends in a ?).

Check your answer. Use the inverse, or estimating, to check it makes sense.

Hiral buys a car costing £12450. He pays £4500 straight away and pays the rest in monthly instalments over a year. How much is each monthly instalment?

Once you have read and understood the problem, look for the important information and underline it.

The numbers are important because they tell you the initial cost and what has already been paid.

Hiral buys a car costing £12450. He pays £4500 straight away and pays the rest in monthly instalments over a year. How much is each monthly instalment?

This will help you work out how many instalments are being paid.

Now you know the important information you need to choose the operations to solve the problem.

1. Work out how much is left to be paid after the £4500 is paid. £12450 − £4500 = £7950

2. Work out how many instalments need to be paid. There are 12 months in a year so 12 instalments.

3. Work out the cost of each instalment by dividing the amount left to be paid (£7950) by 12.

```
        6 6 2.5
1 2 ) 7 ⁷9 ⁷5 ³0.⁶0
```

To check this answer, you could do the inverse.
£662.50 × 12 = £7950, £7950 + £4500 = £12450

Answer: £662.50

Now answer the following questions.

1. Satia has a bookcase with 5 shelves. There are 56 books on the top shelf and twice as many books on each of the other shelves. How many books are there altogether? _____

2. Raniya chooses a number. She multiplies it by 6 then subtracts 11. Her answer is 295. Which number did Raniya choose? _____

3. A teacher needs to buy enough pencils so that each child in her school has 3 each. There are 12 classes each with 31 children in. How many pencils does she need to buy? _____

4. A shop has 18 boxes of milk chocolate bars, 12 boxes of white chocolate bars and 2 boxes of plain chocolate bars. If there are 40 bars in each box, how many chocolate bars are there altogether? _____

5. Oliver has 457 toy cars. He gives 231 to his little brother and 136 to his cousin. How many does he have left? _____

6. A rugby team wants to transport its 2314 supporters to a match. Each coach seats 48 people and costs £398. How much will it cost to transport all the supporters? _____

Function machines

Function machines take numbers in, perform calculations on them and then send out the answers. The first number into the machine will always be the first number out.

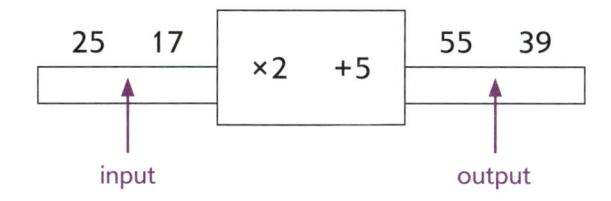

```
25  17  [×2  +5]  55  39
    ↑              ↑
  input          output
```

17 and 25 go in on the left. They are both multiplied by 2 (17 × 2 = 34, 25 × 2 = 50) and then 5 is added (34 + 5 = 39, 50 + 5 = 55). The answers come out on the right.

BODMAS rules do not apply because each calculation within the machine is done separately. You must do the calculations in the order specified on the machine.

If the missing numbers are at the entrance to the machine, you need to work backwards, applying the inverse of the calculation to work out what they are.

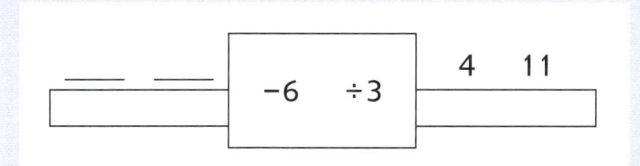

```
__  __  [−6  ÷3]  4  11
```

6 was subtracted from the starting number, then the result was divided by 3 to give the answer 4. Let's work backwards. If we multiply 4 by 3, we get the number that was divided by 3. The number is 12. If we then add 6, we will know what the start number was before subtracting 6. The start number is 18.

Let's try it with 11. 11 × 3 = 33, 33 + 6 = 39. The start number is 39.

Answer: 18 and 39

Now answer the following questions.

1. 12 23 [+12 ×3] __ __

2. 2 8 [×4 −25] __ __

3. −3 −12 [+13 ×9] __ __

4. __ __ [÷2 +7] 37 51

5. __ __ [−16 ×5] 95 30

6. __ __ [×4 ÷6] 8 14

TIP Once you have worked out what the start number is, start the calculation from the beginning to check it works.

Algebra

Algebra is the use of letters or symbols to represent numbers in calculations. You have been doing algebra since you first started maths. 1 + ? = 3 is a sort of algebra because a question mark is used instead of a number. The equals sign tells us that the values to the left equal the values to the right.

Sometimes, you will be given the value of the letters or symbols that have been used and you will need to use these to work out the calculation.

If $a = 8$ and $b = 5$ what is $a + b$?

Replace the letters in the calculation with the values you have been given.
$8 + 5 = 13$

Answer: 13

> If two letters are placed next to each other, you need to multiply them. For example, if $a = 8$ and $b = 5$, then $ab = 8 \times 5 = 40$. If a letter is written over another number, you need to divide. For example, if $a = 8$, then $\frac{a}{2} = a \div 2 = 8 \div 2 = 4$.

Sometimes, you may not be given the value of the symbols.

If $a + 1 = 2a - 5$, what is a?

TIP The 2 in $2a$ doesn't count as a number on its own. It is telling us there are 2 'a's ($2 \times a$).

Work out what a is by moving some of the letters and numbers so that a is on its own on one side of the = sign and a number is on the other. To move a letter or a number, do the opposite operation to both sides of the **equation**.

$a + 1 = 2a - 5$
$\quad\quad\quad +5$
$a + 6 = 2a$
$\quad\quad\quad -a$
$6 = a$

- We have 1 on the left and −5 on the right.
- We need to have 0 on one side. It's always good to remove any negative numbers, so add 5 to both sides.
- We don't need to write the zero in as it isn't worth anything.
- Now the equation only has numbers on the left, so we need to get all the letters onto the right.
- We can subtract an a from each side.

You can double check the answer is correct by putting it into the original equation: $6 + 1 = 12 - 5$. The values to the left and to the right of the equals sign are equal (7), so the answer is correct.

Answer: 6

✎ Now answer the following questions. BODMAS rules apply.

If $a = 3$, $b = 6$ and $c = 7$, work out the answer to these equations.

1. $3c - (a + b) = $ _____

2. $a^2 + (b \div a) + c = $ _____

3. $\frac{bc}{7} + a = $ _____

Solve these equations.

4. If $3a + 6 = 5a - 4$, then $a = $ _____

5. If $4c - 2 = 3c + 1$, then $c = $ _____

6. A baker bases her cake prices (P) on this equation: $P = 35 + 8h + i$, where h is the number of hours taken and i is the cost of the ingredients. If she spends £25 on ingredients and 5 hours making the cake, how much will she charge her client? _____

Number sequences

In order to find missing numbers in number sequences, you first need to identify the rule.

Write the missing numbers in this sequence.

1, 4, 7, 10, 13, _____, _____

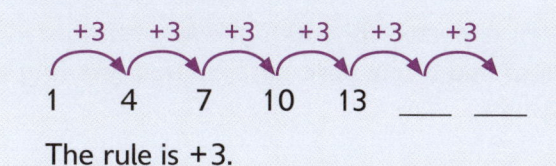

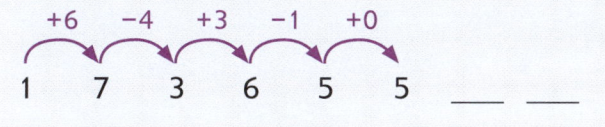

+3 +3 +3 +3 +3 +3
1   4   7   10 13 ___ ___

The rule is +3.

Answer: 1, 4, 7, 10, 13, __16__, __19__

The rule will not always be as simple as adding the same number.

Write the missing numbers in this sequence.

2, 4, 7, _____, 16, 22, _____

+2 +3 +? +? +6 +?
2   4   7   ___ 16 22 ___

The gap between the third number and the fifth number is +9. If this was a +4 jump followed by a +5 jump, it would fit the pattern of the jumps increasing by 1 each time. 7 + 4 is 11, so this is the first missing number. The second missing number will be 22 + 7, which is 29.

Answer: 2, 4, 7, __11__, 16, 22, __29__

Sometimes, you might just recognise the rule. For example, you should recognise 1, 4, 9, 16 and 25 as the first 5 square numbers, which means that the next two numbers in the sequence will be square numbers.

Cube numbers and prime numbers also often appear in number sequences. Some sequences may include **triangular numbers**. These add 1, then 2, then 3, and so on: 1, 3, 6, 10, 15, 21, 28.

In all of the examples above, there is a single rule. Sometimes, there will be more than one rule.

Write the missing numbers in this sequence.   1, 7, 3, 6, 5, 5 _____, _____

+6 −4 +3 −1 +0
1   7   3   6   5   5   ___ ___

There isn't an obvious pattern here so try looking at every second number.

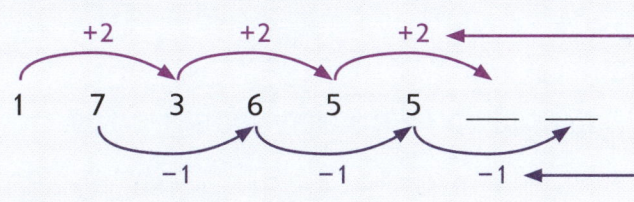

+2   +2   +2
1   7   3   6   5   5   ___ ___
    −1   −1   −1

The first rule is +2 to alternate numbers.

The second rule is −1 to alternate numbers.

Answer: 1, 7, 3, 6, 5, 5, __7__, __4__

Write the missing numbers in these sequences.

1. 6, 13, 20, _____, 34, 41, _____
2. 35, 28, _____, 17, 13, _____, 8
3. 1, _____, 27, 64, _____, 216
4. 5, 6, 10, 9, 15, _____, _____
5. 7, 9, 13, 19, _____, 37, _____
6. 5, _____, −1, −9, −25, −57, _____

Finding the nth term

Sometimes, you won't be asked to find the next number in the sequence but maybe the 100th number or 'term'.

You are not expected to work out every number in the sequence until you get to the 100th one. You need to find a rule that can help you find any number in the sequence. This is known as 'finding the **nth term**'.

> What would the 100th number in this sequence be?
>
> 2, 5, 8, 11, 14, ...

Here, the rule is +3, but we don't want to have to keep adding 3 until we get to the 100th number.

Instead, we can use the number 3 to help us write a formula. You need to give each number in the sequence a position number (n), so for example the number 2 is the 1st number in the sequence and the number 5 is the 2nd number in the sequence.

Position in the sequence	1	2	3	4	5
Number	2	5	8	11	14

Whatever the position of the number is, we multiply that by 3. Look at the answer you get to decide what the next step should be.

Position in the sequence	1 × 3 = 3	2 × 3 = 6	3 × 3 = 9	4 × 3 = 12	5 × 3 = 15
Number	2	5	8	11	14

For the 1st number we have got the answer 3. In order to get the nth term number, which is 2, we need to subtract 1 from 3. Therefore, our formula for finding the number is to multiply it by 3 and then subtract 1. So the formula is $3n - 1$. (We use the letter n to stand for the sequence position, which is why it is called finding the nth term. It is a type of algebra.)

Try the formula with all the other numbers in the sequence.

The 2nd number in the sequence: 2 × 3 = 6,   6 − 1 = 5

The 3rd number in the sequence: 3 × 3 = 9,   9 − 1 = 8

The 4th number in the sequence: 4 × 3 = 12,   12 − 1 = 11

The 5th number in the sequence: 5 × 3 = 15,   15 − 1 = 14

Therefore, to find the 100th number we just follow the formula: 100 × 3 = 300, 300 − 1 = 299.

Answer: 299

> **TIP** Remember that the **nth term** means **any** position in the sequence. You can check your formula with terms you know before you use it to find the term you don't know.

Finding the nth term

It is not just number sequences that need formulas. There will often be questions relating to a number of objects. These work in exactly the same way. Work out the sequence and then apply the formula.

How many lines are needed to make 12 triangles?

1 triangle — 3 lines
2 triangles — 5 lines
3 triangles — 7 lines
4 triangles — 9 lines

The number of lines gives the sequence 3, 5, 7, 9. The rule is +2, so the formula will start with $2n$.

With 1 triangle, $2n = 2 \times 1 = 2$. As there are 3 lines in the triangle, we need to add an extra 1. Therefore, the formula is $2n + 1$.

The calculation to work out the lines needed to make 12 triangles is therefore $2 \times 12 + 1$.

Answer: 25 lines

Now answer the following questions.

1. Look at this sequence.   4, 9, 14, 19, 24, ...

    i)   Write the formula for the nth term.   _____

    ii) What will the 10th number in the sequence be?   _____

2. Look at this sequence.   11, 15, 19, 23, 27, ...

    i)   Write the formula for the nth term.   _____

    ii) What will the 25th number in the sequence be?   _____

3. Look at this sequence.   1, 10, 19, 28, 37, ...

    i)   Write the formula for the nth term.   _____

    ii) What will the 14th number in the sequence be?   _____

4. Look at this sequence.   3, 10, 17, 24, 31, ...

    i)   Write the formula for the nth term.   _____

    ii) What will the 100th number in the sequence be?   _____

5. How many lines are needed to make 16 squares?   _____

6. How many white squares will be in the 99th pattern?   _____

11+ Maths Study and Practice Book

Calculations, algebra and number sequences practice page 1

Now test your skills with these practice pages. If you get stuck, go back to pages 25 to 43 for some reminders.

Addition

1. 72 + 59 = _____
2. 215 + 125 = _____
3. 3735 + 2908 = _____
4. 74 591 + 67 215 = _____
5. Alisha was counting the stickers in her sticker books. She had 25 in one book, 37 in another, 63 in another and 111 in the final book. How many stickers did she have altogether? _____
6. Fern was counting seeds at the garden centre. There were 562 sunflower seeds, 1289 poppy seeds and 351 pumpkin seeds. How many seeds were there altogether? _____

Subtraction

7. 99 − 47 = _____
8. 700 − 251 = _____
9. 4721 − 2067 = _____
10. 5000 − 2467 = _____
11. Kenzo made 126 cupcakes for a cake sale. He sold 78 in the first hour. How many did he have left to sell? _____
12. Naya counted how many steps it took to walk to Poppy's house and back again. She counted 1534 steps on the way there. On the way home, she counted 1386 steps. How many fewer steps did she take on the way home? _____

Multiplying and dividing by 10, 100 and 1000

13. 3.7 × 100 = _____
14. 456 ÷ 1000 = _____
15. 2.06 × 10 = _____
16. 52.8 ÷ 1000 = _____
17. How many times larger than 0.036 is 36? _____
18. Tarek's pet snail weighs 31.08 grams. His pet cat weighs 100 times as much. How much does his cat weigh? _____

Calculations, algebra and number sequences practice page 2

Multiplication

1. 70 × 9 = _____
2. 24 × 4 = _____
3. 45 × 8 = _____
4. 62 × 17 = _____
5. 126 × 23 = _____
6. There are 32 daffodils in Ahmed's garden and 5 times as many snowdrops. How many snowdrops are there? _____

Division and remainders

7. 240 ÷ 8 = _____
8. 360 ÷ 60 = _____
9. 435 ÷ 5 = _____
10. 2954 ÷ 7 = _____
11. There are 360 children in Preena's school. They are spilt evenly across 12 classes. How many children are in each class? _____
12. In a game of cricket, 6 players together scored 456 runs. If the players scored the same number of runs, how many runs did they each score? _____

For questions 13 to 16, write each remainder as a number, a fraction and a decimal.

13. 96 ÷ 5 = _____
14. 374 ÷ 10 = _____
15. 531 ÷ 2 = _____
16. 1067 ÷ 5 = _____
17. An ice cream factory makes 1475 ice creams an hour. They are packed into boxes of 4. How many ice creams will be left over? _____
18. Taxis can hold 6 passengers. If there are 297 people getting taxis to the same venue, how many taxis are needed? _____

Order of operations

19. 4 (3 × 6) + 7 = _____
20. 4 + 9 − 3 × 2 = _____
21. 15 × 2^2 − 6 = _____
22. $(9 + 2)^2$ − 17 = _____
23. 12 × 3 ÷ 2 + (3 − 1) = _____
24. 5^2 − 4 × 3 = _____

11+ Maths Study and Practice Book

Calculations, algebra and number sequences practice page 3

Word problems

1. Tia found 15 dozen balls on the golf course. How many did she find? _____

2. Puja picks 397 plums and needs to pack them up equally into 26 crates. How many plums will go in each crate and how many will be left over? _____

3. At an international netball tournament, the 7 matches are all sell-outs. If the stadium can hold 2327 spectators, how many tickets are sold? _____

4. A house cost £145 614 in 2009 and £307 129 in 2019. By how much has the value of the house increased? _____

5. Fran and her friends go litter picking on the beach. Fran picks up 164 pieces of litter, and her friends both pick up 97 pieces of litter. How many pieces of litter have they collected between them? _____

6. Jenifer is 39 years older than Audrey, who is 12 years older than Christopher. If Christopher is 12, how old is Jenifer? _____

Function machines

7. 16 24 → [+4 ×5] → ___ ___

8. 18 36 → [−14 ×2] → ___ ___

9. ___ ___ → [×3 ÷2] → 15 36

10. 4 15 → [×12 −7] → ___ ___

11. ___ ___ → [+17 −4] → 19 42

12. ___ ___ → [÷5 +9] → 23 17

Algebra

If $a = 5$, $b = 12$, $c = 9$ and $d = 3$, work out the answer to these equations.

13. $3c + b =$ _____

14. $\frac{c}{d} + ab =$ _____

15. $ad - b + c =$ _____

16. $b^2 - d + bc =$ _____

Solve these equations.

17. If $5a + 3 = 3a + 11$, then $a =$ _____

18. If $6b + 9 = 9b - 12$, then $b =$ _____

Calculations, algebra and number sequences practice

Number sequences

Write the missing numbers in these sequences.

1. 3, 7, 11, 15, 19, _____, _____
2. 56, 48, 41, 35, 30, _____, _____
3. 3, 6, 12, 24, 48, _____, _____
4. 81, 64, 49, 36, 25, _____, _____
5. 5, 4, 10, _____, 15, 16, _____, 32
6. 1, 2, _____, 5, 8, 13, _____

Finding the nth term

7. Look at this sequence. 4, 7, 10, 13, 16, ...

   i) Write the formula for the nth term. _____

   ii) What will the 100th number in the sequence be? _____

8. Look at this sequence. 9, 16, 23, 30, 37, ...

   i) Write the formula for the nth term. _____

   ii) What will the 38th number be? _____

9. Look at this sequence. 19, 21, 23, 25, 27, 29, ...

   i) Write the formula for the nth term. _____

   ii) What will the 67th number be? _____

10. Look at this sequence. 13, 19, 25, 31, 37, ...

    i) Write the formula for the nth term. _____

    ii) What will the 98th number be? _____

11. Circle which of the following sequences can be formed from the given rule for the nth term.
    nth term = −6n

    A. −3, −6, −9, −12, −15
    B. −6, −12, −18, −24, −30
    C. −1, −7, −13, −19, −25
    D. 60, 54, 48, 42, 36

12. How many lines will be in the 99th pattern? _____

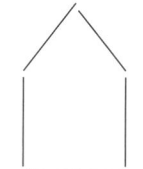

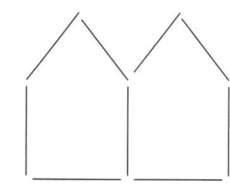

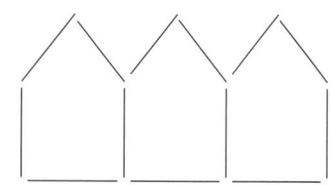

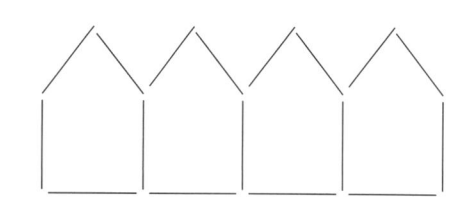

Fractions of shapes

...ts a part of a whole. When a whole is divided into equal parts, each of the parts is a ...ole.

...ten with a top number (numerator) and a bottom number (denominator).

$\frac{1}{2}$ ...umerator tells you how many of those equal parts you have got.
denominator tells you how many equal parts the whole has been divided into.

(!) A **unit fraction** is a fraction where the numerator is 1, for example $\frac{1}{3}$ or $\frac{1}{4}$.

This square has been divided into four equal parts of size $\frac{1}{4}$.

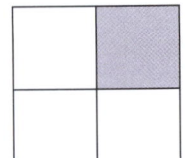

$\frac{1}{4}$ is shaded.

$\frac{3}{4}$ is unshaded.

Sometimes, the shape may not be divided into equal parts. Therefore, you need to work out what equal parts would look like.

What fraction of this shape is shaded?

Even though the square is split into six parts, they are not equal parts and therefore they are not sixths.

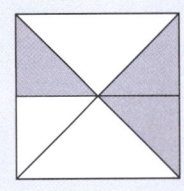

The shaded parts are actually eighths as you can see by adding lines to show the equal fractions.

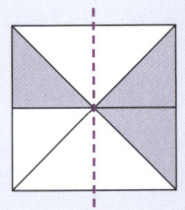

Answer: $\frac{3}{8}$ of the shape is shaded.

What fraction of each shape is shaded?

1. _____

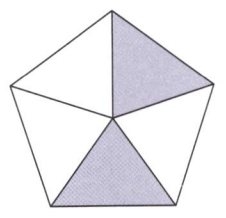

2. _____

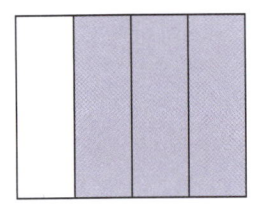

3. _____

4. _____

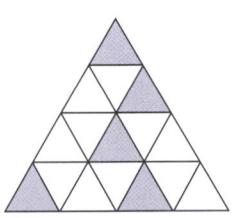

5. _____

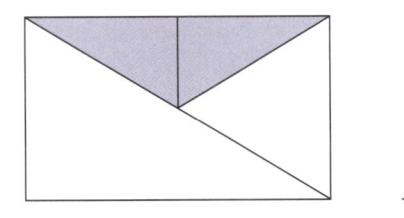

6. _____

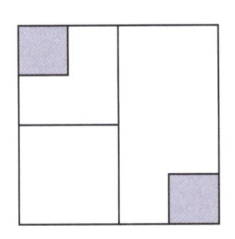

Fractions of quantities

To find a fraction of a quantity, you must first find the unit fraction (the fraction where the numerator is 1). For example, if you need to find $\frac{3}{4}$ of 8, first you need to find $\frac{1}{4}$ of 8. You do this by dividing the number by the denominator. $\frac{1}{4}$ of 8 = 8 ÷ 4 = 2.

If $\frac{1}{4}$ of 8 = 2 then $\frac{3}{4}$ of 8 will be 3 times that. 2 × 3 = 6, so $\frac{3}{4}$ of 8 = 6.

Imagine this square is worth 8.

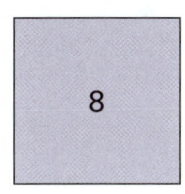

When it is cut into quarters, each quarter will be worth 2.

Three of those quarters will total 6.

You can do this for any number and any fraction. All you have to do is follow the same steps: divide by the denominator and then multiply by the numerator. For example, you can use it to find $\frac{2}{3}$ of 15.

Imagine the square is now worth 15.

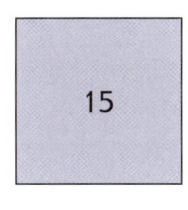

When it is cut into thirds, each third will be worth 5.

Two of those thirds will total 10.

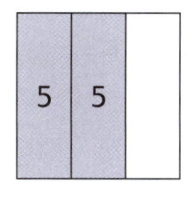

15

15 ÷ 3 = 5

5 × 2 = 10

! To find a fraction of a quantity, divide by the denominator and then multiply by the numerator.

If you are working with measures, it can sometimes be easier to convert the measurement into a different unit of measure first.

What is $\frac{4}{5}$ of 1m?

It's not that easy to divide 1 by 5, so instead think of 1m as 100cm. It is much easier to divide 100 by 5.

100 ÷ 5 = 20   20 × 4 = 80

Answer: 80cm or 0.8m

! If you are trying to find a fraction of a measure (length, mass, capacity, money, time), you must remember to include the unit of measure. Always check whether the question specifies which unit of measure the answer should be written in.

Fractions of quantities

Always read the question carefully so that you know which part of the fraction you are looking for.

> In a class of 30 pupils, $\frac{3}{5}$ are girls. How many are boys?

The question is asking for the number of boys. If $\frac{3}{5}$ of the pupils are girls, then $\frac{2}{5}$ must be boys. You therefore need to work out $\frac{2}{5}$ of 30.

If $\frac{1}{5}$ of 30 = 6 (30 ÷ 5 = 6), then $\frac{2}{5}$ of 30 = 12 (6 × 2 = 12).

TIP While you could work out the number of girls ($\frac{3}{5}$ of 30 = 18) and then subtract that from 30 (30 − 18 = 12), it involves doing two calculations. This will take you longer and also give you more opportunity to make a mistake.

Answer: 12

Sometimes, you may not be told what the whole amount is, but only what the fraction amount is.

> $\frac{5}{9}$ of Harry's friends have brown eyes and the rest have blue. If 25 of Harry's friends have brown eyes, how many have blue eyes?

You are not told how many friends Harry has, only how many a fraction of his friends are. To work out the answer, you need to work in the same way as before and find the unit fraction first.

If 5 of the $\frac{1}{9}$s are worth 25, then dividing 25 by 5 will give you the value of $\frac{1}{9}$.

As $\frac{4}{9}$ of Harry's friends have blue eyes, this must be 20 people because each $\frac{1}{9}$ is worth 5. 5 × 4 = 20

Answer: 20

Now answer the following questions.

1. What is $\frac{5}{6}$ of 30? _____

2. Dania spent 45 minutes doing gymnastics. $\frac{2}{9}$ of the session was spent stretching. How long did Dania spend stretching? _____

3. Anna had a 12m long piece of wool. She used $\frac{2}{3}$ of it. How much did she have left? _____

4. Johnny weighed $\frac{7}{12}$ as much as his dad. If his dad weighed 72kg, how much did Johnny weigh? _____

5. $\frac{5}{8}$ of the animals in a rescue centre were dogs and the rest were cats. If there were 45 dogs, how many cats were there? _____

6. A television was priced at £360. The shop had a $\frac{1}{3}$ off promotion. What was the discounted price? _____

Equivalent fractions

The word equivalent means equal. **Equivalent fractions** are equal (have the same value). Unlike whole numbers, lots of fractions can have the same value.

$\frac{2}{4}$ is equivalent to $\frac{1}{2}$.

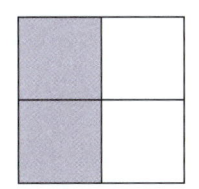

$\frac{2}{3}$ is equivalent to $\frac{8}{12}$.

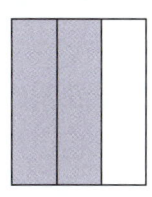

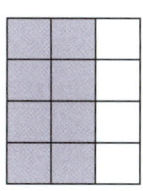

Imagine a cake when thinking of equivalent fractions. If you eat half a cake that is cut into 6 equal pieces, you eat 3 pieces, $\frac{3}{6}$. If the cake was cut into 8 equal pieces you would need to eat 4 pieces, $\frac{4}{8}$, to eat half. Whether you eat $\frac{3}{6}$ or $\frac{4}{8}$ of the cake, you have still eaten the same amount: $\frac{1}{2}$.

When creating an equivalent fraction, the same process must be applied to both the numerator and the denominator. In the example, both the numerator and the denominator have been divided by 2.

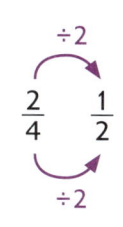

Sometimes you will need to find an equivalent fraction where the numerator and denominator are larger, and sometimes you will need to find an equivalent fraction where the numerator and denominator are smaller.

$\frac{3}{4} = \frac{}{12}$

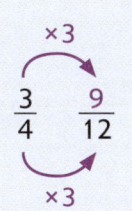

The denominator has changed from a 4 to a 12.

It has been multiplied by 3.

That means the numerator needs to be multiplied by 3 as well.

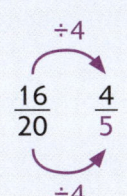

Answer: $\frac{3}{4} = \frac{9}{12}$

$\frac{16}{20} = \frac{4}{}$

The numerator has changed from a 16 to a 4.

It has been divided by 4.

That means the denominator needs to be divided by 4 as well.

Answer: $\frac{16}{20} = \frac{4}{5}$

Write the missing numerator or denominator in each fraction pair.

1. $\frac{3}{8} = \frac{}{24}$

2. $\frac{6}{15} = \frac{2}{}$

3. $\frac{}{7} = \frac{16}{28}$

4. $\frac{18}{} = \frac{9}{10}$

TIP Start by looking at just one fraction and see if any of the other fractions are equivalent.

Circle the two equivalent fractions in each group.

5. $\frac{1}{2}$ $\frac{6}{8}$ $\frac{5}{10}$ $\frac{4}{5}$ $\frac{3}{8}$

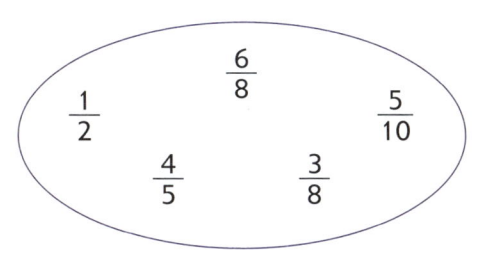

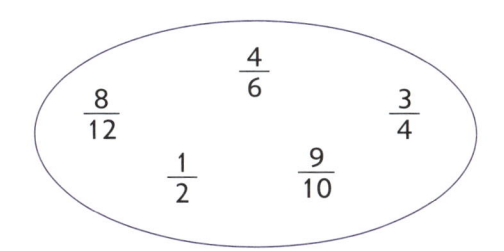

6. $\frac{8}{12}$ $\frac{4}{6}$ $\frac{3}{4}$ $\frac{1}{2}$ $\frac{9}{10}$

Improper fractions and mixed numbers

Improper fractions are fractions where the numerator is larger than the denominator. This means that the fraction is worth more than 1.

For example, if you had 4 cakes cut into halves you would have 8 halves, which you could write as $\frac{8}{2}$. $\frac{8}{2}$ is an improper fraction because the numerator (8) is larger than the denominator (2).

Mixed numbers include a whole number as well as a fraction. For example, $2\frac{1}{2}$ is a mixed number.

It is important that you know how to convert improper fractions into mixed numbers and vice versa.

Write $\frac{8}{5}$ as a mixed number.

First, divide the numerator by the denominator. $8 \div 5 = 1 r.3$

Then put the remainder over the denominator: $1\frac{3}{5}$

Answer: $1\frac{3}{5}$

Write $1\frac{3}{5}$ as an improper fraction.

First, multiply the whole number by the denominator. $1 \times 5 = 5$

Then add the numerator. $5 + 3 = 8$

Then put the answer over the denominator: $\frac{8}{5}$

Answer: $\frac{8}{5}$

> A proper fraction is a fraction in which the numerator is smaller than the denominator (for example, $\frac{1}{8}$). Proper fractions are worth less than one whole.
>
> In an improper fraction, the numerator is larger than the denominator (for example, $\frac{7}{3}$). Improper fractions are worth more than one whole.

Convert these improper fractions into mixed numbers.

1. $\frac{14}{5}$ _____

2. $\frac{9}{4}$ _____

Convert these mixed numbers into improper fractions.

3. $4\frac{1}{6}$ _____

4. $6\frac{3}{8}$ _____

5. How many thirds are there in $16\frac{2}{3}$? _____

6. How many fifths are there in $100\frac{4}{5}$? _____

Simplifying fractions

Knowing how to identify equivalent fractions is very important as you will use it in lots of aspects of fraction work. In particular, when you have worked out a problem involving fractions you will often be asked to write the answer as a fraction in its 'simplest form' or 'lowest terms'. This means that you need to find the equivalent fraction that can be made using the smallest digits. To do this you need to find the largest number that can be divided into both the numerator and the denominator – this is known as the highest common factor (HCF).

Write $\frac{35}{60}$ in its lowest terms.

$\frac{35}{60}$ ← Both the numerator and denominator can be divided by 5.

$\frac{35}{60} \xrightarrow{\div 5} \frac{7}{12}$

7 and 12 have no common factors, so they cannot be made smaller. So $\frac{35}{60}$ can be written as $\frac{7}{12}$ in its lowest terms.

Answer: $\frac{7}{12}$

> Remember to divide the numerator and the denominator by the same number.

Sometimes, you might not know the HCF. Don't worry – you can keep dividing the numerator and the denominator until you find the simplified fraction.

Simplify $\frac{56}{84}$.

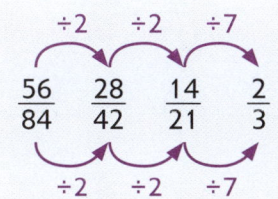

$\frac{56}{84} \xrightarrow{\div 2} \frac{28}{42} \xrightarrow{\div 2} \frac{14}{21} \xrightarrow{\div 7} \frac{2}{3}$

2 and 3 have no common factor, so they cannot be made any smaller.

Answer: $\frac{2}{3}$

> Sometimes, the fraction you are working with may already be written in its simplest form, so you will not be able to find a common factor.

Simplify these fractions.

1. $\frac{24}{28}$ _____
2. $\frac{25}{45}$ _____
3. $\frac{17}{68}$ _____
4. $\frac{12}{19}$ _____
5. $\frac{42}{56}$ _____
6. $\frac{45}{126}$ _____

TIP If the numerator is a prime number, try dividing the denominator by it. For example, $\frac{13}{39} = \frac{1}{3}$.

Ordering fractions

You may be asked to put a group of fractions in order of size – either in ascending or descending order. If all of the fractions have the same denominator, this is straightforward.

> Write these fractions in ascending order. $\frac{1}{8}$ $\frac{4}{8}$ $\frac{3}{8}$ $\frac{7}{8}$ $\frac{2}{8}$
>
> As the denominators are all the same, you need to look at the numerator to determine the size of each fraction.
>
> **Answer:** $\frac{1}{8}$ $\frac{2}{8}$ $\frac{3}{8}$ $\frac{4}{8}$ $\frac{7}{8}$

You are more likely to be asked to order fractions that have different denominators. To do this, you need to convert the fractions so that they all have the same denominator. You need to find the **common denominator** – the common multiple of all the denominators.

When looking for the common denominator, always start with the biggest denominator you have. Do all the other numbers go into it? If not, count up in that number until you find the number that can be divided by all the other denominators.

> Write these fractions in ascending order. $\frac{2}{5}$ $\frac{12}{20}$ $\frac{3}{10}$ $\frac{1}{2}$ $\frac{3}{4}$
>
> There are lots of possible common denominators: 20, 40, 60, 80. It's a good idea to use the lowest common denominator so that the calculations will be easier. In this case 20 is divisible by all the denominators.
>
> Now convert all the fractions into fractions with a denominator of 20. Remember, whatever you do to the bottom you do to the top.
>
> $\frac{2}{5} \xrightarrow{\times 4} \frac{8}{20}$ $\frac{12}{20} \xrightarrow{\times 1} \frac{12}{20}$ $\frac{3}{10} \xrightarrow{\times 2} \frac{6}{20}$ $\frac{1}{2} \xrightarrow{\times 10} \frac{10}{20}$ $\frac{3}{4} \xrightarrow{\times 5} \frac{15}{20}$
>
> It is now much easier to put them in order. Starting with the smallest:
>
> $\frac{6}{20}$ $\frac{8}{20}$ $\frac{10}{20}$ $\frac{12}{20}$ $\frac{15}{20}$
>
> You must write your answer with the fractions in their original form.
>
> **Answer:** $\frac{3}{10}$ $\frac{2}{5}$ $\frac{1}{2}$ $\frac{12}{20}$ $\frac{3}{4}$

> ❗ Remember that you must always write the fractions in your answers in the same form that they were written in the question. Go back and check them if you have time.

Ordering fractions

If the numbers you need to order are mixed numbers, there are two things you need to do.

1. Look at the whole number. For example, for the fractions $1\frac{1}{5}$, $5\frac{4}{6}$ and $3\frac{2}{5}$, it is clear from the value of the ones (the whole number in the mixed number) that $1\frac{1}{5}$ is the smallest and $5\frac{4}{6}$ is the largest.

2. If the whole numbers are all the same or some of the whole numbers are the same, then just the fraction parts need to be converted into equivalent fractions.

> When ordering fractions, you do not need to find the common denominator of all the fractions, just the ones with the same whole numbers.

Write these fractions in ascending order. $1\frac{2}{3}$ $2\frac{4}{5}$ $1\frac{3}{8}$ $2\frac{5}{6}$ $2\frac{3}{4}$

The two mixed numbers that have 1 as the whole number are smaller than the three mixed numbers with 2 as the whole number. You can work out which of the mixed numbers starting with 1 is the smaller just by comparing the fraction parts, $\frac{2}{3}$ and $\frac{3}{8}$. The lowest common denominator is 24. $\frac{2}{3} = \frac{16}{24}$ (×8) and $\frac{3}{8} = \frac{9}{24}$ (×3). Since $\frac{9}{24}$ is smaller than $\frac{16}{24}$, then $1\frac{3}{8}$ is smaller than $1\frac{2}{3}$.

Now compare the fraction parts of the mixed numbers beginning with 2. The lowest common denominator is 60, so $\frac{4}{5} = \frac{48}{60}$ (×12), $\frac{5}{6} = \frac{50}{60}$ (×10) and $\frac{3}{4} = \frac{45}{60}$ (×15). Since $\frac{45}{60}$ is the smallest, followed by $\frac{48}{60}$ and then by $\frac{50}{60}$, the order of the mixed numbers is $2\frac{3}{4}$, $2\frac{4}{5}$, $2\frac{5}{6}$.

Answer: $1\frac{3}{8}$ $1\frac{2}{3}$ $2\frac{3}{4}$ $2\frac{4}{5}$ $2\frac{5}{6}$

Write these fractions in ascending order.

1. $\frac{2}{3}$ $\frac{6}{8}$ $\frac{11}{12}$ $\frac{5}{6}$ $\frac{1}{2}$ _____

2. $3\frac{1}{4}$ $3\frac{5}{8}$ $3\frac{4}{7}$ $2\frac{3}{4}$ $3\frac{9}{14}$ _____

3. $\frac{4}{6}$ $\frac{5}{9}$ $\frac{1}{3}$ $\frac{1}{2}$ $\frac{1}{4}$ _____

> **TIP** There are lots of numbers that can be the common denominator. You will still get the right answer no matter which common denominator you use. However, the calculations will be simpler if you try to find the lowest common denominator.

Write these fractions in descending order.

4. $\frac{9}{10}$ $\frac{3}{4}$ $\frac{16}{25}$ $\frac{7}{20}$ $\frac{3}{5}$ _____

5. $6\frac{5}{6}$ $5\frac{2}{3}$ $6\frac{1}{2}$ $5\frac{3}{5}$ $5\frac{7}{10}$ _____

6. $10\frac{2}{11}$ $12\frac{1}{10}$ $10\frac{11}{12}$ $10\frac{7}{9}$ $10\frac{1}{6}$ _____

Adding and subtracting fractions

To add and subtract fractions, the denominators must be the same. You can then add or subtract the numerators. For example:

$\frac{1}{5} + \frac{2}{5} = \frac{3}{5}$

If the denominators are not the same, you first need to convert the fractions into equivalent fractions that have a common denominator.

$\frac{3}{4} - \frac{1}{3} =$

$\frac{3}{4} - \frac{1}{3}$ → $\frac{3}{4}$ ×3→ $\frac{9}{12}$; $\frac{1}{3}$ ×4→ $\frac{4}{12}$ → $\frac{9}{12} - \frac{4}{12} = \frac{5}{12}$

The common denominator is 12 as 12 can be divided by both 3 and 4.

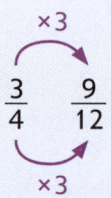

As $\frac{5}{12}$ cannot be simplified, it is the answer.

Answer: $\frac{5}{12}$

> You should always give the answer in its lowest terms.

When adding fractions, you may end up with an improper fraction as an answer. If this happens, you should convert the improper fraction into a mixed number.

$\frac{5}{6} + \frac{5}{8} =$

$\frac{5}{6} + \frac{5}{8}$ → $\frac{5}{6}$ ×4→ $\frac{20}{24}$; $\frac{5}{8}$ ×3→ $\frac{15}{24}$ → $\frac{20}{24} + \frac{15}{24} = \frac{35}{24}$ → So $\frac{5}{6} + \frac{5}{8} = 1\frac{11}{24}$

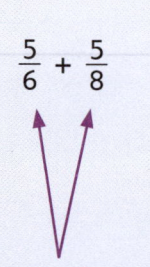

The common denominator is 24 as 24 can be divided by both 6 and 8.

This is an improper fraction, as the numerator is bigger than the denominator.

Simplify $\frac{35}{24}$ by dividing the numerator by the denominator: 35 ÷ 24 = 1r.11. Put the remainder over the denominator to get $1\frac{11}{24}$.

Answer: $1\frac{11}{24}$

Adding and subtracting fractions

If you are adding mixed numbers, you can add the whole numbers first, then add the fractions. If adding the fractions gives you an improper fraction, don't forget to add on the whole number once you have converted it into a mixed number.

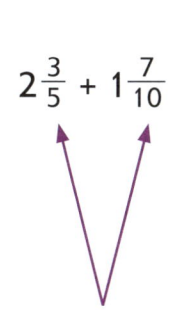

$2\frac{3}{5} + 1\frac{7}{10}$ → $2 + 1 = 3$ → $\frac{3}{5} \xrightarrow{\times 2} \frac{6}{10}$ → $\frac{6}{10} + \frac{7}{10} = \frac{13}{10} = 1\frac{3}{10}$ → $3 + 1\frac{3}{10} = 4\frac{3}{10}$

- The common denominator is 10 as 10 can be divided by both 5 and 10.
- Add the whole numbers.
- Convert the fraction.
- Add the two fractions.
- Add the whole number to the mixed number.

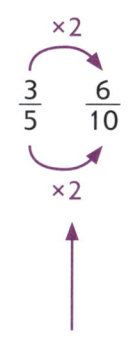

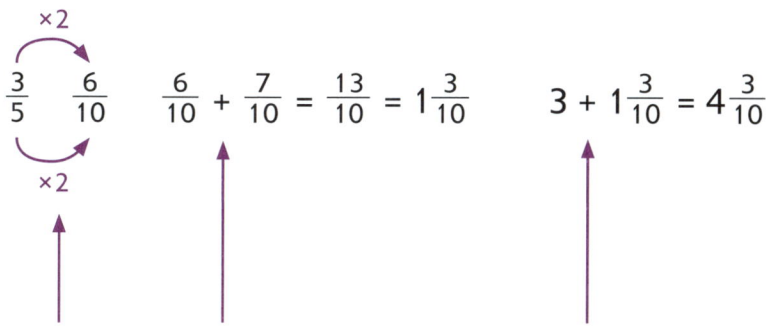

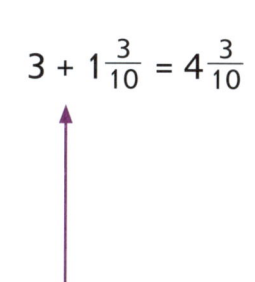

If you are subtracting mixed numbers, you need to convert them into improper fractions before trying to do the subtraction calculation. This is because the fraction in the first mixed number may be smaller than the second fraction, so you would not be able to carry out the subtraction.

$3\frac{1}{4} - 1\frac{3}{4} =$

You could subtract the whole numbers (3 − 1 = 2), but you cannot subtract the fractions because $\frac{1}{4}$ is smaller than $\frac{3}{4}$. Instead, you will need to convert the mixed numbers into improper fractions before you carry out the subtraction.

$3\frac{1}{4} = \frac{13}{4}$ $1\frac{3}{4} = \frac{7}{4}$

Now that you have two improper fractions you can carry out the subtraction.

$\frac{13}{4} - \frac{7}{4} = \frac{6}{4}$

After you have finished your calculation, you will need to convert your improper fraction back into a mixed number. Remember to simplify the mixed number if it can be simplified.

$\frac{6}{4} = 1\frac{2}{4}$, which can be simplified to $1\frac{1}{2}$.

Answer: $1\frac{1}{2}$

Now answer the following questions.

1. $\frac{2}{7} + \frac{3}{9} =$ _____

2. $\frac{4}{8} - \frac{1}{5} =$ _____

3. $\frac{5}{6} + \frac{9}{10} =$ _____

4. $2\frac{2}{5} - 1\frac{10}{12} =$ _____

5. $5\frac{1}{2} + 2\frac{5}{8} =$ _____

6. $4\frac{1}{4} - 2\frac{8}{9} =$ _____

Multiplying and dividing fractions

When you multiply and divide fractions, it doesn't matter if they have different denominators.

To multiply fractions, you simply multiply the numerators and multiply the denominators.

$\frac{1}{3} \times \frac{3}{4} =$

Start by multiplying the numerators. $1 \times 3 = 3$

Then multiply the denominators. $3 \times 4 = 12$

Now you know that $\frac{1}{3} \times \frac{3}{4} = \frac{3}{12}$. However, both 3 and 12 are divisible by 3, so this fraction can be simplified. Divide both the numerator and the denominator by 3 to get $\frac{1}{4}$.

Answer: $\frac{1}{4}$

⚠ When you multiply whole numbers, the answers are always bigger than the numbers you start with (unless you multiply by 1, in which case the answer will stay the same). When multiplying proper fractions, the answers will be smaller.

When you divide fractions, the process is similar.

You flip the second fraction and then multiply them.

$\frac{4}{5} \div \frac{2}{3} =$

First, you need to rearrange this so that you are multiplying rather than dividing. Flip the second fraction upside down.

$\frac{4}{5} \times \frac{3}{2} =$

Then multiply the numerators and the denominators to get your new fraction.

$4 \times 3 = 12$

$5 \times 2 = 10$

$\frac{12}{10}$ is an improper fraction because the numerator is bigger than the denominator. It needs to be turned into a mixed number and simplified.

$\frac{12}{10} = 1\frac{2}{10} = 1\frac{1}{5}$

Answer: $1\frac{1}{5}$

⚠ When you divide whole numbers, the answers are always smaller than the numbers you start with. When dividing fractions, the answers will be bigger.

✏ Now answer the following questions.

1. $\frac{3}{4} \times \frac{5}{7} =$ _____

2. $\frac{1}{9} \times \frac{4}{6} =$ _____

3. $\frac{2}{5} \times \frac{8}{10} =$ _____

4. $\frac{6}{9} \div \frac{1}{4} =$ _____

5. $\frac{9}{14} \div \frac{2}{7} =$ _____

6. $\frac{2}{3} \div \frac{1}{6} =$ _____

Fraction sequences

As with number sequences (see page 41), it is important to find the rule when looking to see what the next fraction in a sequence is going to be.

Write the next two fractions in the sequence. $\frac{1}{8}, \frac{2}{8}, \frac{3}{8}, \frac{4}{8}, \frac{5}{8},$ _____ , _____

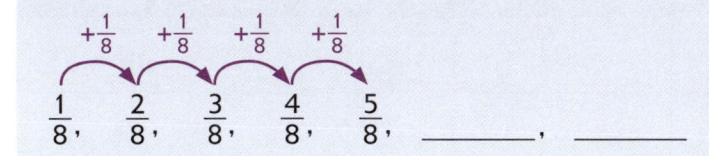

$\frac{1}{8}, \frac{2}{8}, \frac{3}{8}, \frac{4}{8}, \frac{5}{8},$ _____ , _____ (with $+\frac{1}{8}$ jumps shown)

$\frac{1}{8}$ is being added each time. Continue the pattern from the last term you are given.

Answer: $\frac{1}{8}, \frac{2}{8}, \frac{3}{8}, \frac{4}{8}, \frac{5}{8}, \underline{\frac{6}{8}}, \underline{\frac{7}{8}}$

You may need to convert the fractions into equivalents before you are able to identify the rule.

Write the next two fractions in the sequence. Write your answers in their simplest form.

$\frac{1}{12}, \frac{1}{6}, \frac{1}{4}, \frac{1}{3}, \frac{5}{12},$ _____ , _____

$\frac{1}{12}, \frac{2}{12}, \frac{3}{12}, \frac{4}{12}, \frac{5}{12},$ _____ , _____

In order to make it easier to identify the rule, you need to convert the fractions so that they all have the same denominator. The common denominator is 12.

Now the denominators are the same, it is much easier to spot the rule. $\frac{1}{12}$ is being added each time but a simplified fraction is being written down.

Answer: $\frac{1}{12}, \frac{1}{6}, \frac{1}{4}, \frac{1}{3}, \frac{5}{12}, \underline{\frac{1}{2}}, \underline{\frac{7}{12}}$

Write the missing fractions in these sequences. Write your answers in their simplest form.

1. $\frac{1}{4}, \frac{1}{2}, \frac{3}{4}, 1,$ _____ , _____

2. $5, 4\frac{2}{3}, 4\frac{1}{3}, 4,$ _____ , _____

3. $\frac{1}{10}, \frac{1}{5}, \frac{3}{10}, \frac{2}{5},$ _____ , _____

4. $1\frac{7}{16}, 1\frac{3}{8}, 1\frac{5}{16}, 1\frac{1}{4},$ _____ , _____

5. _____ , $\frac{3}{4},$ _____ , $1\frac{3}{4}, 2\frac{1}{4}, 2\frac{3}{4}$

6. $5\frac{5}{6},$ _____ , $5\frac{1}{2}, 5\frac{1}{3},$ _____ , 5

11+ Maths Study and Practice Book

Decimal fractions

Decimal fractions are more commonly referred to simply as decimals.

They are the digits located to the right of the decimal point. They are called decimal fractions because their values are fractions whose denominators are powers of 10. The value of each digit is 10 times greater than the digit to the right.

	T	O	.	$\frac{1}{10}$	$\frac{1}{100}$	$\frac{1}{1000}$
2 =	0	2	.	0	0	0
$\frac{2}{10}$ =	0	0	.	2	0	0
$\frac{2}{100}$ =	0	0	.	0	2	0
$\frac{2}{1000}$ =	0	0	.	0	0	2

You may be asked to identify a decimal on a number line. It is very important that you look carefully at the start and finish numbers on the line and the number of points along the number line.

There are 10 'spaces' between the 0 and the 1, so each point along the number line is worth $\frac{1}{10}$.

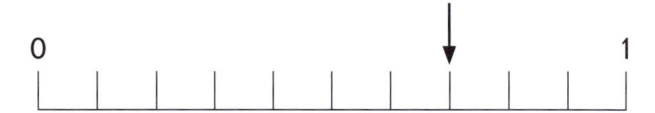

The arrow is therefore pointing to 0.7 on the number line.

You will also need to know what each digit within a decimal fraction is worth.

Give the values of the underlined digits.   1.3<u>4</u>2

The 4 is in the $\frac{1}{100}$ column, so it is worth $\frac{4}{100}$.

Answer: $\frac{4}{100}$

✏️ What decimal fraction is each arrow pointing at?

1. _____ (between 1 and 2)

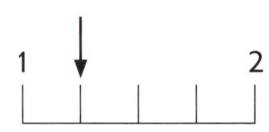

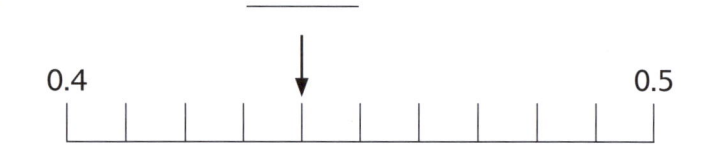

2. _____ (between 0.4 and 0.5)

Give the values of the underlined digits.

3. 19.7<u>3</u>6 _____

4. 3.<u>1</u>09 _____

Write these decimal fractions as fractions.

5. 6.78 _____

6. 17.891 _____

Ordering decimals

It is important to understand the value of each digit in a decimal fraction. However, when ordering decimals, there is a much easier way to work out which numbers are larger or smaller.

> Write these decimals in ascending order.   3.12   3.01   3.11   3.31   3.03
>
> To work out the order from smallest to largest, ignore the decimal point and read them as whole numbers.
>
> 312   301   311   331   303
>
> This makes it a lot easier to see the order in which they should be written.
>
> 301   303   311   312   331
>
> **Answer: 3.01   3.03   3.11   3.12   3.31**

! Don't forget to put the decimal points back in when you write the answer.

In the example above, all the numbers have 2 digits after the decimal place. It is important that all the numbers have the same number of decimal places. If some of the numbers have fewer digits after the decimal place, you need to add zeros to the end. This will not change the value of the decimal.

> Write these decimals in ascending order.   2.011   2.1   2.11   2.01   2.001
>
> Two of these numbers (2.011 and 2.001) have 3 digits after the decimal place, so you need to make sure all the numbers are written to 3 decimal places.
>
> 2.011   2.100   2.110   2.010   2.001   ← Add on zeros so that all the numbers have the same number of digits after the decimal point.
>
> 2011   2100   2110   2010   2001   ← Now you can ignore the decimal points and read them as whole numbers.
>
> 2001   2010   2011   2100   2110   ← Put them in order.
>
> 2.001   2.010   2.011   2.100   2.110   ← Add back in the decimal points.
>
> 2.001   2.01   2.011   2.1   2.11   ← Remember to take off any extra zeros you added.
>
> **Answer: 2.001   2.01   2.011   2.1   2.11**

Write these decimals in ascending order.

1. 6.34   6.304   6.341   6.43   0.6   _____
2. 1.011   1.101   0.1   1.1   1.111   _____
3. 12.3   1.23   12.03   10.23   1.3   _____

Write these decimals in descending order.

4. 9.07   90.7   9.7   9.701   9.17   _____
5. 1.851   1.58   1.815   1.18   8.1   _____
6. 34.7   34.07   34.73   37.4   34.3   _____

Rounding decimals

Rounding decimals uses exactly the same rules as rounding whole numbers.

Look at the digit in the column to the right of the number you are rounding to. If the digit is less than 5, you round down. If the digit is 5 or more, you round up.

> Round 1.46 to the nearest $\frac{1}{10}$.

1.46   Look at the digit to the right of the $\frac{1}{10}$ column. It's a 6, which is greater than 5, so the $\frac{1}{10}$ digit needs to round up to 5.

Use this digit to decide whether to round up or down.

Answer: 1.5

Rather than being asked to 'round to the nearest $\frac{1}{10}$', you will usually be asked to write a number 'correct to 1 decimal place', and, rather than 'rounding to the nearest $\frac{1}{100}$', you may be asked to write a number 'correct to 2 decimal places'.

Whether you are asked to round a number or write the number correct to a certain number of decimal places, you must make sure you write your answer with any zeros there might be to show you are working with decimals.

> Write 3.04 correct to 1 decimal place.

Don't write this as 3. You should keep the 0 to show you have rounded to 1 decimal place.

Answer: 3.0

> Write 6.001 correct to 2 decimal places.

Don't write this as 6. You should keep the two 0s to show you have rounded to 2 decimal places.

Answer: 6.00

! The exception to this rule is if you are asked to write your answer as a whole number, in which case you should not include a decimal point.

✎ Now answer the following questions.

1. Round 7.37 to the nearest $\frac{1}{10}$.   _____

2. Round 14.672 to the nearest $\frac{1}{100}$.   _____

3. Write 5.173 correct to 1 decimal place.   _____

4. Write 18.429 correct to 2 decimal places.   _____

5. Write 6.99 correct to 1 decimal place.   _____

6. Write 21.133 correct to 2 decimal places.   _____

Adding and subtracting decimals

As with adding and subtracting whole numbers, when adding and subtracting decimals you need to decide whether to carry out a mental or a written calculation.

The most important thing to remember is the value of the decimals. Sometimes, it might help to think about how many tenths, hundredths or thousandths they are worth (see page 60).

> 0.8 + 0.6 =
>
> 0.8 + 0.6 does not equal 0.14 just because 8 + 6 = 14. Think carefully about the value of the decimals.
>
> 0.8 is the same as $\frac{8}{10}$ and 0.6 is the same as $\frac{6}{10}$. $\frac{8}{10} + \frac{6}{10}$ would not equal $\frac{14}{100}$.
>
> Instead it equals $\frac{14}{10}$ which, as an improper fraction, is equal to the mixed number $1\frac{4}{10} = 1.4$.
>
> **Answer: 1.4**

As long as you remember that, then the same types of rules apply, such as looking for number bonds. For example, 2.8 + 3.2 = 6. You know that 0.8 + 0.2 = 1.0, so you can add on the whole numbers.

When you add and subtract decimals, the answers will have the same digits as if you were adding or subtracting whole numbers. For example, 26 − 11 = 15 and 2.6 − 1.1 = 1.5.

The easiest and most accurate way to add or subtract decimals, especially when working with hundredths and thousandths, is to carry out a vertical calculation. You use the same method that you would use to add or subtract whole numbers. Keep the decimal points in the same column.

```
  3.6 7 1          By lining up the decimal
+ 2.9 2            points you can be sure that
---------          all the other digits are in the
  6.5 9 1          correct columns.
    1
```

```
    3 12
  7.⁴4 ³3 ¹0       If necessary, put a 0 at
− 4.2 7 4          the end of decimals when
---------          subtracting to make them
  3.1 5 6          the same length.
```

! As long as you line up the decimal points in your calculation, then all the other digits will line up in the correct place.

Now answer the following questions.

1. 2.6 + 2.6 = _____

2. 3.7 − 2.9 = _____

3. 4.783 + 2.96 = _____

4. 18.09 − 13.046 = _____

5. 12.7 + 8.455 = _____

6. 56.01 − 23.743 = _____

Multiplying and dividing decimals

Multiplying decimals

Regardless of whether you are planning to multiply decimals mentally or using a written method, the easiest way to work out the answer is to multiply the decimals by 10, 100 or 1000 in order to create whole numbers. Once you have multiplied the whole numbers, you then need to divide the answer by the same factor that was used to multiply.

9.6 × 7 =

9.6 × 10 = 96 and 96 × 7 = 672

Then divide this answer by 10: 672 ÷ 10 = 67.2

Answer: 67.2

If you have to multiply both numbers, then you have to divide the answer by both factors.

0.8 × 0.4 =

0.8 × 10 = 8
0.4 × 10 = 4   8 × 4 = 32

As you multiplied two numbers by 10, you have to then divide the answer by 10 twice.

32 ÷ 10 = 3.2 and 3.2 ÷ 10 = 0.32 (the same as dividing by 100)

Answer: 0.32

An easier way to work this out is to remember that the number of digits after the decimal points in the question will be the same as in the answer.

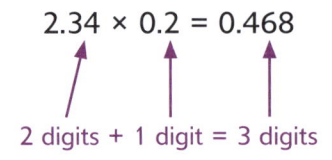

1.1 × 1.2 = 1.32
1 digit + 1 digit = 2 digits

2.34 × 0.2 = 0.468
2 digits + 1 digit = 3 digits

You can also estimate the answer in order to check that you have got the decimal point in the correct place. Ignore the digits after the decimal point and just multiply the whole numbers.

4.9 × 3.4 =   4 × 3 = 12, so the answer will be approximately 12.

49 × 34 = 1666

The answer needs to be approximately 12. Putting the decimal point after the first 6 gives the answer closest to 12. Putting the decimal point in the other positions gives 1.666, 166.6 or 1666, none of which are close to 12.

Answer: 16.66

✏️ Now answer the following questions.

1. 0.9 × 0.5 = _____
2. 12 × 0.6 = _____
3. 2.4 × 0.8 = _____
4. 13.2 × 7 = _____
5. 15.6 × 1.6 = _____
6. 9.6 × 4.12 = _____

Multiplying and dividing decimals

Dividing decimals

Dividing decimals works in a similar way. The division is much easier if you multiply the decimals first so that they are whole numbers. However, you only need to divide the answer if you have only multiplied one of the numbers.

> 4.2 ÷ 7 =
>
> 4.2 × 10 = 42, so work out 42 ÷ 7 = 6. Then divide the answer by 10, which gives 6 ÷ 10 = 0.6.
>
> **Answer: 0.6**

! As with multiplying, the order of the digits will always stay the same when you reintroduce the decimal point.

If you have to multiply both numbers by the same amount, then you don't have to change the answer at all.

> 4.5 ÷ 0.9 =
>
> 4.5 × 10 = 45 and 0.9 × 10 = 9, so work out 45 ÷ 9 = 5.
>
> If 45 ÷ 9 = 5, then 4.5 ÷ 0.9 = 5 as well, as you have multiplied both numbers by 10.
>
> **Answer: 5**

TIP Because the numbers in the first part of the calculation are always multiplied by the same amount, the answer remains the same when they are then divided.

If the numbers have to be multiplied by different amounts to become whole numbers, it is a better idea to multiply both by the same amount.

> 5.5 ÷ 0.11 =
>
> 5.5 only needs to be multiplied by 10 to become a whole number, but 0.11 needs to be multiplied by 100. As you need to multiply both numbers by the **same** amount and you want both numbers to become whole numbers, you need to multiply both by 100.
>
> 5.5 × 100 = 550 and 0.11 × 100 = 11, so work out 550 ÷ 11 = 50.
>
> **Answer: 50**

Now answer the following questions.

7. 2.5 ÷ 5 = _____
8. 8.1 ÷ 9 = _____
9. 4.8 ÷ 0.08 = _____
10. 5.1 ÷ 0.17 = _____
11. 4.48 ÷ 1.4 = _____
12. 10.12 ÷ 0.22 = _____
13. Jacob has £13.25. A bag of oranges costs £1.29. How many bags of oranges can Jacob buy? _____

Percentages

The words 'per cent' mean 'out of 100'. A per cent is a fraction out of 100. The symbol for per cent is %. This grid is made up of 100 squares. Each tinted shape makes up a **percentage** of the grid.

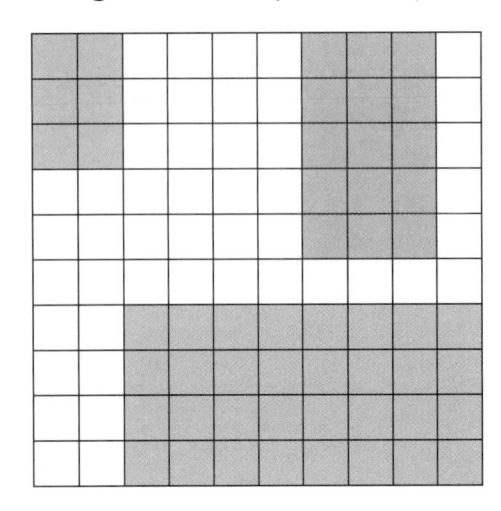

The top-left rectangle contains 6 squares. $\frac{6}{100}$ = 6%.
The top-left rectangle takes up 6% of the grid.

The top-right rectangle contains 15 squares. $\frac{15}{100}$ = 15%.
The top-right rectangle takes up 15% of the grid.

The bottom rectangle contains 32 squares. $\frac{32}{100}$ = 32%.
The bottom rectangle takes up 32% of the grid.

1% is 1 out of 100   50% is 50 out of 100   100% is 100 out of 100

The easiest way to find a percentage of a number is to find 10% first.

10% = $\frac{10}{100}$ = $\frac{1}{10}$ so 10% is $\frac{1}{10}$, which is the same as dividing by 10.

10% of 60 = 6 because 60 ÷ 10 = 6.

Once you have found 10%, you can find other percentages.

20%	20% is 2 lots of 10%. 20% of 60 = **12** (as 6 × 2 = 12)
30%	30% is 3 lots of 10%. 30% of 60 = **18** (as 6 × 3 = 18)
5%	You can use 10% to find 5% as 5% is half of 10%. 5% of 60 = **3** (as 6 ÷ 2 = 3)
15%	To find 15% of 60, add together 10% and 5%. 15% of 60 = **9** (as 6 + 3 = 9)
1%	You can also use 10% to find 1%. 10% ÷ 10 = 1%. 1% of 60 = **0.6** (as 6 ÷ 10 = 0.6)
2%	2% would be 2 lots of 1%. 2% of 60 = **1.2** (as 2 × 0.6 = 1.2)

TIP To find 1%, you can divide the number by 100 as 1% is $\frac{1}{100}$. However, it is much easier to find 10% first, then adjust.

There are some percentages you should recognise:
10% = $\frac{1}{10}$ 20% = $\frac{1}{5}$ 25% = $\frac{1}{4}$ 50% = $\frac{1}{2}$ 75% = $\frac{3}{4}$

Percentages

You will need to be able to use percentages to work out word problems. When you are asked to solve a word problem, make sure that you read the question carefully so that you know what it is asking you. You can then identify the important information in the question and work out the correct answer.

> 70% of the children in Jamie's class have brown hair. If there are 30 children in his class altogether, how many do not have brown hair?

First, read the question carefully. You need to work out the **number** of children who do **not** have brown hair, but you are only given the **percentage** of children who **do** have brown hair.

You can start by working out the percentage of children who do not have brown hair. If 70% have brown hair, then 30% do not have brown hair.

You now know you need to find 30% of the total number of children in the class, which is 30. Remember that you always find 10% first.

10% of 30 = 3

30% of 30 = 9 (because 3 × 3 = 9), so 9 children do not have brown hair.

Answer: 9

TIP You could have worked out how many children have brown hair and then subtracted that from the whole class to find out how many do not have brown hair. However, you run the risk of writing down how many have brown hair as you may forget that you then have to work out how many don't have brown hair.

Now answer the following questions.

1. What is 35% of 20? __7__

2. What is 20% of 56? __11.2__

3. What is 62% of 80? __49.6__

4. Milly has 80 sweets. 45% of them are red. How many red sweets does she have? __36__

5. A supermarket puts 120 boxes of washing powder on the shelves first thing on Monday morning. By lunchtime, 65% have been sold. How many boxes are left on the shelf? __42__

6. The price of a jumper is £32. It is reduced by 15% in the sales. What is its new price? __£27.20__

7. The cost of a TV increases by 17%. It was originally £450. What is its new price? __£526.50__

TIP Remember that it is often a good idea to start by working out 10%.

Converting between fractions, decimals and percentages

Fractions, decimals and percentages can all be linked by common denominators. This helps when you need to convert between them.

Fractions can have any denominator.

Decimals have denominators that are powers of 10. For example, 10, 100, 1000.

Percentages only have 100 as a denominator.

To convert between them, you just need to find the common denominator

Fraction to decimal – the denominator needs to become a power of 10.

$$\frac{1}{4} = \frac{25}{100} = 0.25 \quad (\times 25) \qquad \frac{2}{5} = \frac{4}{10} = 0.4 \quad (\times 2)$$

Fraction to percentage – the denominator needs to become 100.

$$\frac{3}{4} = \frac{75}{100} = 75\% \quad (\times 25) \qquad \frac{13}{20} = \frac{65}{100} = 65\% \quad (\times 5)$$

Decimal to fraction – whichever column the final digit is in, that is the denominator. You may then need to simplify your answer.

$$0.6 = \frac{6}{10} = \frac{3}{5} \quad (\div 2) \qquad 0.37 = \frac{37}{100}$$

Decimal to percentage – turn the decimal into a fraction, then convert the denominator to 100 if necessary.

$$0.66 = \frac{66}{100} = 66\% \qquad 0.175 = \frac{175}{1000} = \frac{17.5}{100} = 17.5\% \quad (\div 10)$$

Percentage to fraction – turn the percentage into a fraction over 100, then simplify if necessary.

$$47\% = \frac{47}{100} \qquad 84\% = \frac{84}{100} = \frac{21}{25} \quad (\div 4)$$

Percentage to decimal – the percentage can be turned straight into a decimal in the $\frac{1}{100}$ column.

$$35\% = 0.35$$

> **!** It is a good idea to memorise certain conversions.
>
> $\frac{1}{2} = 0.5 = 50\%$ $\frac{1}{4} = 0.25 = 25\%$ $\frac{3}{4} = 0.75 = 75\%$ $\frac{1}{10} = 0.1 = 10\%$ $\frac{1}{8} = 0.125 = 12.5\%$
>
> Some conversions will require rounding to a certain number of decimal places, for example $\frac{1}{3} = 0.33 = 33.3\%$.

Complete the table below to show equivalent fractions, decimals and percentages.

1.

Fractions	Decimals	Percentages
$\frac{7}{10}$		
$\frac{1}{5}$		
	0.8	
	0.56	
		45%
		3%

Word problems

When you come across word problems relating to fractions, decimals and percentages, it is really important that you read the question carefully and know exactly what it is you are looking for. Remember that you can use RUCSAC (see page 38) to help you.

Remember to use all the skills you have learnt working with fractions, decimals and percentages, including finding equivalent fractions, when you are solving word problems.

> A T-shirt was reduced in price by 10% to £9.90. What was the original price?
>
> Start by identifying what the question is asking you to do. It is asking you to find the original price and it has given you the reduced price and the percentage that the original price was reduced by.
>
> You need to think about the percentage that is left. If 10% has been taken off, then the remaining price is 90% of the original. You now know that £9.90 is 90% of the original.
>
> **TIP** Instead of adding 10% to 90%, you could find 10% and multiply it by 10 to get 100% (£1.10 × 10 = £11.00). Both methods will give you the correct answer, so you can choose either one.
>
> If you work out how much 10% is, you will know how much was taken off. You can then add this on to the 90% you already have to make 100%.
>
> To find 10% of the original, you divide 90% by 9. Therefore, you also divide £9.90 by 9 to get 10%.
>
> £9.90 ÷ 9 = £1.10
>
> You now know that £1.10 is 10%. Add this to £9.90, which is 90%, to make 100% of the original price.
>
> £1.10 + £9.90 = £11.00
>
> **Answer: £11.00**

Now answer the following questions.

1. Amy had some sweets. She gave $\frac{1}{3}$ to Matilda, $\frac{1}{5}$ to Evie and $\frac{1}{4}$ to Lloyd. If she kept 26 for herself, how many did she have to start with? _____

2. $\frac{2}{7}$ of the people on a train are children. If there are 78 more adults on the train than children, how many people are on the train? _____

3. 15% of the children at a school have blue eyes. If 66 have blue eyes, how many don't? _____

4. A television was reduced by 20% in the sale to a new price of £432. What was the original price? _____

5. I think of a number and multiply it by 3. I then subtract 5.1. My answer is 7.5. What number did I start with? _____

6. The product of two numbers is 13.44. If one of the numbers is 2.4, what is the other number? _____

7. Aditi bought a jar of marbles. 20% of the marbles were red. What fraction of the marbles were not red? _____

8. $\frac{1}{2}$ of Rakesh's socks are red, 15% are blue, $\frac{1}{5}$ are green and the rest are black. What percentage of his socks are black? _____

11+ Maths Study and Practice Book

Ratio and proportion

Ratios compare one amount to another amount.

Proportions are parts of a total amount.

If you are making orange squash and you mix one part orange to four parts water, then the ratio of orange to water will be 1:4. This is read as '1 to 4'.

If you use 1 litre of orange, you will need 4 litres of water.

If you use 2 litres of orange, you will need 8 litres of water.

If you use $\frac{1}{2}$ litre of orange, you will need 2 litres of water.

These ratios are all equivalent. Both sides of the ratio can be multiplied or divided by the same number to give an equivalent ratio (much like equivalent fractions).

To find the proportion you need to think about fractions, because proportion looks at a part of the whole. The above ratio is 1:4 so, in total, there are 5 parts. You would say that one part in every five ($\frac{1}{5}$) of the orange squash is orange and four parts in every five ($\frac{4}{5}$) are water.

> **TIP** Ratio is also commonly used to show the scale of maps. Scale will be covered on page 82.

Ratio

Sometimes, you will be given the individual parts of the ratio and asked to find equivalent parts.

> Robin has 7 stickers to every 5 that Jenny has. If Robin has 49 stickers, how many does Jenny have?

First, identify the important information. Robin has 7 stickers when Jenny has 5. This information can be written as a ratio of 7:5.

Once you have that written as a ratio, you can look at the next piece of information. Robin actually has 49 stickers. This is seven times more stickers than Robin has in the ratio. You know that what is done to one side of a ratio must be done to the other side, so Jenny's side of the ratio must also be multiplied by seven.

If you multiply 5 and 7, you get 35. Jenny must have 35 stickers when Robin has 49, so this must be the answer.

```
       Robin   Jenny
         7  :   5
   ×7 (              ) ×7
        49  :  35
```

Answer: 35

> **TIP** You can only use multiplication or division with ratios and proportion – never addition or subtraction. You must always do exactly the same process to both sides.

Ratio and proportion

Sometimes, the question will be related not only to the ratio but also to the total.

> Maisie, Ethan and Jim were given birthday money by their aunt in the ratio of 5:2:1. If their aunt gave them a total of £48, how much did each child receive?

Imagine each child received the initial ratio amount. That would be a total of £8 (5 + 2 + 1). Their aunt gave them 6× that (8 × 6 = 48), therefore each child will receive 6× the ratio amount. To check your answer, add the amounts. £30 + £12 + £6 = £48

	Maisie	Ethan	Jim	
×6	£5	£2	£1	= £8
	£30	£12	£6	= £48	×6

Answer: Maisie received £30, Ethan received £12 and Jim received £6

❗ With ratio the terms 'to every' and 'for every' are used. With proportion the term 'in every' is used.

Proportion

> There are 42 sweets in a jar. 2 in every 7 were mint flavoured. How many were not mint flavoured?

2 in every 7 means $\frac{2}{7}$. If $\frac{2}{7}$ were mint flavoured that means $\frac{5}{7}$ are not. $\frac{5}{7}$ of 42 is 30.

Answer: 30

✏️ Now answer the following questions.

1. For every 6 steps Hannah takes, Maya takes 11. If Hannah takes 42 steps, how many does Maya take? _____

2. There were 4 red balls to every 5 blue balls in the ball pit. If there were 234 balls altogether, how many were blue? _____

3. 3 in every 4 cows in a field are brown. If there are 232 cows, how many are brown? _____

4. Indira, Sara and Vicky were comparing how many pairs of earrings they owned. For every pair that Indira had, Sara had 3 and Vicky had 6. If there were a total of 120 earrings, how many did Vicky have? _____

5. 3 in every 7 people on the bus are children. If there are 32 adults on the bus, how many children are there? _____

6. Rashid, Edward and Cameron were comparing the number of shells they had collected. Rashid had collected twice as many as Edward, who had collected three times as many as Cameron. If Edward had 54 shells, how many shells did they have altogether? _____

Fractions, decimals and percentages practice page 1

Now test your skills with these practice pages. If you get stuck, go back to pages 48 to 71 for some reminders.

Fractions of shapes

What fraction of each shape is shaded?

1. 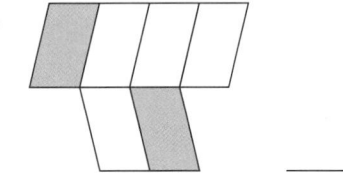 _____
2. 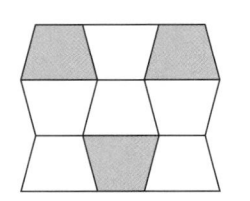 _____
3. 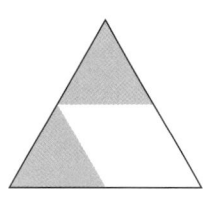 _____
4. 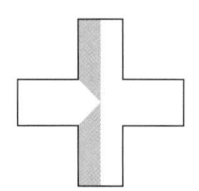 _____
5. _____
6. _____

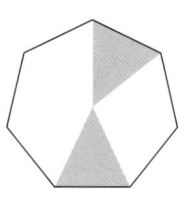

Fractions of quantities

7. What is $\frac{1}{9}$ of 63? _____

8. What is $\frac{2}{3}$ of 126? _____

9. There are 72 rabbits in a field. $\frac{2}{3}$ are brown. How many are not brown? _____

10. Rebecca sorted her sweets into colours. $\frac{2}{5}$ were red. If there were 40 red sweets, how many sweets did she have altogether? _____

Equivalent fractions

11. $\frac{3}{5} = \frac{}{30}$

12. $\frac{}{9} = \frac{3}{27}$

13. $\frac{7}{12} = \frac{42}{}$

14. $\frac{8}{} = \frac{48}{72}$

Circle the two equivalent fractions in each group.

15. $\frac{5}{6}$ $\frac{9}{24}$ $\frac{2}{3}$ $\frac{7}{14}$ $\frac{4}{7}$ $\frac{6}{16}$ $\frac{1}{5}$

16. $\frac{1}{2}$ $\frac{3}{16}$ $\frac{2}{5}$ $\frac{5}{8}$ $\frac{4}{6}$ $\frac{14}{35}$ $\frac{6}{10}$

Improper fractions and mixed numbers

Convert these improper fractions into mixed numbers.

17. $\frac{34}{12}$ _____

18. $\frac{19}{9}$ _____

19. $\frac{23}{5}$ _____

Convert these mixed numbers into improper fractions.

20. $2\frac{3}{4}$ _____

21. $6\frac{2}{7}$ _____

22. $5\frac{4}{9}$ _____

Simplifying fractions

Simplify these fractions.

23. $\frac{18}{45} =$ _____

25. $\frac{15}{60} =$ _____

27. $\frac{16}{44} =$ _____

24. $\frac{7}{28} =$ _____

26. $\frac{12}{36} =$ _____

28. $\frac{17}{54} =$ _____

Fractions, decimals and percentages practice page 2

Ordering fractions

Write these fractions in ascending order.

1. $\frac{1}{3} \quad \frac{1}{7} \quad \frac{1}{4} \quad \frac{1}{8} \quad \frac{1}{10}$

2. $\frac{1}{5} \quad \frac{2}{8} \quad \frac{7}{20} \quad \frac{3}{5} \quad \frac{3}{8}$

3. $\frac{3}{4} \quad \frac{3}{12} \quad \frac{5}{6} \quad \frac{2}{9} \quad \frac{5}{8}$

Write these fractions in descending order.

4. $2\frac{3}{4} \quad 4\frac{2}{9} \quad 2\frac{6}{14} \quad 2\frac{4}{7} \quad 4\frac{1}{6}$

5. $1\frac{1}{2} \quad 1\frac{5}{6} \quad 1\frac{3}{8} \quad 1\frac{1}{3} \quad 1\frac{7}{12}$

6. $\frac{32}{5} \quad \frac{27}{4} \quad \frac{13}{3} \quad \frac{13}{2} \quad \frac{27}{6}$

Adding and subtracting fractions

7. $\frac{1}{3} + \frac{2}{5} =$ _____

8. $\frac{4}{7} - \frac{1}{4} =$ _____

9. $\frac{1}{9} + \frac{5}{6} =$ _____

10. Isaac spent $\frac{1}{4}$ of his birthday money on toys, $\frac{1}{5}$ on sweets and the rest he saved. What fraction of his birthday money did he save? _____

11. $\frac{3}{4}$ of Andy's birthday cake was left after his party. If Andy ate a further $\frac{1}{6}$ of the original cake, how much of the cake was left? _____

Multiplying and dividing fractions

12. $\frac{1}{3} \times \frac{2}{5} =$ _____

14. $\frac{4}{3} \times \frac{9}{5} =$ _____

16. $\frac{5}{8} \div \frac{1}{3} =$ _____

13. $\frac{3}{4} \times \frac{3}{7} =$ _____

15. $\frac{4}{5} \div \frac{3}{7} =$ _____

17. $\frac{6}{1} \div \frac{14}{9} =$ _____

Fraction sequences

Write the missing fractions in these sequences. Write your answers in their simplest form.

18. $\frac{1}{8}, \frac{1}{4}, \frac{3}{8}, \frac{1}{2},$ _____, _____

20. $\frac{1}{3}, 1,$ _____, $2\frac{1}{3}, 3,$ _____

19. $\frac{4}{5}, \frac{70}{100}, \frac{6}{10},$ _____, $\frac{2}{5},$ _____

21. $9, 8\frac{1}{2}, 7\frac{1}{2},$ _____, $4,$ _____

Decimal fractions

What decimal fraction is each arrow pointing at?

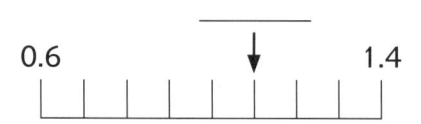

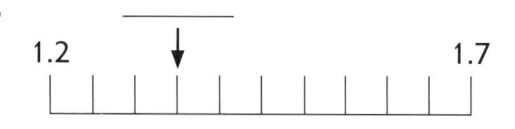

22. _____
0.6 ↓ 1.4

23. _____
1.2 ↓ 1.7

Give the values of the underlined digits.

24. 6.1<u>3</u>6 _____

25. 8.10<u>9</u> _____

Write these decimal fractions as fractions.

26. 4.24 _____

27. 7.135 _____

Fractions, decimals and percentages practice page 3

Ordering decimals

Write these decimals in descending order.

1. 0.34   0.43   0.04   0.33   0.44   _____

2. 0.56   0.561   0.65   0.615   0.506   _____

Write these decimals in ascending order.

3. 0.977   0.979   0.97   0.799   0.79   _____

4. 1.342   1.432   1.24   1.234   1.43   _____

Rounding decimals

5. Round 19.842 to the nearest $\frac{1}{10}$.   _____

6. Round 1.042 to the nearest $\frac{1}{100}$.   _____

7. Write 4.221 correct to 1 decimal place.   _____

8. Write 29.97 correct to 1 decimal place.   _____

9. Write 5.499 correct to 2 decimal places.   _____

Adding and subtracting decimals

10. 13.7 + 9.9 =   _____

11. 152.846 + 121.94 =   _____

12. 15.71 − 12.96 =   _____

13. An estate agent in London is selling 4 mansions. They are priced at £2.61 million, £7.4 million, £1.87 million and £3.9 million. What is the total value of all 4 mansions?   _____

14. Dolly was racing her pet snails. One finished in 19.47 seconds and the other one finished in 13.6 seconds. What was the difference in their times?   _____

Multiplying and dividing decimals

15. 0.7 × 0.3 = _____   17. 2.23 × 1.7 = _____   19. 3.6 ÷ 0.6 = _____

16. 1.2 × 0.9 = _____   18. 4.9 ÷ 7 = _____   20. 1.21 ÷ 0.11 = _____

Percentages

21. What is 30% of 90?   _____   22. What is 15% of 20?   _____

23. There are 720 passengers on the train. 60% of them are adults. How many are children?   _____

24. A coat was reduced by 20%. The original price was £42. What was the sale price?   _____

25. A car costing £12 500 is increased in price by 5%. What is the new price?   _____

Fractions, decimals and percentages practice page 4

Converting between fractions, decimals and percentages

1. In a class of 30 children, 40% walk to school, $\frac{1}{3}$ are driven to school and the rest take the bus. How many take the bus? _____

Write these in ascending order.

2. $\frac{1}{2}$ 55% $\frac{9}{20}$ 0.9 25% 0.2 _____

3. 0.4 20% $\frac{2}{3}$ 45% 0.7 $\frac{4}{5}$ _____

4. Jenna achieved $\frac{13}{20}$ in her spelling test. What is this as a percentage? _____

Are these statements true or false?

5. 0.6 < 65% _____

6. 20% > $\frac{1}{4}$ _____

Word problems

7. 37% of visitors to a zoo bought a slice of cake from the café. If 962 people bought cake, how many people visited the zoo? _____

8. A newsagents makes $\frac{1}{3}$ of its money from selling newspapers, $\frac{1}{4}$ of its money from selling sweets and the rest from groceries. If £1065 is made from groceries, how much is made from newspapers? _____

9. I decide to have some fun around a 1km running track. I run for $\frac{2}{5}$ of it, I hop for $\frac{1}{4}$ of it, I skip for $\frac{3}{10}$ of it and do forward rolls around the rest. For what fraction of the track am I doing forward rolls? _____

10. Kerry makes 6 dozen cookies. $\frac{4}{9}$ are eaten. How many are left? _____

11. Ritu is 180cm tall. Zara is 32% shorter. How tall is Zara? _____

12. Ed swims 5 mornings a week. On Monday he swam 1.26 miles. On Tuesday he swam 1.08 miles. On Wednesday he swam 0.87 miles. On Thursday he swam 1.4 miles and on Friday he swam 1.6 miles. How far did Ed swim? _____

Ratio and proportion

13. There are 3 pink pigs for every 2 brown pigs. If there are 75 pigs altogether, how many pink pigs are there? _____

14. To make 12 cupcakes, Eloise needs 150g of flour. How much flour does she need to make 20 cupcakes? _____

15. To make 1 litre of lemonade, Ivy needs 3 lemons and 140g of sugar. If she uses 350g of sugar, how many litres of lemonade can she make? _____

16. Pete answered 150 maths questions in 100 minutes. If he worked at the same speed, how many questions could he answer in half an hour? _____

17. It takes 3 workers 4 hours to do a job. How long would it take 2 workers to do the same job? _____

18. Jasper has three times as many toy cars as Faith who has twice as many as Sunhil. If they have a total of 90 toy cars, how many cars do they each have?

_____

Length, mass and capacity

There are different units of measure for quantities of length, mass and capacity. These quantities can be measured in metric and imperial units. You will learn more about imperial measures on page 79. Metric measures are the units of measure that we currently use in the UK.

It is important to be able to switch between the different units of measure within length, mass and capacity.

Length
10mm = 1cm
100cm = 1m
1000m = 1km

Mass
1000g = 1kg
1000kg = 1t (tonne)

Capacity
1000ml = 1l

TIP You can look at your ruler to help you remember how many mm are in a cm. Try to picture a metre stick when trying to remember how many cm are in 1m.

You will often hear the same prefixes when talking about measure:

milli = $\frac{1}{1000}$

centi = $\frac{1}{100}$

kilo = 1000

When put together with the unit of measure, the prefix helps you work out the relationship.

millimetre	1000mm in a metre		**centi**metre	100cm in a metre
millilitre	1000ml in a litre		**centi**litre	100cl in a litre
milligram	1000mg in a gram		**centi**gram	100cg in a gram

With 'kilo' measurements you are actually saying the amount.

kilometre = 1000m   There are 1000m in a km.
kilolitre = 1000l   There are 1000l in a kl.
kilogram = 1000g   There are 1000g in a kg.

You do not need to know all of these conversions but knowing the relationship between the words and the amounts will help you understand how the conversions work and make remembering them much easier.

It is also very useful to know some common fractions of measures.

$\frac{1}{2}$km = 500m	$\frac{1}{2}$l = 500ml	$\frac{1}{2}$kg = 500g	$\frac{1}{2}$m = 50cm
$\frac{1}{4}$km = 250m	$\frac{1}{4}$l = 250ml	$\frac{1}{4}$kg = 250g	$\frac{1}{4}$m = 25cm
$\frac{3}{4}$km = 750m	$\frac{3}{4}$l = 750ml	$\frac{3}{4}$kg = 750g	$\frac{3}{4}$m = 75cm
$\frac{1}{10}$km = 100m	$\frac{1}{10}$l = 100ml	$\frac{1}{10}$kg = 100g	$\frac{1}{10}$m = 10cm

Length, mass and capacity

You need to be able to work with different measures when they are written in fractions.

$1\frac{3}{4}$ m = _____ cm

If you know there are 100cm in 1m, then you can work out that $\frac{3}{4}$ = 75cm.

Answer: 175cm

Knowing how many of a smaller measurement go into a larger measurement will also enable you to do conversions with decimals.

1267g = _____ kg

You know that 1000g = 1kg, so you need to divide the number by 1000.

$\frac{1267}{1000}$ = 1.267

Answer: 1.267kg

TIP If you know that 1000g = 1kg, then you know the answer will be just over 1kg because there is only 1 thousand in 1267. The rest, 267, will be worth less than 1kg.

! Can you see how the digits have stayed exactly the same and in the same order? This will always happen when converting between metric units of measure.

3.456l = _____ ml

1l = 1000ml, so you need to multiply the number by 1000.

3.456 × 1000 = 3456

Answer: 3456ml

TIP You know 3l = 3000ml, so the answer must be just over 3000ml. You also know the digits will stay in the same order, so the answer must be 3456ml.

45cm = _____ m

100cm = 1m, so this is less than 1m. We need to divide the number by 100.

$\frac{45}{100}$ = 0.45

Answer: 0.45m

✎ Convert these measurements.

1. 2804m = _____ km
2. $3\frac{1}{2}$ cm = _____ mm
3. 1129ml = _____ l
4. $7\frac{1}{2}$ l = _____ ml
5. 119g = _____ kg
6. $6\frac{1}{4}$ kg = _____ g

Length, mass and capacity

With measurement problems, it is very important to make sure you are using the same units of measure throughout the question. If there is more than one type of unit, convert them all to the same unit first.

> Remember to use **RUCSAC** when solving any type of word problem involving measures. Look back at page 38 for a reminder about what the acronym stands for.

Ravi has a 5m length of wood. First he cuts off 1.2m, then he cuts off 80cm and finally he cuts off 130cm. How much wood does Ravi have left?

TIP It is usually better to convert the units so that any numbers are whole numbers rather than decimals, as it is easier to work with whole numbers than with decimals.

In the word problem, the lengths are in cm and m. Change them into cm.

So, the wood is initially 500cm long. First 120cm is cut off, then 80cm and finally 130cm.

500 − 120 = 380, 380 − 80 = 300, 300 − 130 = 170cm

Answer: 170cm

Now answer the following questions.

7. Glasses hold 0.2l and mugs hold 250ml. Grace has 4l of water and wants to share it between an equal number of glasses and mugs. How many glasses and mugs in total will she be able to fill?

8. The keepers at a safari park are weighing the meerkats. They take the following 5 measurements: 0.93kg, 780g, 0.74kg, 0.913kg and 816g. What is the total weight of the heaviest 4 meerkats in kg?

9. Look at this map. How far in km is the shortest route between Rantop and Selmore by road?

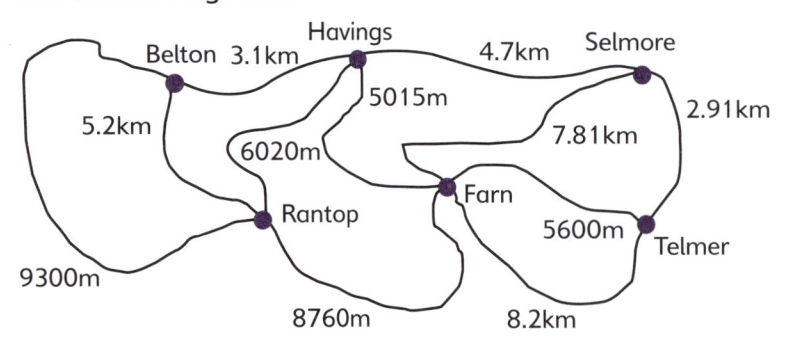

   Belton 3.1km — Havings — 4.7km — Selmore
   5.2km, 5015m, 2.91km
   6020m, 7.81km
   Rantop — Farn
   9300m, 5600m, Telmer
   8760m, 8.2km

10. A farmer measures the perimeter of his field for new fencing. He measures the four sides as 682m, 0.51km, 406m and 0.627km. He buys 3km of fencing. How many metres of fencing will be left over?

11. Nancy lives 4.7km away from the park and Angus lives 3.72km from the park. They both cycle there and back. How many more metres has Nancy cycled compared to Angus?

12. Nina needs to take 0.015l of medicine twice a day. She has to take it for 30 days. How many ml of her 1-litre bottle of medicine will she have left at the end of the 30 days?

Imperial measures

The imperial system of measures was developed in Great Britain, but towards the end of the last century the UK moved over to the metric system. Many people felt that the metric system was more convenient to use as the units are all based on tens, hundreds and thousands (just like place value).

While we no longer officially use the imperial system, many of the measures are still in common use. It is important to recognise them and know approximately what they are worth compared to metric measures.

Imperial measures that are still commonly used today

Length: inches (in), feet (ft), yards (yd) and miles (mi although mph stands for miles per hour)

12 inches = 1 foot
3 feet = 1 yard
1760 yards = 1 mile

> Miles are still used in the UK to measure long distances. Feet and inches are still commonly used to measure people's heights.

Mass: ounces (oz), pounds (lb), stones (st)

16 ounces = 1 pound
14 pounds = 1 stone

Capacity: pints (pt), gallons (gal)

8 pints = 1 gallon

Look at all the different numbers in use compared to the 10s, 100s and 1000s used in metric measurements.

Here are the most important conversions between imperial and metric measures.

Note that the symbol ≈ means approximately.

1in ≈ 2.5cm	1oz ≈ 30g	1pt ≈ 0.5l
1ft ≈ 30cm	1lb ≈ 0.5kg	1gal ≈ 4l
1yd ≈ 90cm	1st ≈ 6kg	
1mi ≈ 1.6km		

Convert these measurements.

1. 15cm ≈ _____ in
2. 5pt ≈ _____ l
3. 16mi ≈ _____ km
4. 14l ≈ _____ gal
5. 12lb ≈ _____ g
6. 4.5kg ≈ _____ lb

Reading scales

Measurements are often read from scales. Scales can take many different forms.

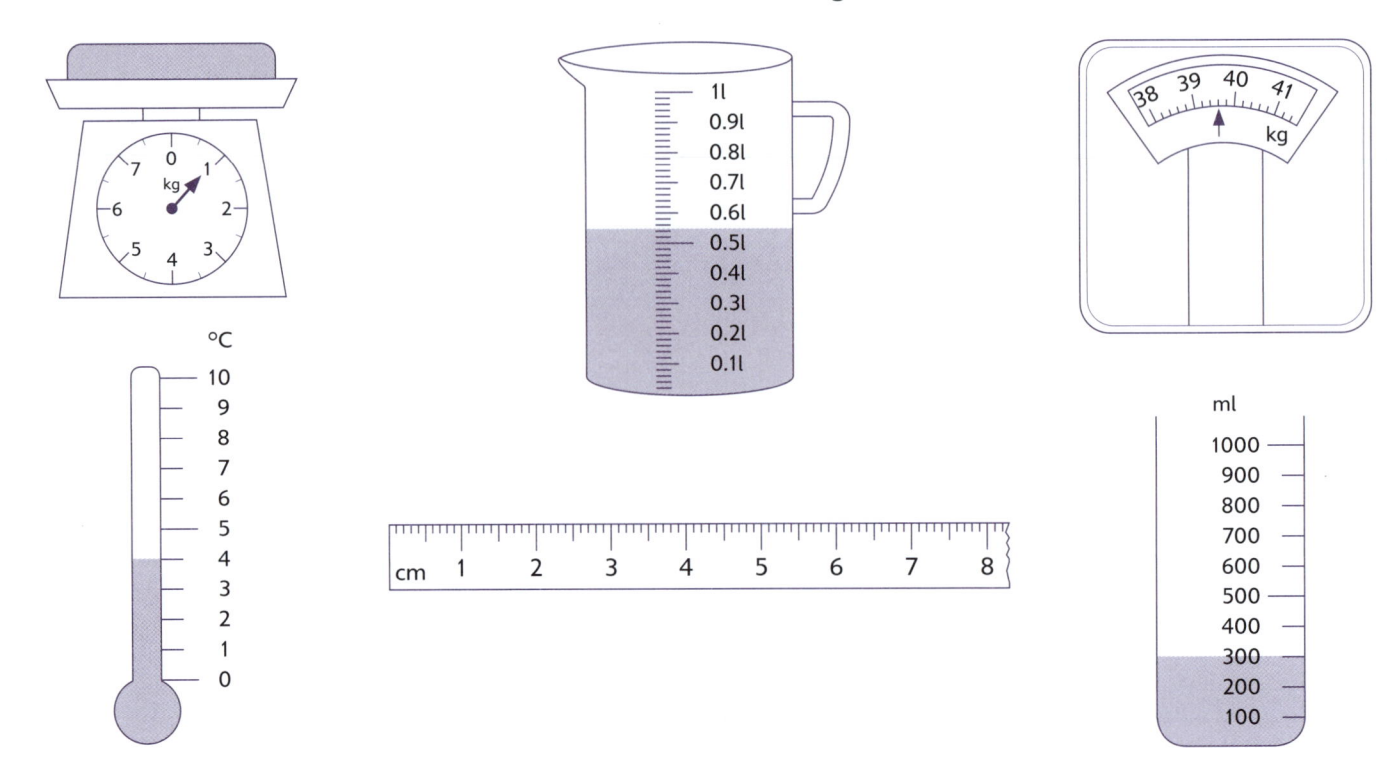

Regardless of the measuring device you need to look at three things:

1. The units of measure.
2. Where the measurements begin and end.
3. The value of each interval/increment on the scale.

Record the measurement shown on the spring balance.

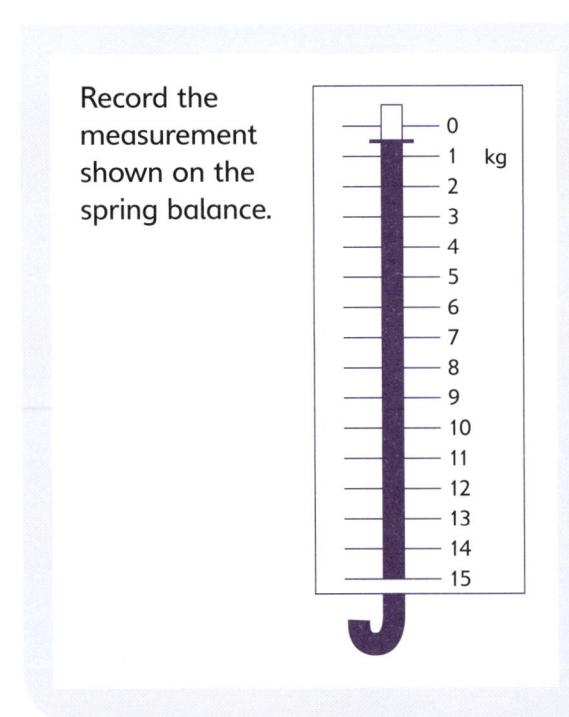

Remember the three things you need to look at.

1. The units of measure are kg.
2. The measurement starts at the top at 0 and goes down to 15.
3. The measurements increase in 1kg increments.

The pointer is half-way between 0 and 1.

Answer: 0.5kg

Reading scales

Record the measurement shown on each scale.

1.

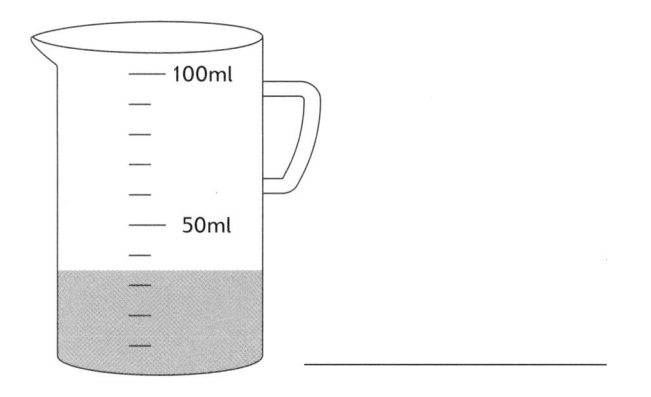

2.

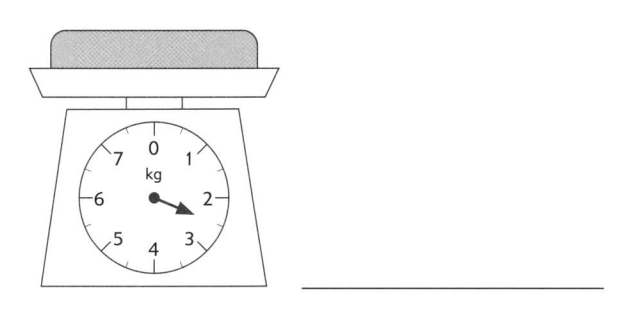

3.

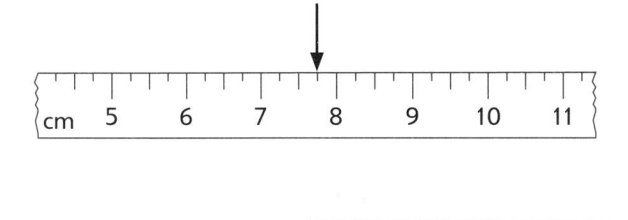

4.

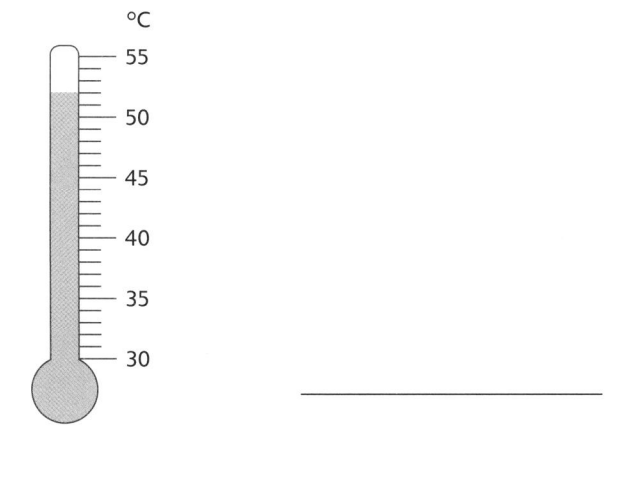

5.

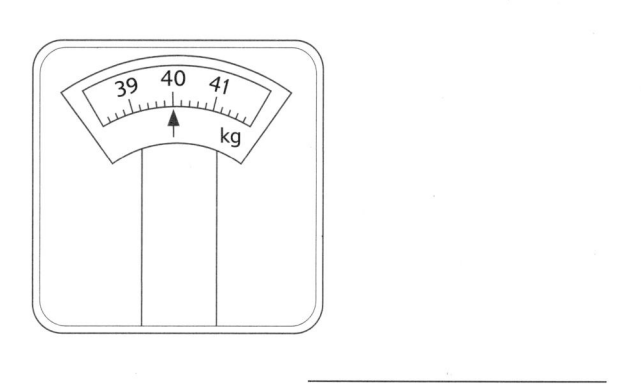

6.

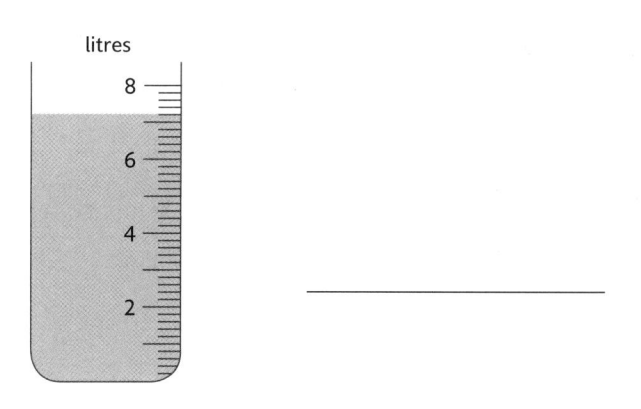

7.

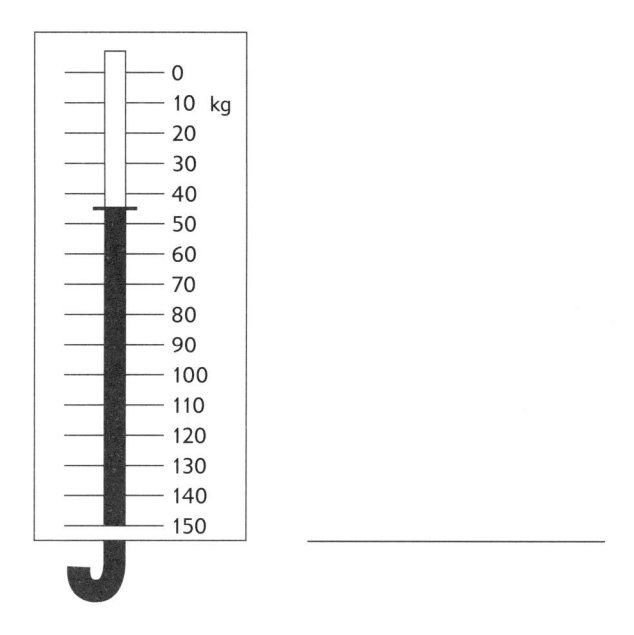

8.

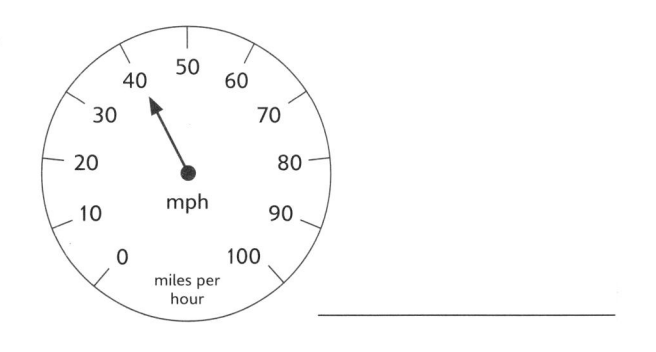

11+ Maths Study and Practice Book

Scale

Scale is the ratio of the size of a drawing, model or map compared to the size of the real thing.

Scale is usually written as a ratio and does not use any units of measure. It is assumed that whichever measurement is relevant will be used, so, for example, a scale of 1:20 could be 1cm:20cm, 1m:20m or 1km:20km. The unit of measure will always be the same on both sides of the ratio.

> A map has a scale of 1:200. If the distance on the map is 5cm, what is the actual distance?
>
> As the question is in cm, then so is the scale. Multiply both sides of the scale by 5.
> 5:1000. 1000cm = 10m
> **Answer: 10m**

You will need to be able to work out the scale based on given distances.

> Jay walks 250m. On a map this is shown as 5cm. What is the scale on the map?
>
> Convert the measurements so they both use the same units. 250m = 25000cm, so the scale is 5:25000. You now need to simplify this ratio to find the scale.
>
> **Answer: 1:5000**
>
> 5:25000 ÷5 → 1:5000

You may also be asked to change the size of a shape by a certain **scale factor**.

> A rectangle is 2cm × 4cm. It is increased by a scale factor of 3. What is the area of the new rectangle?
>
> Increasing it by a scale factor of 3 means making each dimension 3 times bigger, so it would become a 6cm × 12cm rectangle. The **area** of the new rectangle would therefore be 6 × 12 = 72cm².
>
> **Answer: 72cm²**

TIP See page 94 for more detail on how to find the area of a rectangle.

Now answer the following questions.

1. Malik sails his dinghy 1km down the river. On his map the distance measures 2cm. What is the scale of the map? _____

2. A map has a scale of 1:300. If a path is 12cm long on the map, how long is it in real life? _____

3. Lily measured the length of her road as 2km. After drawing it to scale, it measured 5cm on her map. What is the scale of her map? _____

4. A rectangle is increased by a scale factor of 4. Its new dimensions are 16cm × 4cm. What were the dimensions of the original rectangle? _____

5. A rectangle measuring 7cm × 3cm is increased by a scale factor of 5. What is the area of the new rectangle? _____

Time

There are two types of clock (analogue and digital) and two types of number system to tell the time (12-hour and 24-hour).

Analogue clocks have hands which move around a face and point at numbers. They show the minutes past the hour and the minutes to the next hour.

Digital clocks only have numbers. They only show minutes past the hour.

> ❗ There are 60 seconds in one minute, 60 minutes in one hour and 24 hours in one day.

12-hour clock

This splits the day into two parts based on the hours between 12 midnight and 12 midday (a.m.) and 12 midday and 12 midnight (p.m.). There are two times each day when the same number is used. For example, there are two 8 o'clocks – 8.00 a.m. in the morning and 8.00 p.m. in the evening. This is the time system used by analogue clocks because they only have numbers that go up to 12.

24-hour clock

This runs from midnight all the way round to the next midnight with each of the 24 hours having a different number. Only 8 o'clock in the morning will be written as 08:00. 8 o'clock in the evening will be written as 20:00 because by this time 20 hours will have gone past since the day started. Digital clocks can use either the 24-hour clock or the 12-hour clock.

> ❗ Many people refer to 12.00 a.m. as midnight and 12.00 p.m. as midday, but in order to avoid confusion it is best to use '12 midnight' and '12 noon'. On a digital clock 12:00 is midday and 00:00 is midnight.

What is the difference between the time shown on the clocks?

afternoon

The analogue clock reads twenty-five minutes to four (3.35 p.m.) in the afternoon and the digital clock reads twenty-two minutes past six in the evening (6.22 p.m.).

The easiest way to work out the duration between two times is to use a timeline. You can either write it down or imagine it in your head.

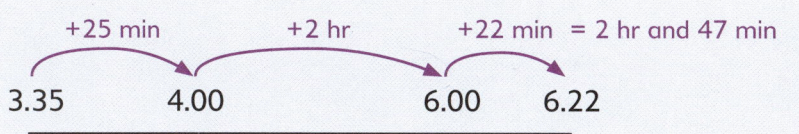

```
   +25 min      +2 hr       +22 min   = 2 hr and 47 min
3.35         4.00         6.00     6.22
```

Answer: 2 hours and 47 minutes

11+ Maths Study and Practice Book

Time

You will often have to solve problems relating to time. These could be linked to timetables (such as bus, train or television timetables) or to how long something takes.

Look at this bus timetable.

	A	B	C	D
Tring	08:34	09:39	10:33	10:48
Aldbury	08:39	09:44	10:37	10:53
Pitstone	08:45	09:50	10:43	10:59
Ivinghoe	08:51	09:56	10:49	11:06
Cheddington	09:07	10:14	11:04	11:24

! Look carefully at timetables and make sure you know which way the times are going. They may have the times written going across the page, going down the page or going up the page.

If I need to be in Pitstone by 10:30, at what time do I need to catch the bus from Aldbury?

The 10:37 from Aldbury doesn't arrive in Pitstone until 10:43, which is too late, so you'd need to catch the bus that leaves Aldbury at 09:44, which is bus B.

Answer: 09:44

Which is the quickest bus for getting from Tring to Cheddington?

To find this out you need to work out how long each journey takes. Use a timeline.

Bus A

+26 min   +7 min   = 33 min

08:34   09:00   09:07

Bus B

+21 min   +14 min   = 35 min

09:39   10:00   10:14

Bus C

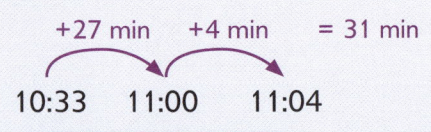

+27 min   +4 min   = 31 min

10:33   11:00   11:04

Bus D

+12 min   +24 min   = 36 min

10:48   11:00   11:24

Answer: Bus C

Jane took the first bus to Ivinghoe and her friend then picked her up at 11:15 to take her home. How long did Jane spend in Ivinghoe?

The first bus gets Jane to Ivinghoe at 08:51. Use a timeline to work out the duration between then and 11:15.

+9 min   +2 hr   +15 min   = 2 hr and 24 min

08:51   09:00   11:00   11:15

Answer: 2 hours and 24 minutes

Time

Now answer the following questions.

Write these times in words and in figures using both 12- and 24-hour notation.

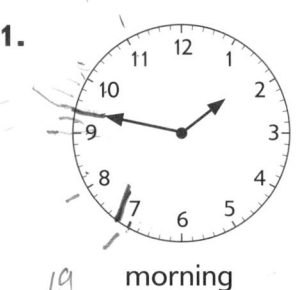

1. morning — ~~thirteen~~ ~~quarter~~ to ~~to~~ two in the morning   01:47   1:47

2. 19:36 — 7:36 pm   24 to 8

3. evening — half past seven / 07:30 / 19:28   [correction: 28]

4. Seb finished watching a film at 3.24 p.m. If the film was 1 hour and 35 minutes long, at what time did it start?   1.49 pm ✓

5. Rihanna put a cake in the oven at 12.46 p.m. It needed to cook for 55 minutes. At what time did she take it out of the oven?   1:51 pm   1:41   13:46

6. Here is part of the day's television schedule.

   News: 10.43 a.m.
   Cartoons: 11.05 a.m.
   Doctor Alice: 11.34 a.m.
   Film: 11.49 a.m.
   Weather: 1.58 p.m.
   Children's hour: 2.06 p.m.

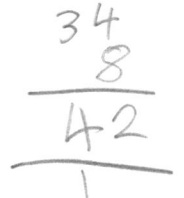

   i) Remi turns the television on at 10.52 a.m. How long does she have to wait until she can watch *Doctor Alice*?   42 mins ✓

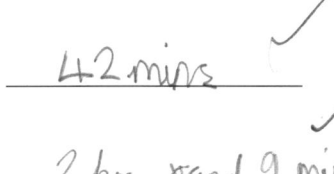

   ii) How long does the film last?   2 hrs and 9 mins ✓

   iii) Dave turns on the television at 1.02 p.m. How much of the film has he missed?   1 hr and 13 mins ✓

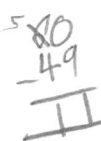

Time zones

A time zone is a region that shares the same time. Because Earth rotates every 24 hours, there are different time zones around the world.

The UK is the centre of the time zones and is classed as 0. This is because this is where the zero meridian, the imaginary line between east and west, is located. The meridian runs through Greenwich in London. 'Greenwich Mean Time' or 'GMT' is the standard time against which all the time zones are measured. Countries to the east of the UK are ahead in time. Countries to the west of the UK are behind in time.

The table shows the differences between the time in London and in other cities around the world.

TIP When answering questions about travelling to other countries, it is always best to keep to the time of the initial country and then adjust the timings to the new country at the end.

City	Time difference to London
Los Angeles	−8
Sydney	+10
Tokyo	+9
Toronto	−5
Athens	+2
Delhi	+4.5
Rio de Janeiro	−4
Lima	−6

If it was 3 p.m. in Athens, what time would it be in Lima?

Athens is 2 hours ahead of London and London is 6 hours ahead of Lima. Therefore, Athens is 8 hours ahead of Lima. If it is 3 p.m. in Athens then it is 7 a.m. in Lima.

Answer: 7 a.m.

Owen left Delhi at 7 a.m. and flew for 14 hours to Toronto. What was the time in Toronto when he landed?

If Owen left at 7 a.m. and flew for 14 hours, it would be 9 p.m. Delhi time when he arrived in Toronto. Toronto is 9.5 hours behind Delhi, so the time in Toronto would be 11.30 a.m.

Answer: 11.30 a.m.

Now answer the following questions using the table above.

1. When it is 16:30 in London, what time will it be in Tokyo? _____

2. When it is 04:20 in Lima, what time will it be in Delhi? _____

3. Alex is in Los Angeles. She calls Susie in London. Susie asked Alex to call her at 14:15 London time. At what time does Alex make her phone call? _____

Complete the table showing arrival and departure times of international flights from London.

	Depart	Flight duration	Arrive	Local time
4.	13:30	4 hours	Athens	
5.	05:15	12 hours	Rio de Janeiro	
6.		22 hours	Sydney	19:00

Days, weeks, months and years

As well as telling the time, time also includes measures such as days in a week, weeks in a year, years in a decade, and so on.

Remember!

7 days	= 1 week
2 weeks	= a fortnight
12 months	= 1 year
52 weeks	= 1 year (a year is actually a few days over 52 weeks, but there are 52 whole weeks)
365 days	= 1 year
366 days	= a leap year (a leap year has an extra day at the end of February. Earth takes 365 days and 6 hours to orbit the sun, so every four years the extra 6 hours are put together to make an extra day)
10 years	= a decade
100 years	= a century
1000 years	= a millennium

TIP Leap years always fall on years that are divisible by 4, so 1988, 1996, 2008, 2020, and so on are leap years.

It is also important to know the number of days in each month. You can do this by remembering this rhyme.

> 30 days has September,
> April, June and November.
> All the rest have 31
> Except for February alone.
> And that has 28 days clear
> And 29 in each leap year.

Some questions will simply require you to convert measurements.

> How many months are there in a decade?
>
> There are 12 months in a year and 10 years in a decade, so 12 × 10 = 120.
> **Answer: 120 months**

11+ Maths Study and Practice Book

Days, weeks, months and years

Other questions about time will involve a bit more depth. You may need to use your knowledge of days, weeks, months and years, and also do some working out. You might also find it helpful to make a timeline.

> Kitty was born on 18th February 2016. Alfie was born a fortnight later.
> On what date was Alfie born?

There are several things to consider in this question.

1. How many days are there in February?   28, or 29 in a leap year
2. Was 2016 a leap year?   Yes, the number 2016 is divisible by 4.
3. How many days in a fortnight?   14

You can use a timeline to help work out the answer.

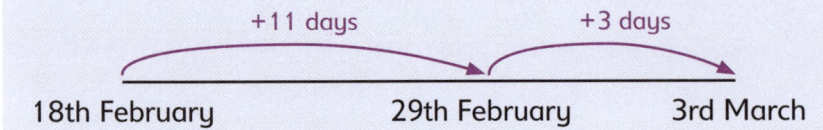

+11 days   +3 days
18th February   29th February   3rd March

Adding 11 days to 18th February takes you to 29th February (the last day of February). As there are 14 days in a fortnight, you need to add another 3 days. The third day of the next month is 3rd March.

Answer: 3rd March

Now answer the following questions.

1. How many weeks are there in half a year? _____

2. How many months are there in 8 years? _____

3. How many fortnights are there in half a year? _____

4. How many days are there altogether in the months of March, April, May and June? _____

5. Ally went travelling for 6 weeks. She left on 15th April. On what date did she return? _____

6. If 9th November 2016 was a Wednesday, what day was 5th January 2017? _____

7. Sam's birthday is on 15th October. If Gabby's birthday is exactly 7 weeks before Sam's, when is Gabby's birthday? _____

8. If 31st January 2020 was a Friday, what day would 1st March 2020 be? _____

Speed

Speed is the measure of how fast something travels over a given period of time. It is most commonly measured in mph (miles per hour) but a combination of any measurement of length and time can be used, such km/h (kilometres per hour) or m/s (metres per second).

Speed problems will tend to involve working out how far something has travelled or how long something has been travelling based on a given speed, or working out what speed something was travelling based on how far it has gone in a given time.

> Martha travels to her friend's house on her bike. It takes her 20 minutes to cycle the 4-mile journey. At what speed is she travelling?

If it takes her 20 minutes to travel 4 miles, you can multiply this by 3 to find out how many miles she would travel in 1 hour, as 20 minutes × 3 = 60 minutes (1 hour). 4 miles × 3 = 12 miles

Answer: 12mph

> Jonah is travelling at an average speed of 36mph. His journey lasts for 40 minutes. How far has he travelled?

40 minutes is $\frac{2}{3}$ of an hour. If he is travelling at 36mph then $\frac{2}{3}$ of that is 24.

Answer: 24 miles

You will often need to read graphs that show time and distance. By seeing how far someone has travelled over a certain distance, it will enable you to work out their speed.

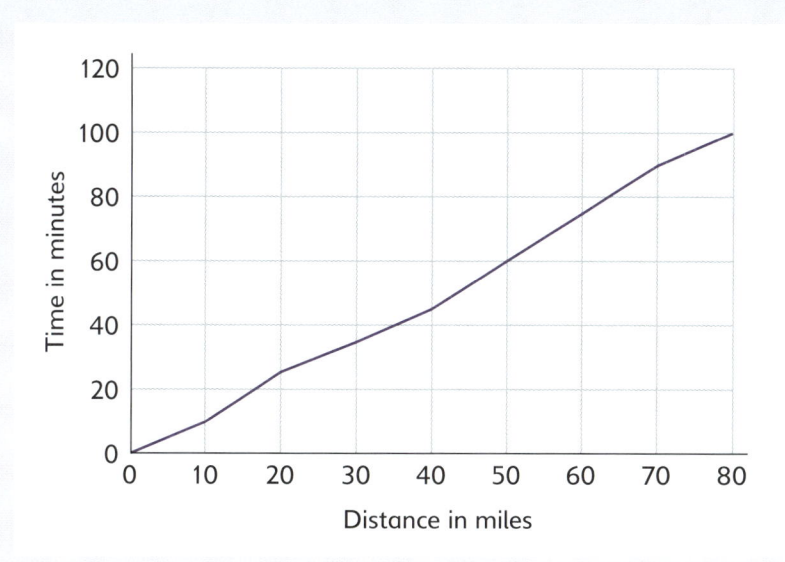

> The graph shows how long it took Farook to drive to his grandma's house. What was his average speed?

He travelled 80 miles in 100 minutes.

To get from 100 minutes to 1 hour (60 minutes), divide 100 by 5 to get 20 minutes, then multiply 20 by 3 to get 60 minutes.

Do the same to the distance, so 80 ÷ 5 = 16, 16 × 3 = 48.

Answer: 48mph

Speed

A useful formula for calculating speed is: | distance (d) = speed (s) × time (t)

This can be represented as a triangle.

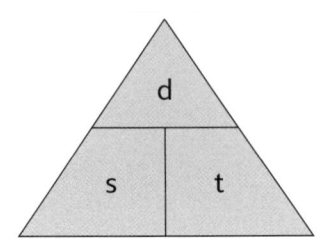

To calculate speed, cover up s and you get $s = \frac{d}{t}$

To calculate time, cover up t and you get $t = \frac{d}{s}$

To calculate distance, cover up d and you get $d = s \times t$

Now answer the following questions.

1. Jo lives 4.25km from town. If she walks at a speed of 5km/h, how long does it take her to walk into town? _____

2. An aeroplane flies at 540mph. How far does it travel in 6 hours and 35 minutes? _____

3. Darren cycles his first 40km in 1 hour and 10 minutes and his next 30km in 1 hour and 20 minutes. What is his average speed? _____

4. Shelley went running with her friend, Abby. Shelley ran 9 miles in 50 minutes while Abby ran 9.1 miles in 1 hour and 5 minutes. Who was faster and by how many mph? _____

This graph shows the time it took Leila to run 4.5km.

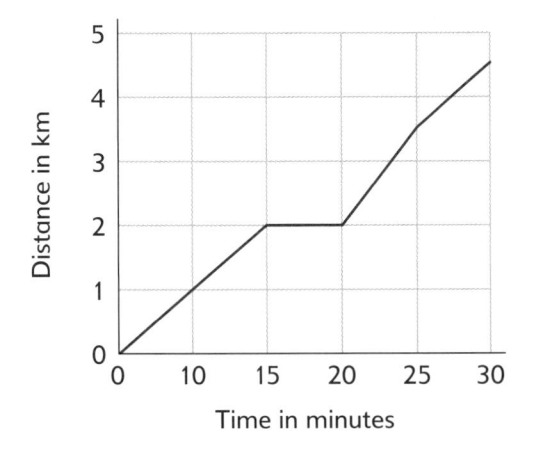

5. What happened after 15 minutes? _____

6. What was Leila's average speed? _____

Money

A lot of money problems will involve adding together several amounts and then subtracting from an amount to find change. It is usually easier and quicker to do vertical calculations, as this way you can make sure the decimal points are always lined up. Look back at pages 27 and 29 if you need a reminder of how to do vertical calculations.

> ! 100 pence = £1

> Adam bought a ball costing £2.45, a pair of football shorts costing £15.98 and a pair of football boots costing £45.20. What change did he get from £100?

First you need to add together the cost of the items to find out how much he spent.

```
   2.4 5
   1 5.9 8
 + 4 5.2 0
   -------
   6 3.6 3
   1 1 1
```

Once you have found the cost of all the items, you need to subtract that from £100 to find the change he will receive.

```
     0 9 9 9
   1 0 0.0 ¹0
 -   6 3.6 3
   ---------
     3 6.3 7
```

Answer: £36.37

You will also need to multiply and divide amounts of money. Once again, it is often easier and quicker to use a written method. Look back at pages 32 to 34 if you need a reminder of how to do these written calculations.

> Chelsea buys 12 boxes of dog food costing £4.53 each. How much does she spend?

```
     4.5 3
   ×   1 2
   -------
   5 4.3 6
     6   3
```

Answer: £54.36

> Eight burger buns cost £2.56. How much does 1 burger bun cost?

```
     0.3 2
   8)2.²5 ¹6
```

Answer: 32p

> **TIP** If you are working with amounts that are nearly a whole pound, such as 98p or 99p, it is easier to round up to the nearest £. For example, 5 × £2.99. Work out 5 × £3 = £15 and then subtract the 5 extra pennies that were added on (1p to each of the £2.99). £15 − 5p = £14.95. So £2.99 × 5 = £14.95.

You may also be asked about which coins will make certain amounts.

> Imani had 4 coins totalling 63p. What coins did she have?

> ! Remember the different coins and notes that are available. Coins: 1p, 2p, 5p, 10p, 20p, 50p, £1, £2. Notes: £5, £10, £20, £50. Notice how they all start with 1, 2 or 5.

Always start with the biggest coin and work backwards.

The biggest coin she could have would be a 50p coin. She couldn't have 2 as that would total £1. The next biggest coin is a 20p coin but that would total 70p. The next biggest coin is a 10p coin. A 50p and a 10p totals 60p, which leaves 3p that can be made from a 2p and a 1p.

Answer: 50p, 10p, 2p and 1p

Money

You also need to understand how to use currency conversion tables. These show what different currencies around the world are worth compared to others.

UK (pound) £	USA (dollar) $	France (euro) €	Japan (yen) ¥
1	1.5	1.2	146

! The exchange rate between currencies changes all the time, so don't expect to always see the same conversion amounts.

The table above shows that £1 is worth the same as $1.5, €1.2 or 146¥.

> Freddie had £50. How many US$ could he exchange this for?

If £1 = $1.5 then you will need to multiply $1.5 by 50 to find the value of £50. $1.5 × 50 = $75.

Answer: $75

> Ekene has €120 and wants to exchange it for Japanese yen. How many yen will he receive?

You can see from the table that €1.2 = 146¥. To get to €120 we need to multiply by 100, so we need to do the same with the yen. 146¥ × 100 = 14 600¥.

Answer: 14 600¥

Now answer the following questions.

1. Natalie bought 3 skirts costing £7.99 each. What was her change from £25? _____

2. Roopa bought a coffee costing £2.45, a tea costing £1.99, a muffin costing £3.09 and a flapjack costing £1.79. She only had £6.50 in her purse. How much did she have to borrow from her friend? _____

3. Ali found 5 coins down the back of the sofa that totalled 94p. Which 5 coins did he find? _____

Use the conversion chart below to help you to answer the following questions.

UK (pound) £	New Zealand (dollar) $	India (rupee) ₹	Kenya (shilling) Ksh
1	2	90	130

4. Mali had £40. How many Indian rupees could she exchange this for? _____

5. Brody bought a t-shirt in Kenya for 1235 Kenyan shillings. How much did this cost in £? _____

6. 16 New Zealand dollars is equivalent to how many Indian rupees? _____

Temperature

Temperature is measured in degrees Celsius, which is written as °C. This is the metric measurement for temperature.

You may also see the temperature written as degrees Fahrenheit, °F. This is the imperial measurement for temperature and it was used in the UK before the country adopted metric measures. It is still used in many countries, including the USA.

Temperature is measured on a thermometer.

Temperature is measured in positive and negative numbers.

If it gets very cold and drops below freezing (0°C), the temperature will be in negative numbers, for example −4°C or −9°C.

In some countries the temperature can drop as low as −50°C while in the hottest places it can be as high as 58°C.

To convert from °C to °F you multiply by 1.8 and add 32.

Questions will often involve you working out a difference in temperature.

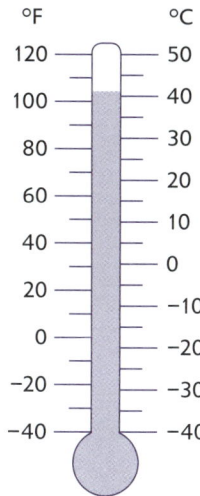

> The temperature on Tuesday was 3°C. By Friday it had fallen by 9°C. What was the temperature on Friday?
>
> 3 − 9 = −6
>
> **Answer: −6°C**

Now answer the following questions.

1. What is the difference in temperature between 26°C and −11°C? _____

2. It is 12°C hotter in Dubai than in New York. If it is 23°C in New York, what is the temperature in Dubai? _____

3. The drop in temperature between 4 p.m. and midnight was 9°C. If the temperature at midnight was 7°C, what was the temperature at 4 p.m.? _____

4. The temperature is −12°C. By how much must it rise to reach 6°C? _____

5. The temperature in the Antarctic dropped from −17°C to −25°C. By how much did the temperature drop? _____

6. The temperature in London rises 8°C from −1°C. What is the approximate new temperature in Fahrenheit? _____

Perimeter and area

Perimeter and area are measurements associated with 2D shapes.

The perimeter is the distance around the outside of a shape. Perimeter can be measured in any unit of length, for example cm, m, km. To work out the perimeter just add together the measurements for every side of the shape.

Find the perimeter of this rectangle.

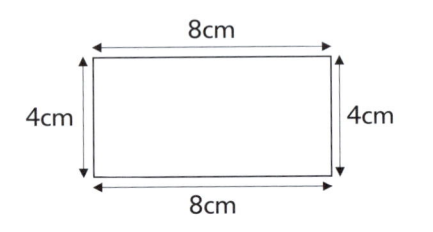

(Rectangle: 8cm by 4cm)

Rather than adding the four measurements together, it is easier to add the length (8cm) and the width (4cm) together and then double it:

perimeter = 2(l + w).

So 8cm + 4cm = 12cm and 12cm × 2 = 24cm

Answer: 24cm

The area is the space inside a 2D shape. It is worked out by imagining how many squares could fit inside. Area can be measured in any unit of length with a little 2 added to the unit, which we read as 'squared', for example cm^2, m^2, km^2.

Find the area of this rectangle.

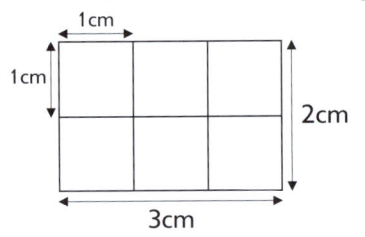

(Rectangle: 3cm by 2cm, divided into 1cm squares)

Each of the squares drawn inside the rectangle has a length and width of 1cm (they are cm squares). As the rectangle is 3cm long you can fit three squares along its length. As it is 2cm wide, you can fit two squares along its width. That makes a total of six squares.

You may have noticed that if you multiply the length of the rectangle by the width of the rectangle you also get an answer of 6. 3 × 2 = 6

For rectangles, this is how you calculate the area: area = length × width (l × w).

Answer: $6cm^2$

TIP The small 2 is used because **2** dimensions are being multiplied in a **2D** shape.

Squares and rectangles

You may be asked questions containing different units of measure. Always look carefully at the units of measure being used. If the units of measure for each side, or for parts of the same question, are different, convert them so that they are the same.

For example, even though 1m = 100cm, $1m^2$ is **not** the same as $100cm^2$. If you convert 1m into cm, 100 × 100 = 10 000, therefore $1m^2$ is the same as $10 000cm^2$.

If a square has sides of 5mm, what is its area in cm^2?

As the measurement is in mm but you are being asked to answer in cm^2, you must turn the measurements into cm first. So, you need to work out 0.5cm × 0.5cm, rather than 5mm × 5mm.

0.5 × 0.5 = 0.25

Answer: $0.25cm^2$

TIP 5mm × 5mm = $25mm^2$. However, that does not convert to $2.5cm^2$ even though 25mm = 2.5cm. The answer to this question is $0.25cm^2$.

Perimeter and area

Sometimes, you will need to work out more than one area to solve a problem.

This is a plan of Leo's garden. The grey area is a vegetable patch and the white area is lawn. What is the area of the lawn?

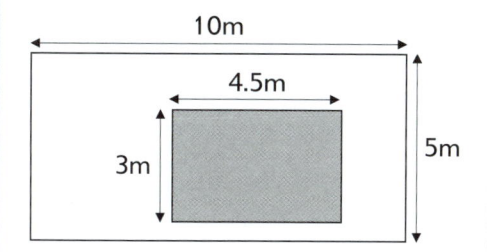

[Diagram: white rectangle 10m × 5m, grey rectangle inside 4.5m × 3m]

To work out the area of the lawn, you need to subtract the area of the vegetable patch (grey rectangle) from the entire area of the white rectangle.

Grey rectangle = 4.5 × 3 = 13.5m^2

White rectangle = 10 × 5 = 50m^2

50m^2 − 13.5m^2 = 36.5m^2

Answer: 36.5m^2

! Make sure you write the answer with the correct unit of measure and the ^{2} symbol. If you forget either, your answer will be incorrect, even if you calculated the number correctly.

Find the perimeter and area of these rectangles.

1. [Rectangle 16cm × 12cm]

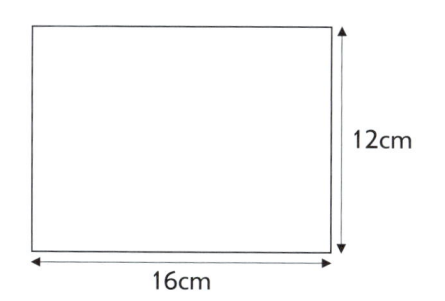

Perimeter: _____

Area: _____

2. [Rectangle 13m × 38m]

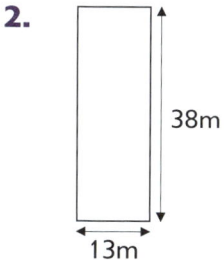

Perimeter: _____

Area: _____

Write in the missing measurements.

	Length	Width	Perimeter	Area
3. Rectangle 1	15cm	12cm		
4. Rectangle 2		8m	52m	
5. Rectangle 3	24mm			768mm^2

6. [Diagram: rectangle 5m × 3.5m with bath 2m × 50cm inside]

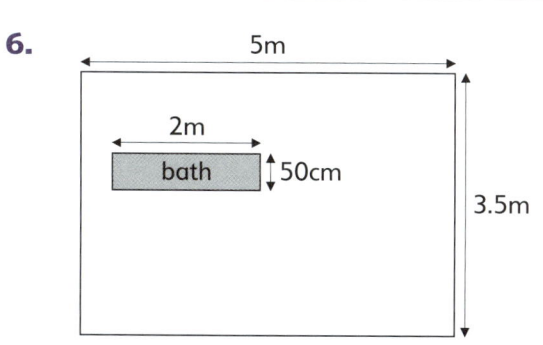

Polly needs to tile the floor around her bath. Using the plan, work out the area of floor that she needs to tile. _____

Perimeter and area

Triangles

To find the perimeter of a triangle, as with rectangles, simply add together the lengths of the three sides.

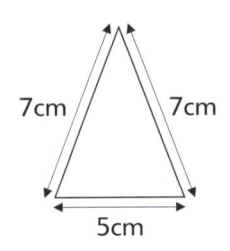

7cm + 7cm + 5cm = 19cm

To calculate the area of a triangle, you first need to think about the rectangle that can be created using the same measurements.

If you find the area of the rectangle (length × width), you then just need to halve it to find the area of the triangle, as a triangle is half the size of a rectangle with the same dimensions. You can also think of it as the triangle's height × base.

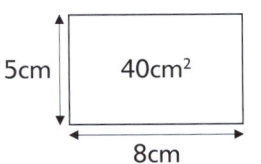

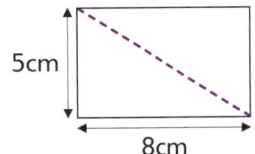

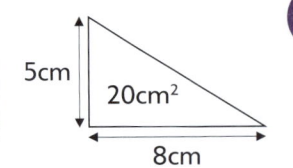

TIP It can sometimes be easier to halve one of the dimensions first and then multiply it by the second. For example, half of 8 is 4, so 4 × 5 = 20.

This works with any type of triangle, not just right-angled triangles.

For any other sort of triangle, you just need to imagine a rectangle being drawn around it that is the same height and width.

A right-angled triangle is a triangle with one 90° angle.

Find the area of this triangle.

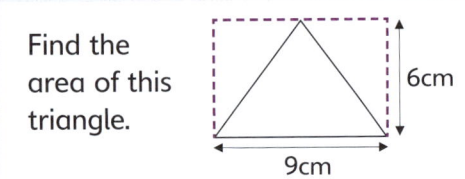

The rectangle will share the same dimensions: 9cm by 6cm. This would give it an area of 54cm².

The area of the triangle will be half that of the rectangle.

Answer: 27cm²

Find the perimeter and the area of these triangles.

7. (9cm, 4cm, 6cm)

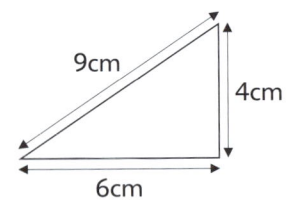

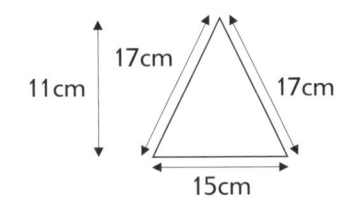

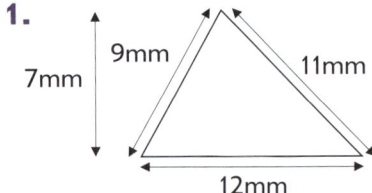

Perimeter: _____

Area: _____

8. (6cm, 6cm, 9cm, 3cm)

Perimeter: _____

Area: _____

9. (17cm, 17cm, 15cm, 11cm)

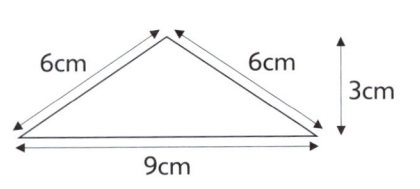

Perimeter: _____

Area: _____

10. (16m, 20m, 4m)

Perimeter: _____

Area: _____

11. (9mm, 11mm, 7mm, 12mm)

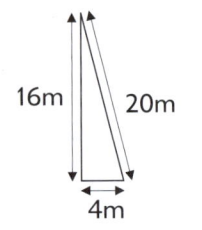

Perimeter: _____

Area: _____

12. (29cm, 33cm, 19cm, 18cm)

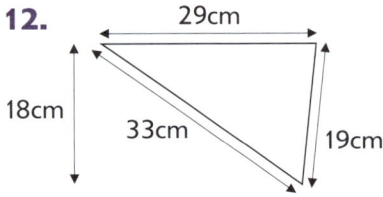

Perimeter: _____

Area: _____

Perimeter and area

Compound shapes

Compound shapes are made up of two or more 2D shapes, such as rectangles and squares.

When working out the perimeter of a compound shape, check that you have been given the measurements for every side. If any are missing, work them out before attempting to calculate the perimeter.

Find the perimeter of this compound shape.

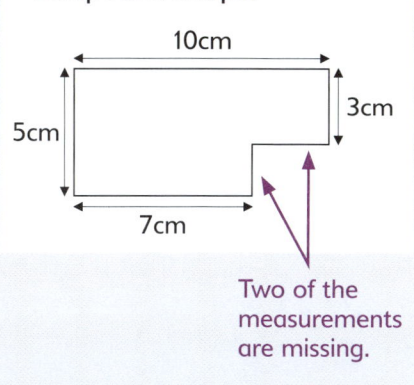

(Shape: 10cm top, 5cm left, 7cm bottom, 3cm right)

Two of the measurements are missing.

The top horizontal measurement shows that the shape is 10cm long. The bottom horizontal measurement is 7cm, so the missing horizontal length must be 3cm as 7cm + 3cm = 10cm.

The left-hand vertical measurement is 5cm. The far-right vertical measurement is 3cm, so the missing vertical measurement must be 2cm as 3cm + 2cm = 5cm.

Now that you have worked out all of the measurements, add them together to find the perimeter. 10cm + 3cm + 3cm + 2cm + 7cm + 5cm = 30cm

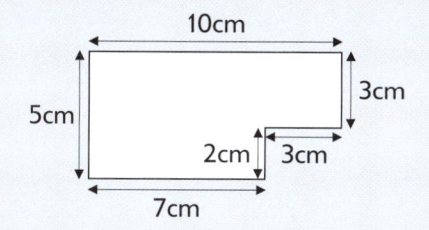

Answer: 30cm

(Shape with all measurements: 10cm, 5cm, 2cm, 3cm, 3cm, 7cm)

> **!** Check that all the measurements are written in the same unit of measure. If there is a mixture, convert some of them so that all of the measurements have the same unit of measure.

Find the area of this compound shape.

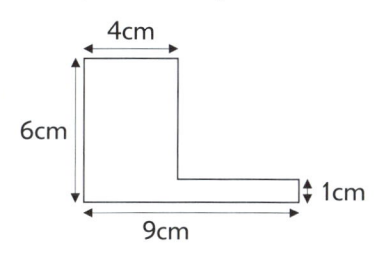

(L-shape: 4cm top, 6cm left, 9cm bottom, 1cm right)

To find the area, first split it into separate basic shapes. They can be split in one of two possible ways.

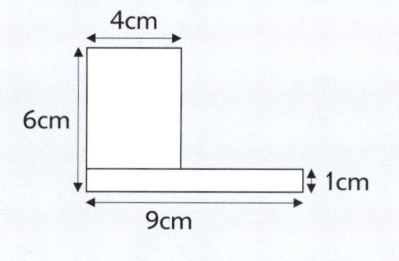

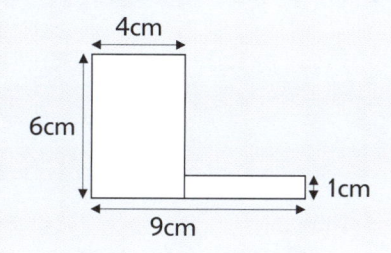

(Two diagrams showing different splits of the L-shape)

Once you have done this, work out the dimensions of each individual rectangle. You need to work out the missing measurements before calculating the area.

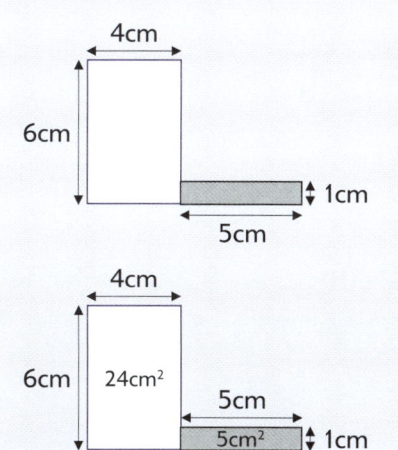

If the base horizontal length is 9cm and part of the top horizontal length is 4cm, then the lower horizontal length must be 5cm.

Multiply the length by the width to find the area of each rectangle. Finally, add the two areas together to get the total area for the compound shape: 24cm² + 5cm².

Answer: 29cm²

11+ Maths Study and Practice Book

Perimeter and area

Find the perimeter and the area of these compound shapes.

13.

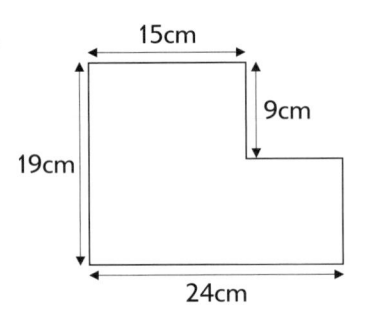

15cm, 9cm, 19cm, 24cm

Perimeter: _____

Area: _____

16.

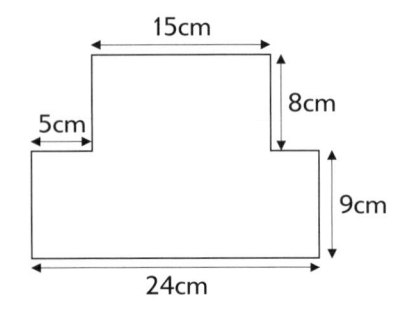

15cm, 8cm, 5cm, 9cm, 24cm

Perimeter: _____

Area: _____

14.

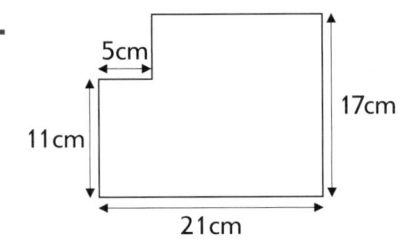

5cm, 17cm, 11cm, 21cm

Perimeter: _____

Area: _____

17.

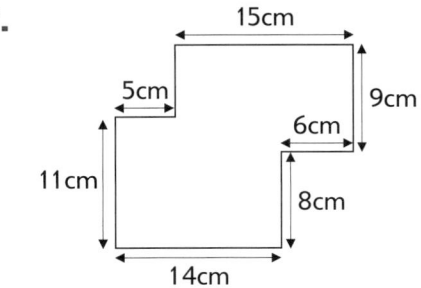

15cm, 5cm, 9cm, 6cm, 11cm, 8cm, 14cm

Perimeter: _____

Area: _____

15.

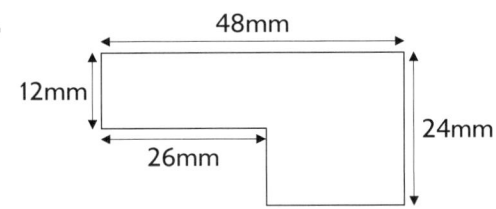

48mm, 12mm, 26mm, 24mm

Perimeter: _____

Area: _____

18.

8m, 3m, 9m, 12m, 5m, 2m

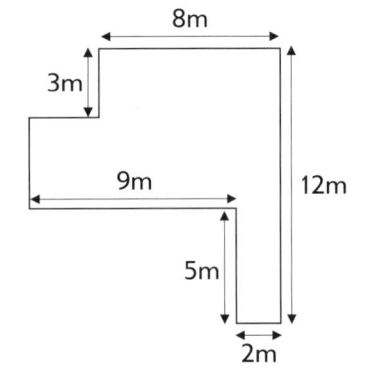

Perimeter: _____

Area: _____

Volume and surface area

The **volume** is the space inside a 3D shape. It is worked out by imagining how many cubes fit inside. Volume can be measured in any unit of length with a little 3 added to it, which we read as 'cubed', for example mm^3, cm^3, m^3.

Each of the cubes inside this cuboid has a length, depth and height of 1cm. As the cuboid is 3cm long, you can fit three cubes along its length. As it is 2cm deep, you can fit two cubes along its width. As it is 2cm high, you can fit two cubes along its height. That makes a total of 12 cubes.

If you multiply the length of the cuboid by the width of the cuboid by the height of the cuboid, you also get an answer of 12. For cuboids, this is how you calculate the volume: volume = length × width × height ($l × w × h$). So the volume of this cuboid is $12cm^3$.

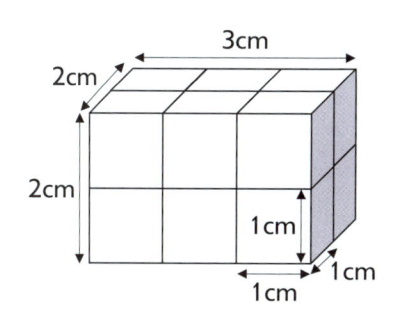

Always look carefully at the units of measure being used. If the units of measure for each side, or for parts of the same question, are different, convert them so that they are the same.

The surface area of a 3D shape is simply the total area of all the **faces** of the shape.

Find the surface area of this cuboid.

The two end faces are both 3cm × 2cm = $6cm^2$ each.

Two of the long rectangular faces are 5cm × 3cm = $15cm^2$ each.

The other two long rectangular faces are 5cm × 2cm = $10cm^2$ each.

So in total the surface area for this cuboid is 6 + 6 + 15 + 15 + 10 + 10 = $62cm^2$.

Answer: $62cm^2$

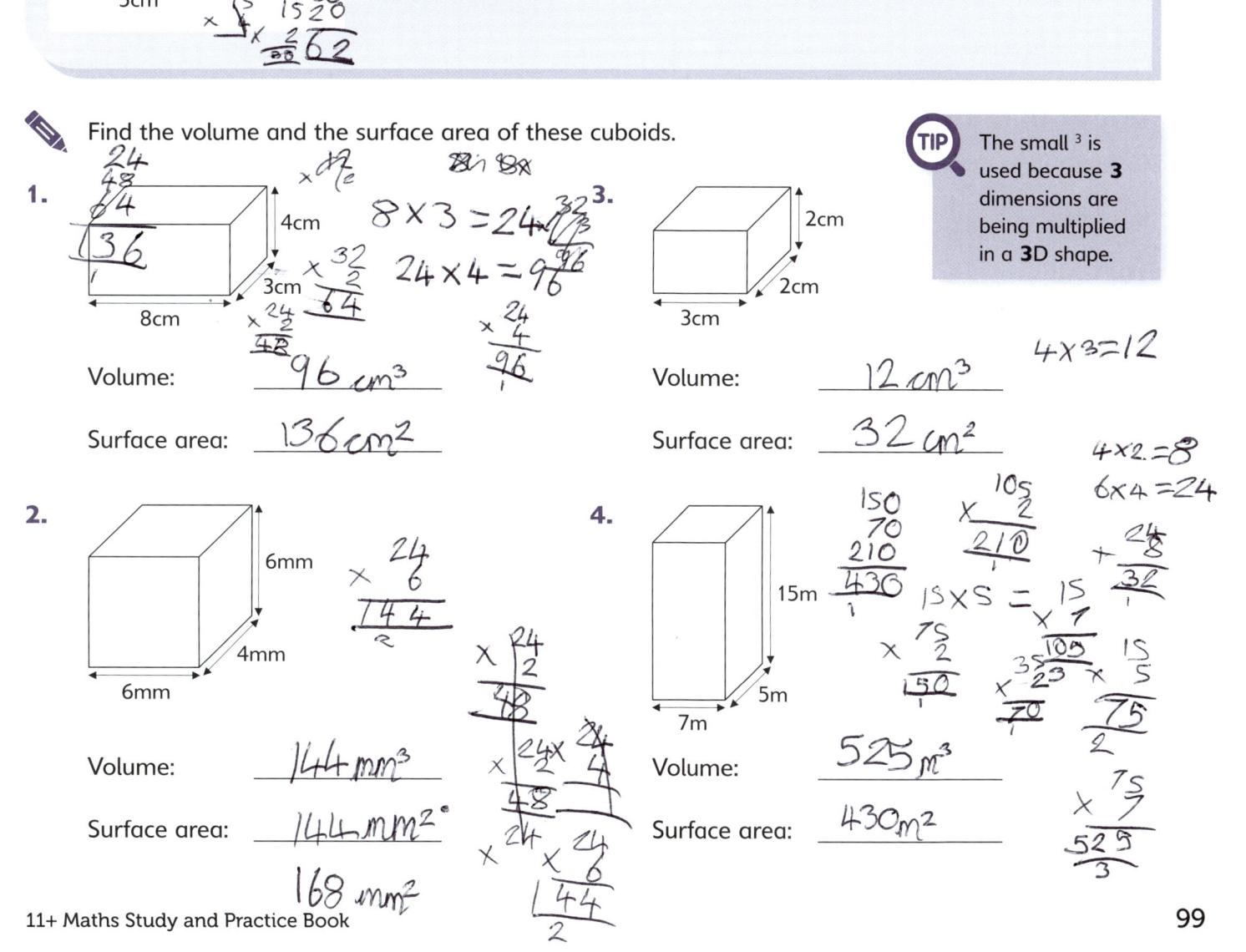

Find the volume and the surface area of these cuboids.

TIP The small ^{3} is used because **3** dimensions are being multiplied in a **3D** shape.

1. (8cm × 3cm × 4cm)
   Volume: _96 cm³_
   Surface area: _136 cm²_

2. (6mm × 6mm × 4mm)
   Volume: _144 mm³_
   Surface area: _144 mm²_

3. (3cm × 2cm × 2cm)
   Volume: _12 cm³_
   Surface area: _32 cm²_

4. (7m × 5m × 15m)
   Volume: _525 m³_
   Surface area: _430 m²_

11+ Maths Study and Practice Book

Measurement practice page 1

Now test your skills with these practice pages. If you get stuck, go back to pages 76 to 99 for some reminders.

Length, mass and capacity

Convert these measurements.

1. _____ g = 16.108kg

2. 34.01km = _____ m

3. _____ mm = 1.2m

4. 37cl = _____ l

5. 0.049l = _____ ml

6. A bottle contained 1.25l of orange squash. If Deeva uses 50ml of squash to make a drink, how many drinks could she make from the whole bottle? _____

7. Stuart drove 556km from Glasgow to London. He then drove 103km to Folkestone and travelled 51km through the Channel Tunnel to France. Once in France he drove a further 1073km down to Marseille. If he followed the same route home, how many km did Stuart travel in total? _____

8. Luke had to collect 8 bags of gravel that each weighed 35kg. What was the total weight of the gravel? _____

Imperial measures

Convert these measurements.

9. 6ft ≈ _____ cm

10. 7oz ≈ _____ g

11. 9pts ≈ _____ l

12. 6yds = _____ ft

13. 30cm ≈ _____ in

14. Abidemi measured the width of her bedroom as 10ft 4in. Approximately how many metres is this? _____

15. William was following a recipe that needed $2\frac{1}{2}$ pints of cream. Approximately how many ml is this? _____

16. Rhys weighs 25kg. Approximately how many stones is this? _____

Measurement practice page 2

Reading scales

What measurements are each of these scales showing?

1. _____ (ruler showing arrow at 18.5 cm)

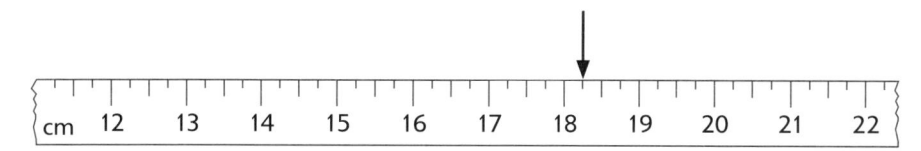

2. _____ (measuring jug showing 130 ml)

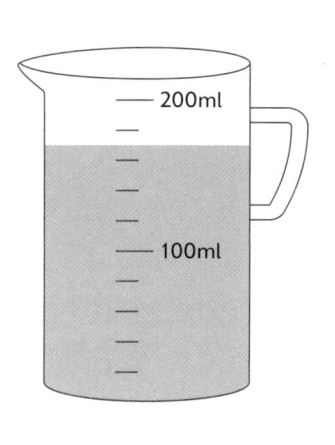

3. _____ (thermometer showing 27 °C)

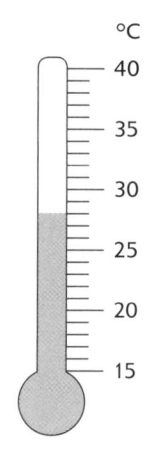

4. _____ (kitchen scale showing 0.5 kg)

What is the difference between the measurements shown on each of these pairs of scales?

5. _____ (bathroom scales: 34 kg and 35.5 kg)

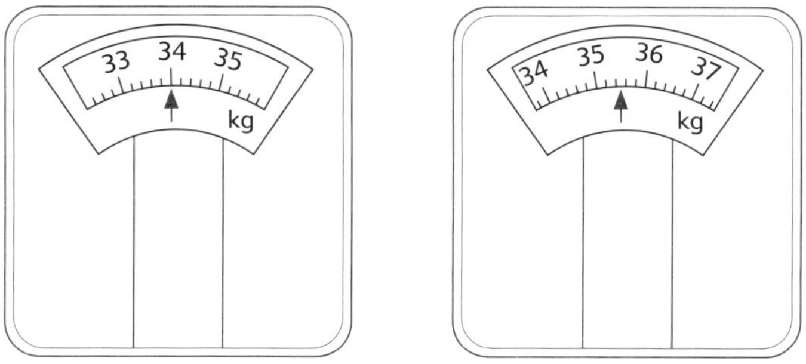

6. _____ (thermometers: −18 °C and 15 °C)

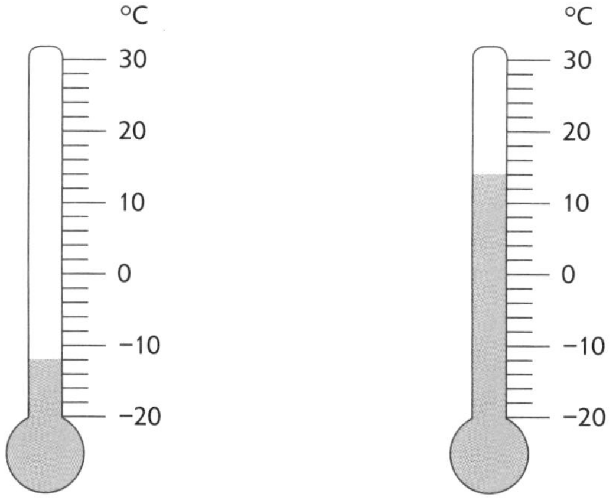

Measurement practice page 3

Scale

1. Jason is going for a hike. The map he is using has a scale of 1:250 000. If the distance he is hiking is 5cm on the map, how many km is it in real life? _____

2. Kalin draws a scale diagram of her garden. If it is 250m long in real life and she draws it as 5cm on her diagram, what scale has she used? _____

3. A map has a scale of 1:325 000. If a road is 13km long, how long will it be on the map? _____

4. A map has a scale of 1:275 000. If I measure the length of a town as 6cm, what is its length in real life? _____

5. A triangle is increased by a scale factor of 6. If the longest side of the original triangle was 5cm, what is the new length? _____

6. A square has a length of 7cm. It increases by a scale factor of 3. What is the area of the new square? _____

Time

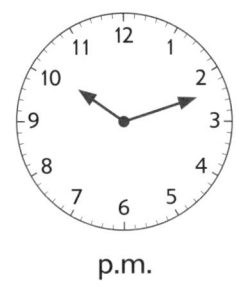

7. The time on this clock is 10 minutes slow. What is the actual time? Write the answer using 24-hour notation. _____

   (clock showing approximately 2:15 p.m.)

8. The time on this clock is 25 minutes fast. What is the actual time? Write the answer using 12-hour notation. _____

   (digital clock showing 16:41)

9. Astrid goes for a run at 18:39 and gets back at 20:14. How long does she go running for? _____

10. Olivia needs to be back home by 1.30 in the afternoon for her grocery delivery. If she goes shopping at 10.55 a.m., how long does she have until she needs to be home? _____

This table shows the times recorded by four children running 100m.

Child	Michael	Asha	Louis	Kai
Time	12.34 sec	13.06 sec	12.29 sec	12.78 sec

11. Which child was the fastest? _____

12. By how much was the fastest child faster than the slowest child? _____

Measurement practice page 4

Time zones

This table shows the time zones of six cities.

City	Time related to GMT
London	0
Amsterdam	+1
San Diego	−8
Honolulu	−10
Calcutta	+5
Samoa	+12

1. When it is 13:30 in Samoa, what time will it be in Honolulu?

2. When it is 19:15 in London, what time will it be in San Diego?

3. New York is 3 hours ahead of San Diego. When it is 12.15 p.m. in Calcutta, what time will it be in New York?

These clocks show the times in five major cities.

17:36	15:36	22:36	10:36	12:36
Helsinki	London	Bangkok	Miami	Buenos Aires

4. What is the time difference between Miami and Bangkok?

5. When it is 13:05 in Buenos Aires, what time will it be in Helsinki?

6. A clock in Helsinki is running 22 minutes slow. When it is 07:54 in Miami, what time will the clock in Helsinki show?

Days, weeks, months and years

7. How many months are there in 7 years?

8. How many decades are there in a millennium?

9. How many days were there in February 1992?

10. How many days are there between September 12th and November 1st?

11. Irfan was born in September 2007, Imogen was born in January 2008, Stevie was born in August 2007 and Laurie was born in March 2008. Who is the oldest?

12. Dylan ordered a new car on December 4th 2015. He had it delivered on March 1st. How many days did he have to wait for his new car?

Measurement practice page 5

Speed

1. Max was cycling at 21mph. If he rode for 2 hours and 20 minutes, how far did he travel?

2. Selma needs to get to Glasgow by 3.00 p.m. If the journey is 330 miles and she leaves at 9.30 a.m., what average speed must she travel at?

3. A passenger train travels at 60mph and a freight train travels at 40mph. If the freight train leaves the station at 10 a.m. and the passenger train leaves at 11 a.m., at what time will the passenger train overtake the freight train?

Money

4. Harper needs to buy a new laptop. She has managed to save £298 and is then given £134 for her birthday. If the laptop costs £499, how much more money does Harper need to save?

5. Zack wants a new car. He can't decide between one costing £11 340 and one costing £15 075. How much will he save if he buys the cheaper car?

Look at this conversion chart.

UK (pound) £	South Africa (rand) R	USA (dollar) $	Sweden (krona) kr
1	18	1.3	12

6. How many South African rand will £30 buy you?

7. I spent $260 while on holiday in America. How much did I spend in pounds?

8. If a TV costs 1800kr, how much would it cost in South Africa?

Temperature

9. The temperature in New York dropped from 28°C to 12.5°C. By how many degrees did the temperature drop?

10. The temperature outside is −24°C and inside is 19°C. What is the difference in temperature?

11. The temperature is −7°C. How much must it rise to reach 15°C?

12. The average temperature for April is 12°C. If the temperature for April one year is on average 3.2°C warmer, what would the average for April that year be?

13. If the temperature reads 12°C, approximately what would this be in °F?

Measurement practice page 6

Perimeter and area

Find the perimeter and the area of these rectangles.

1. 19cm × 6cm

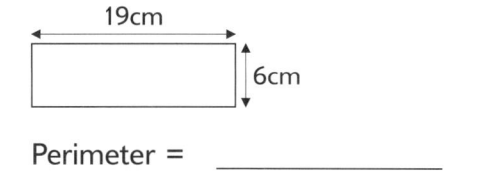

Perimeter = _____

Area = _____

2. 11mm × 18mm

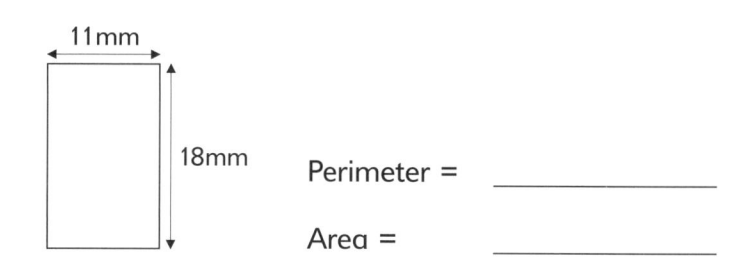

Perimeter = _____

Area = _____

3. If a rectangle has a perimeter of 38cm and a length of 12cm, what would its area be? _____

4. A square has an area of 196mm². What is its perimeter? _____

Find the perimeter of this triangle.

5. Triangle with sides 8cm, 8cm, 4cm _____

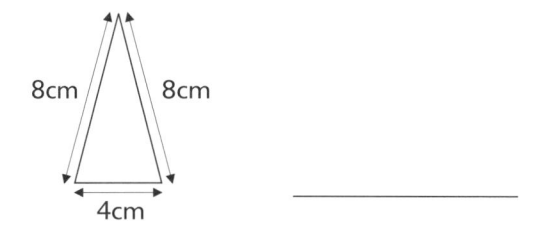

Find the area of this triangle.

6. Triangle with 22m and 13m _____

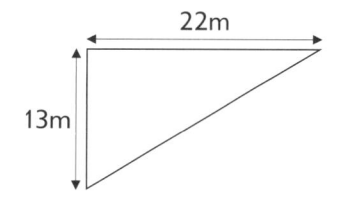

Find the perimeter and the area of these compound shapes.

7. Compound shape: 9cm, 12cm, 10cm, 3cm

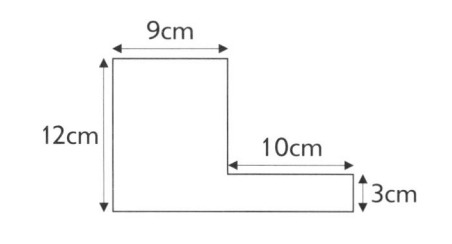

Perimeter: _____

Area: _____

8. Compound shape: 14cm, 21cm, 7cm, 26cm

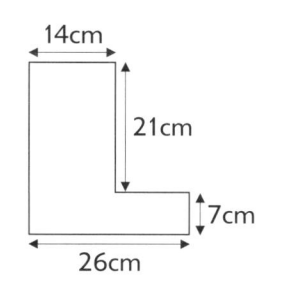

Perimeter: _____

Area: _____

9. Compound shape: 12m, 4m, 13m, 7m

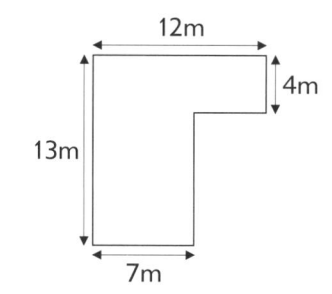

Perimeter: _____

Area: _____

Volume and surface area

Find the volume and the surface area of these cuboids.

10. Cuboid 19cm × 12cm × 10cm

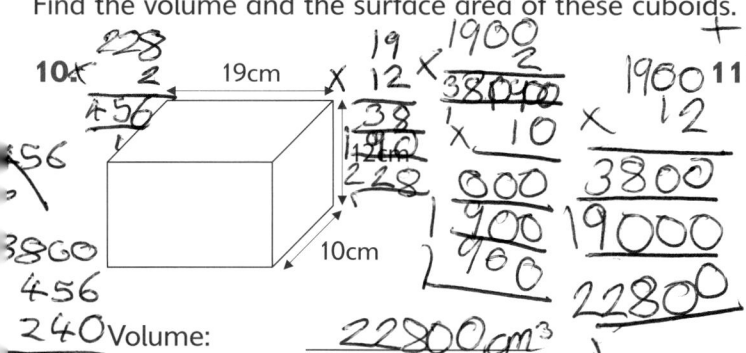

Volume: 22800 cm³

Surface area: 4556 cm²

11. Cuboid 31cm × 6cm × 5cm

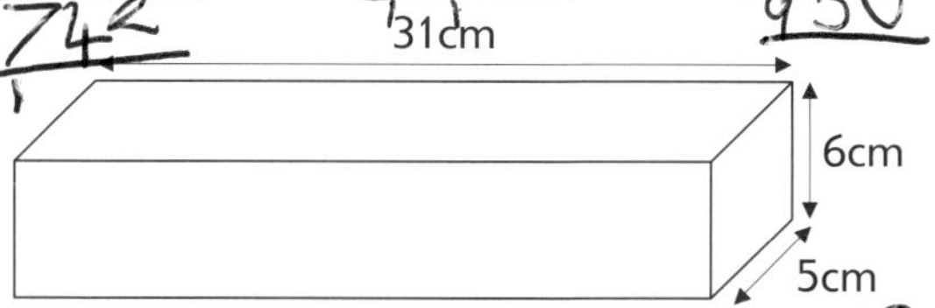

Volume: 930 cm³

Surface area: 742 cm²

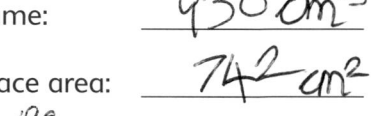

Parallel and perpendicular lines

Parallel and **perpendicular** are words that are used to describe lines.

Parallel lines always stay the same distance apart (think of train tracks).

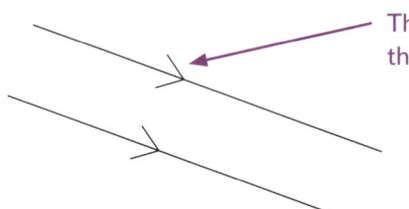

← These arrows show that lines are parallel.

Perpendicular lines cross each other at **right angles**.

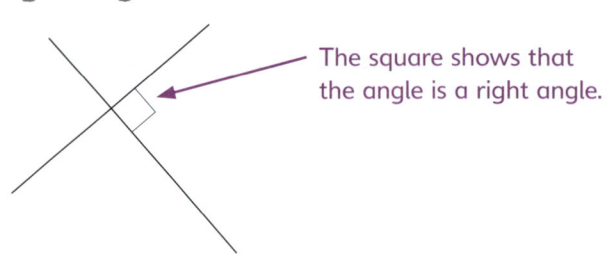

← The square shows that the angle is a right angle.

Parallel lines do not have to be straight. These lines are parallel because they are the same distance apart all along their lengths.

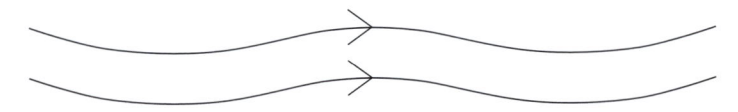

Look at this shape. It contains two pairs of parallel lines and four lines that are perpendicular.

Lines **A** and **C** are parallel and lines **B** and **D** are parallel.

Lines **A** and **B** are perpendicular, lines **B** and **C** are perpendicular, lines **C** and **D** are perpendicular and lines **D** and **A** are perpendicular.

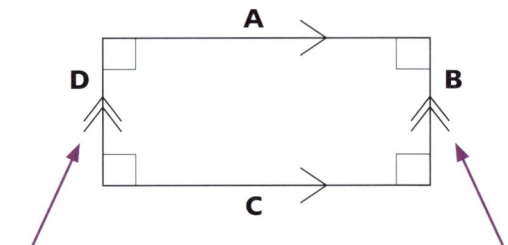

The double arrows just show that while the lines are parallel, they are not parallel with the lines that have a single arrow.

For each pair of lines, write whether they are parallel, perpendicular or neither.

1. _____

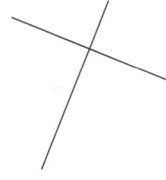

2. _____

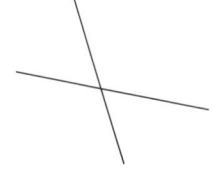

3. _____

4. Draw arrows to show the pair of parallel lines.

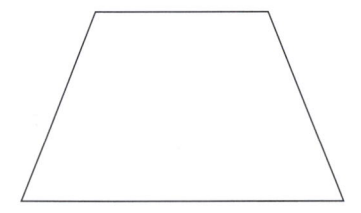

5. Draw squares to show where the perpendicular lines meet.

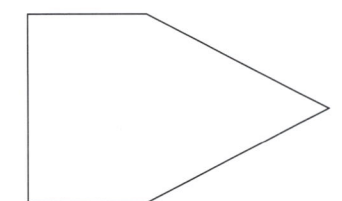

6. Draw arrows and squares to identify the parallel and perpendicular lines.

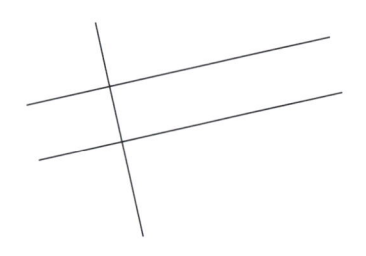

Angles

Different types of angles

Angles measure the amount something turns or rotates. They are measured in degrees (°).

There are six different types of angle:

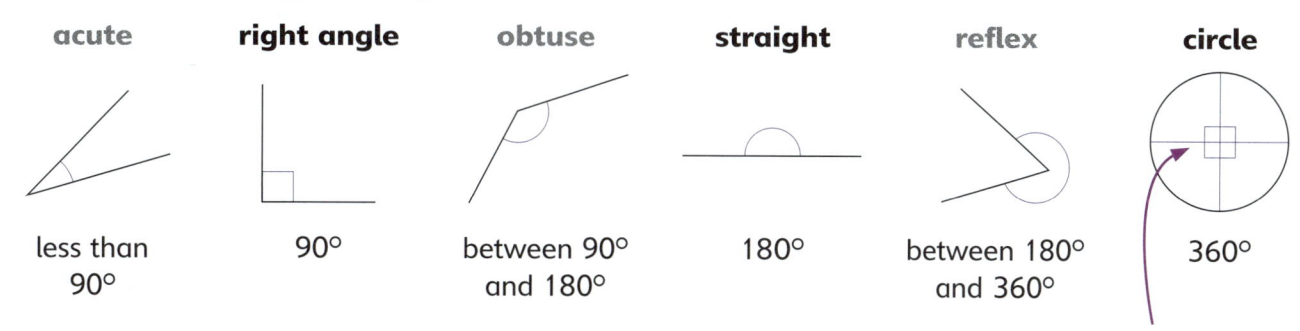

acute	right angle	obtuse	straight	reflex	circle
less than 90°	90°	between 90° and 180°	180°	between 180° and 360°	360°

Notice that the angles in a full circle add up to 360°. Here, four right angles (90° each) add up to 360°.

TIP **A**cute angles are the smallest which makes them **cute** like a small little kitten!
Re**flex** angles are very **flex**ible. They can bend backwards.

You use a protractor when measuring or drawing angles.

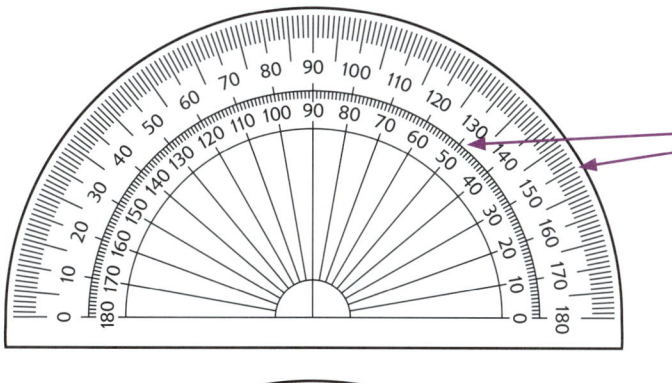

There are two scales of measure on a protractor – an inner and an outer scale. Always start at 0 to make sure you are using the right scale.

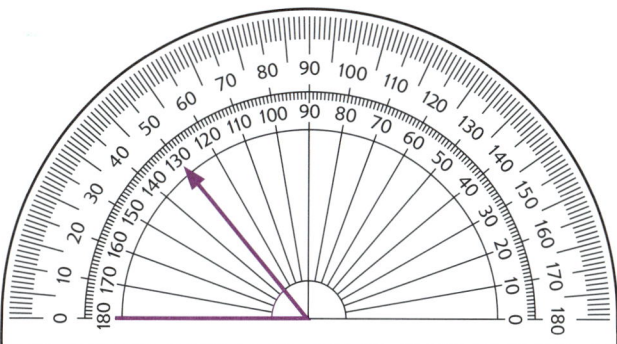

You can always check you have used the correct scale by thinking about the type of angle you are measuring. For example, if it's an acute angle it should be less than 90°, so if you've got an answer greater than 90° you know your measurement is incorrect.

Look at the angle being measured here. The baseline of the angle points to the 0 on the outer scale, so you need to follow the outer scale round, which takes you to the 50° marker. You can be sure that it is 50° and not 130° because it looks like an acute angle.

You will notice that protractors only go up to 180°. Reflex angles are larger than 180°, so you cannot use the protractor to measure them. However, you know that a circle is 360°.

The reflex angle + the internal angle = a full circle = 360°.

To measure a reflex angle, measure the internal angle that goes with it and then subtract that angle from 360°. That will give you the reflex angle.

If the internal angle measures 110°, then the reflex angle must be 250° as 360° − 110° = 250°.

11+ Maths Study and Practice Book

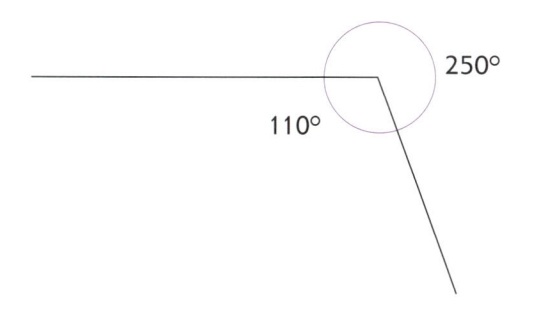

Angles

It is also important to know the points of the compass and the angles between them.
There are eight points that you need to know.

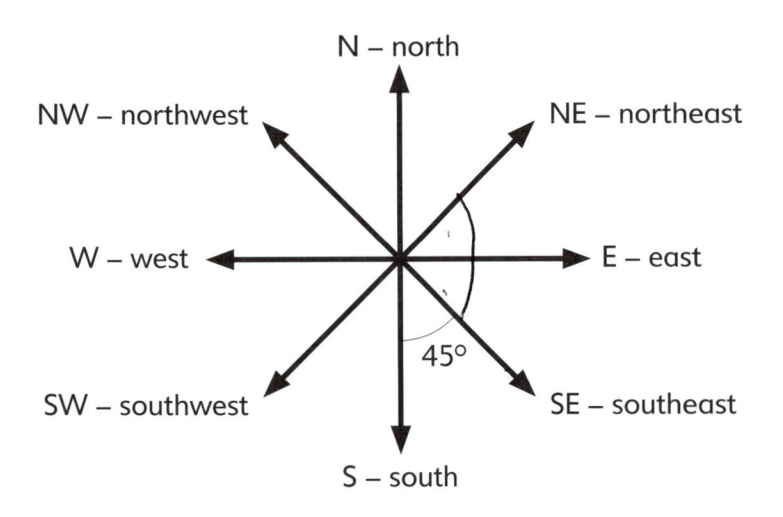

- N – north
- NE – northeast
- E – east
- SE – southeast
- S – south
- SW – southwest
- W – west
- NW – northwest

The angle between each of these points is 45°. Between the main points of N, E, S and W the angle is 90°.

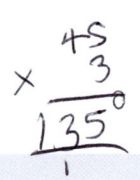

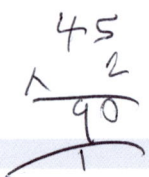

(handwritten calculations: 45 × 3 = 135; 45 × 2 = 90)

What is the size of the angle between E and SW?

There are three 45° angles between E and SW, so the total size of the angle will be 45° + 45° + 45° = 135°.

Answer: 135°

Name the type of angle marked in each of these shapes.

1. _acute_
2. _obtuse_
3. _Right angle_

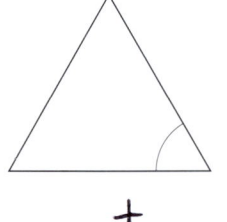

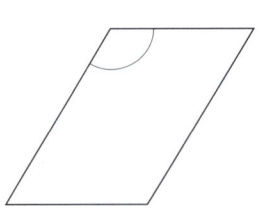

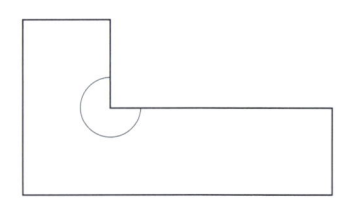

Measure these angles.

4. 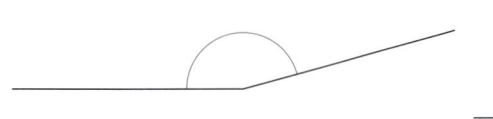
5.

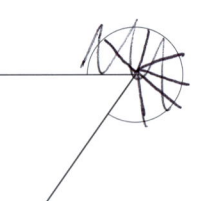

6. Circle the letter of the angle that is approximately 100°.

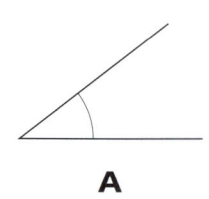

A 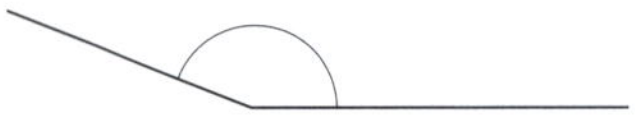   B 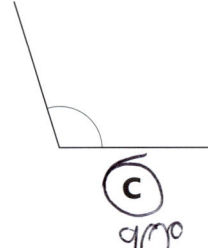   **(C)** 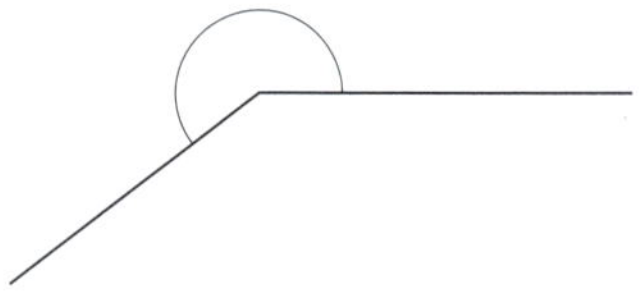   D

7. What is the size of the largest angle between SE and NE? _90°_

Angles

Calculating missing angles

It is important to know the angles of shapes (pages 111 to 113) as well as straight lines and circles (pages 106 and 114) as you will often be asked to fill in missing angles within shapes.

What is the size of angle x?

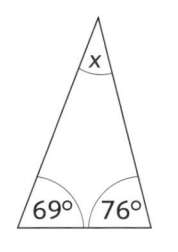

The sum of the angles in a triangle is always 180° (see page 111).

If you know that two of the angles are 69° and 76°, then the third angle must add to them to total 180°.

69° + 76° = 145° and 180° − 145° = 35°

Answer: 35°

When straight lines cross parallel lines, many of the angles will be **congruent** (equal).

These four angles are all the same.

These four angles are all the same.

TIP Angles in a quadrilateral always add up to 360° (see page 111).

By also knowing that a straight line measures 180°, you can work out many missing angles.

What is the size of angle c?

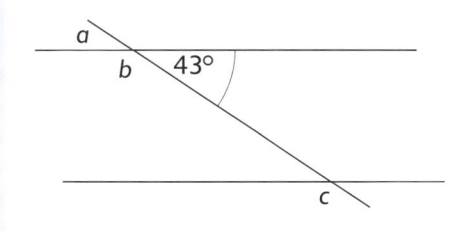

a is opposite the measured angle, therefore $a = 43°$.

b is on a straight line with the measured angle.
180° − 43° = 137°, so $b = 137°$.

c is equal to b.

Answer: 137°

Calculate the angles labelled with letters.

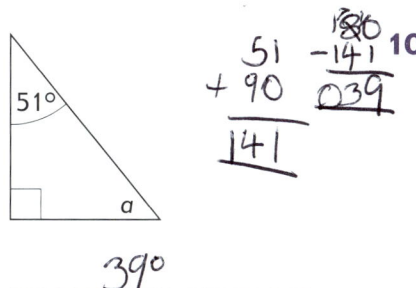

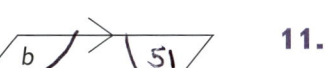

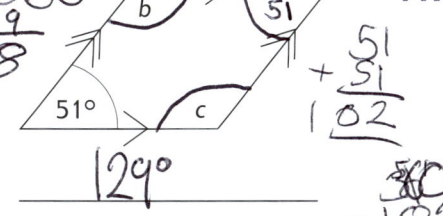

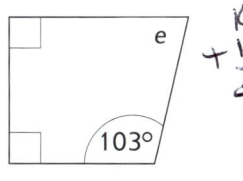

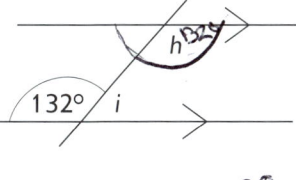

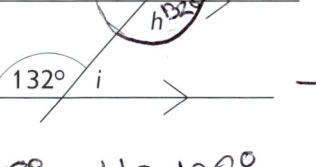

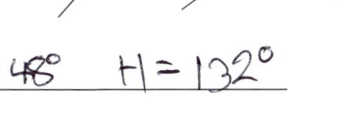

8. (triangle with 51° and right angle, angle a) — 39°

9. (shape with 51°, b, c) — 129°

10. (quadrilateral with 41°, d) — 49°

11. (shape with 103°, e) — 77°

12. (shape with 46°, 51°, f, g) — 46° & 83°

13. (shape with 132°, h, i) — H = 132°, i = 48°

11+ Maths Study and Practice Book

109

Directions of turn

You will need to be able to recognise or describe how a shape has turned or rotated. There are two things that you need to consider: the direction of turn and the size of the turn.

Turns can either be in a clockwise or anticlockwise direction.

Clockwise
This is turning to the right: the same direction as the hands on a clock turn.

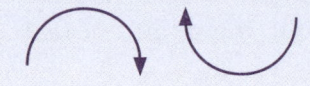

Anticlockwise
This is turning to the left: the opposite direction to which the hands on a clock turn.

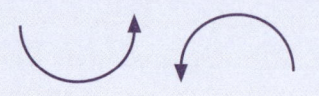

These turns will then be measured in degrees, usually in increments of 45°.

You would normally describe the direction of turn based on the smaller angle of turn, so 45° clockwise rather than 315° anticlockwise. However, always check to see what the question is asking as it may specify the direction you need to go.

Describe the direction and size of turn of this pair of shapes.

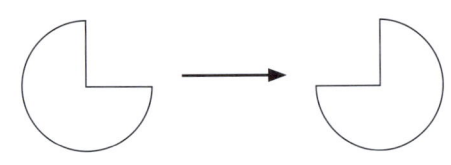

Look at the shape and decide whether you think it has turned clockwise or anticlockwise and by how much. It might help to focus on one part of the shape when you think about how much it has turned. Here, the shape has turned 90° anticlockwise.

If you were required to say how far it had turned clockwise, then it would have rotated 270° clockwise.

Answer: 90° anticlockwise

TIP If you are not sure how a shape has turned, you can always draw it out on a piece of paper and then turn it until it looks like the shape it needs to become.

Describe the direction and size of turn for each pair of shapes.

1.

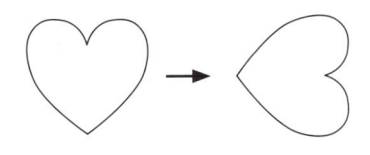

2.

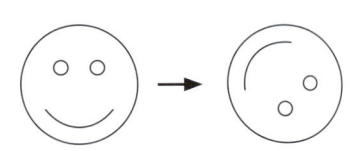

3.

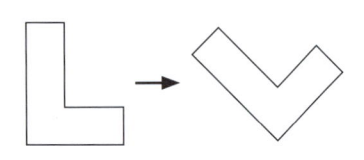

4.

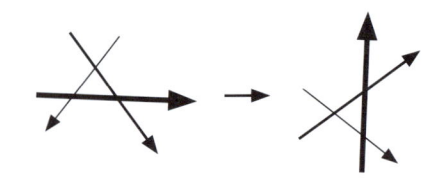

5.

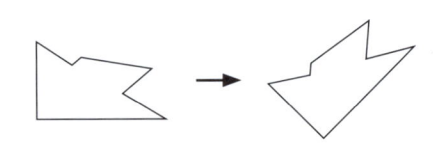

6.

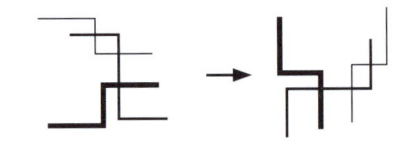

Properties of 2D shapes

2D shapes are flat. 2D is an abbreviation of 2-dimensional. A dimension is something that can be measured. 2D shapes have two dimensions that can be measured: a length and a width.

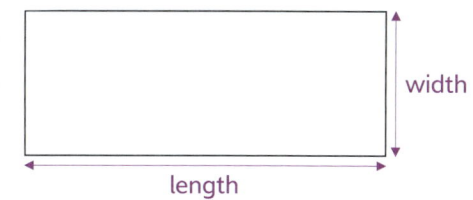

They are made up of sides and angles.

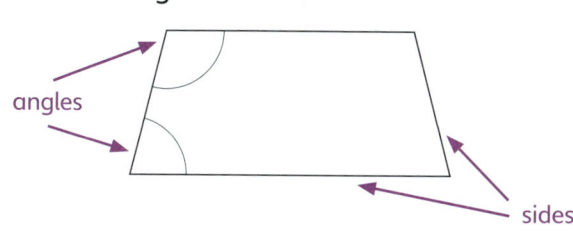

2D shapes can only be drawn. Once they are cut out of a piece of paper, they become 3D as, even though paper is very thin, it still adds a third dimension of height.

Number of sides	Shape name	Total of internal angles
3	triangle	180°
4	quadrilateral	360°
5	pentagon	540°
6	hexagon	720°
7	heptagon	900°
8	octagon	1080°
9	nonagon	1260°
10	decagon	1440°

! The word '**polygon**' is often used when describing some 2D shapes. A polygon is any 2D shape made of straight sides, so not, for example, a circle or oval or any shape with a curved side.

TIP Look at how the total of the internal angles increases by 180° as the number of sides increases by 1.

TIP The word hexagon has an 'x' in it just like the word 'six'. That will help you remember that a hexagon has six sides.

Triangles and quadrilaterals are very common shapes. All the different shapes within these groups have specific names.

Triangles

Equilateral:
three equal sides,
three equal angles (60°)

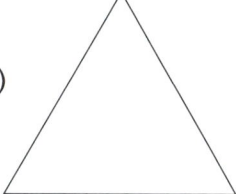

Scalene:
no equal sides
or equal angles

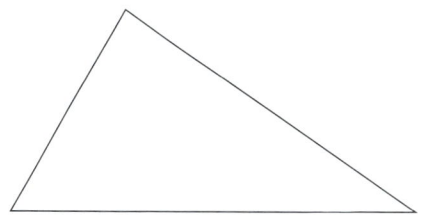

Isosceles:
two equal sides,
two equal angles

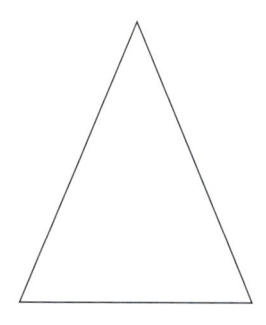

Right-angled: one right angle (90°),
can be isosceles or scalene

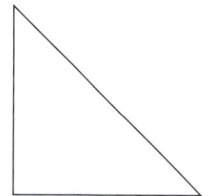

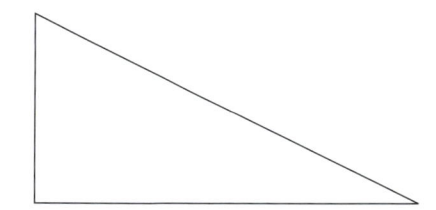

11+ Maths Study and Practice Book

Properties of 2D shapes

Quadrilaterals

A quadrilateral is any shape with four sides.

Square: four equal sides, four right angles (90°), two pairs of parallel sides

Rhombus: four equal sides, opposite sides are parallel and opposite angles are equal

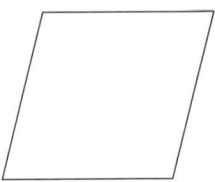

Trapezium: one pair of parallel sides

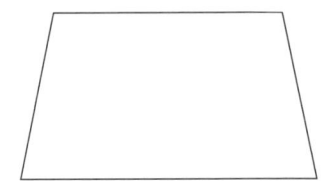

Rectangle: opposite sides are parallel and of equal length, four right angles (90°)

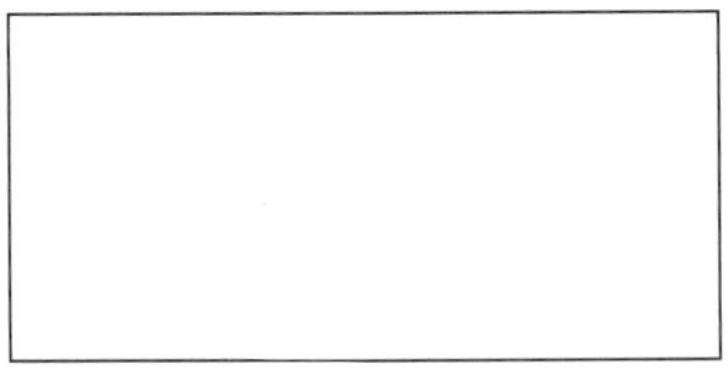

Parallelogram: opposite sides are parallel and of equal length

Kite: two pairs of equal sides, two equal angles

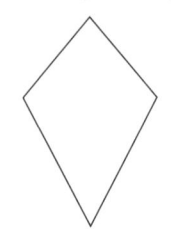

> ❗ A square can be classed as a rectangle, rhombus and parallelogram, but a rectangle, rhombus or parallelogram is not always a square.

For all other shapes, there are simply regular and irregular shapes (see page 113 for definition of regular shapes).

✏️ Now answer the following questions.

1. I have three sides, two of which are equal. What am I? _____

2. I have four sides and one pair of parallel sides. What am I? _____

3. What is the name of this shape?

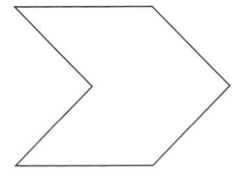

4. What is the name of this shape?

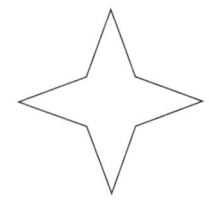

5. How many diagonals are there in a pentagon? Draw them in.

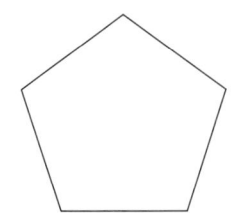

> ❗ Diagonals refer to the lines that join the corners of 2D shapes. They do not need to be slanted. They can be horizontal or vertical.

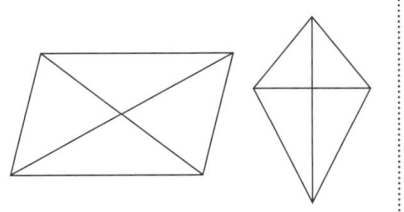

6. Each of my internal angles is 60°. What am I? _____

Regular shapes

These are all regular shapes.

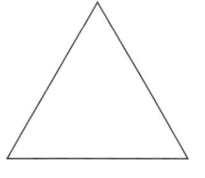

| regular triangle (equilateral) | regular quadrilateral | regular pentagon | regular hexagon | regular heptagon | regular octagon |

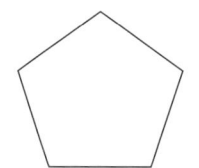

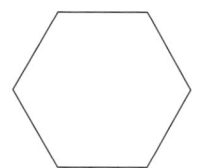

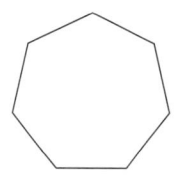

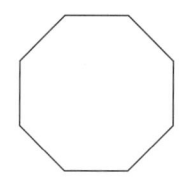

Regular shapes are polygons that have a certain set of properties:
- they have equal length sides
- they have equal size interior angles
- they have the same number of lines of **symmetry** as number of sides
- their order of **rotational symmetry** (see page 116) will equal the number of sides.

> **!** Irregular polygons have at least one angle or side that is different to the others.

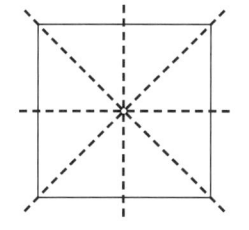

four sides = four lines of symmetry

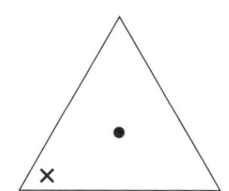

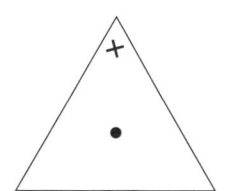

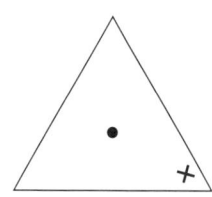

The triangle (three sides) can be rotated 360° around the origin (centre) and look the same three times.

You can also work out the size of the interior angles.

To do this, you first need to work out the exterior angle. This is the angle created between any side of a shape and a line extended from the next side. The key rule to remember is that all of the exterior angles of a polygon add up to 360°.

If the 5 external angles total 360°, then each one must be 72° (360 ÷ 5 = 72).

The interior and exterior angle are measured from the same straight line and so together will add up to 180°. If the exterior angle of a regular pentagon is 72°, then each interior angle must be 180 − 72 = 108°.

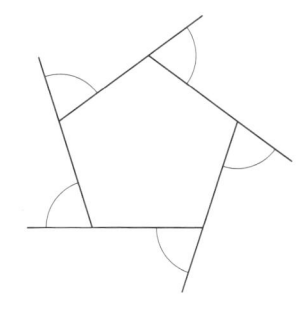

✏️ Now answer the following questions.

1. How many lines of symmetry are there in a regular octagon? _____

2. What is the size of an internal angle within a regular hexagon? _____

3. What is the order of rotational symmetry of a regular pentagon? _____

4. What is the perimeter of this equilateral triangle?

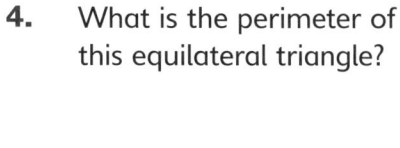

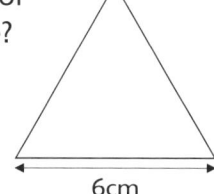

   6cm

5. How many lines of symmetry does this shape have? Draw them in.

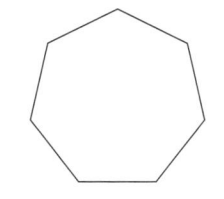

6. What is the total of the interior angles in a regular decagon? _____

11+ Maths Study and Practice Book

Circles

Circles are unlike most shapes because they do not have any straight lines.

Circles have three measurements: the **diameter**, the **radius** and the **circumference**.

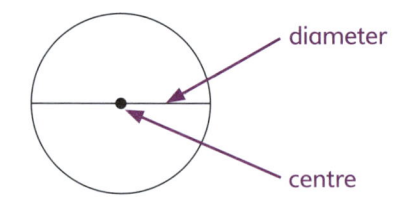

The diameter is the distance from one side of the circle to the other (crossing through the centre).

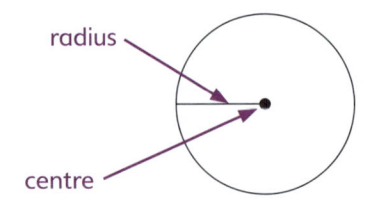

The radius is the distance from the centre of the circle to the edge. It is half the diameter of the circle.

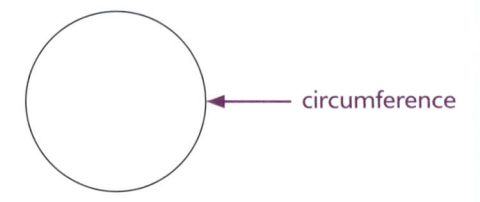

The circumference is the length all the way around the edge (the same as the perimeter in polygons).

To find the circumference of a circle you multiply the radius by 3.14 (π) and then double it ($2\pi r$).

You can find the area of a circle by using the following formula.

area of a circle = $\pi \times radius^2$

You do not need to remember these formulas because, if you are asked to find the circumference or area of a circle, you will be given them in the tests.

What is the area of the circle?

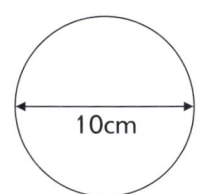

If the diameter of the circle is 10cm, then the radius is 5cm. You will need to use the formula $\pi \times radius^2$ to find the area of the circle.

$3.14 \times 5^2 = 3.14 \times 25 = 78.5cm^2$

Answer: 78.5cm²

Now answer the following questions.

1. The diameter of a circle is 27cm. What is the radius? _____

2. The radius of a circle is 14.25cm. What is the diameter? _____

3. If the radius of a circle is 5cm, what is the circumference? _____

4. Using the formular $2\pi r$ ($\pi = 3.14$), work out the circumference of a circle with a radius of 3cm. _____

5. The length of these three circles is 15cm. What is their radius?

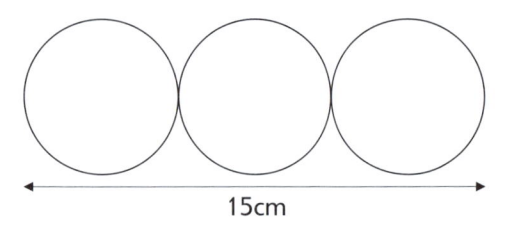

   15cm
   _____

6. Using the formular πr^2 ($\pi = 3.14$), work out the area of a circle with a diameter of 4cm. _____

Symmetry

A shape has a line of symmetry when it can be folded in half and each half can fit exactly together (like a butterfly).

A line of symmetry is also sometimes called a **mirror line** because the two halves of the shape are reflections of each other.

The line of symmetry is usually drawn with either a dotted or dashed line.

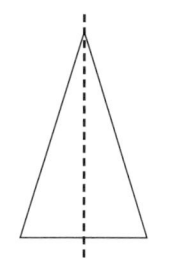

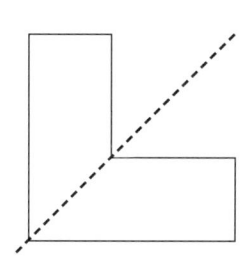

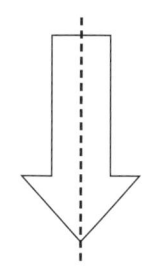

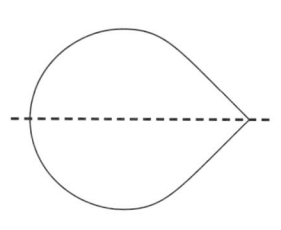

Some shapes may have several lines of symmetry.

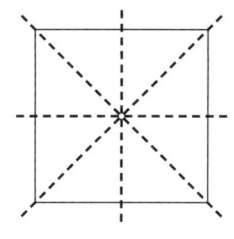

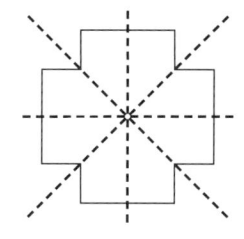

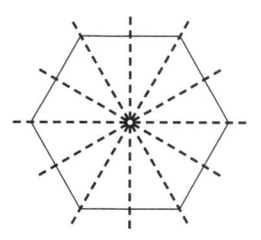

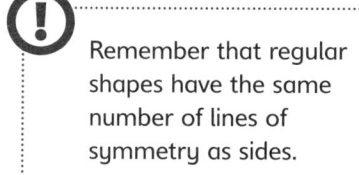

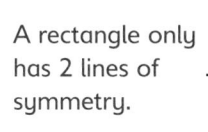

4 lines of symmetry   4 lines of symmetry   6 lines of symmetry

> ❗ Remember that regular shapes have the same number of lines of symmetry as sides.

A rectangle only has 2 lines of symmetry.

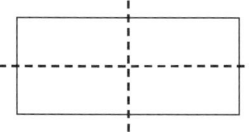

With a diagonal line of symmetry, the symmetrical shape would look like this, not a rectangle.

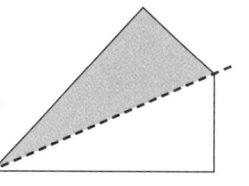

> ❗ Many people make the mistake of thinking that rectangles have four lines of symmetry.

Some shapes have no lines of symmetry.

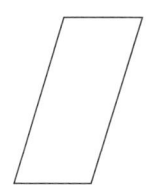

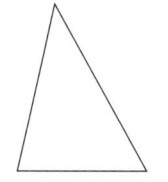

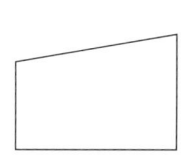

✏️ How many lines of symmetry do each of these shapes have? Draw them in.

1.

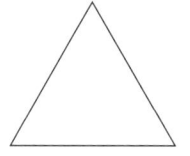

2.

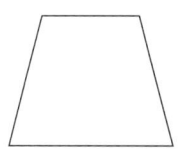

3.

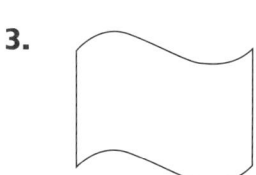

4.

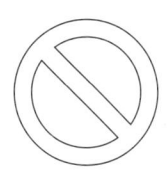

5.

6. Here is half a shape. When it is reflected in the mirror line, what is the name of the whole shape?

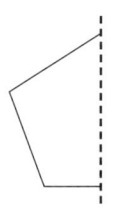

11+ Maths Study and Practice Book

Rotational symmetry

When shapes are rotated, if they appear to look the same at any point while completing a 360° turn, then they are said to have rotational symmetry.

The point around which a shape is rotated is called the centre of rotation.

The number of times a shape looks the same during a 360° turn is called its order of rotational symmetry.

TIP You can add a mark to a shape when trying to work out the order of rotational symmetry. Then turn the page 360° to try to work out what the order would be.

If this rectangle is rotated 360°, it will look exactly the same twice during the rotation.

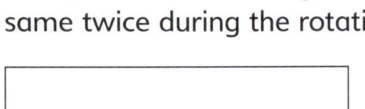

Rotated 180°, the rectangle looks exactly the same.

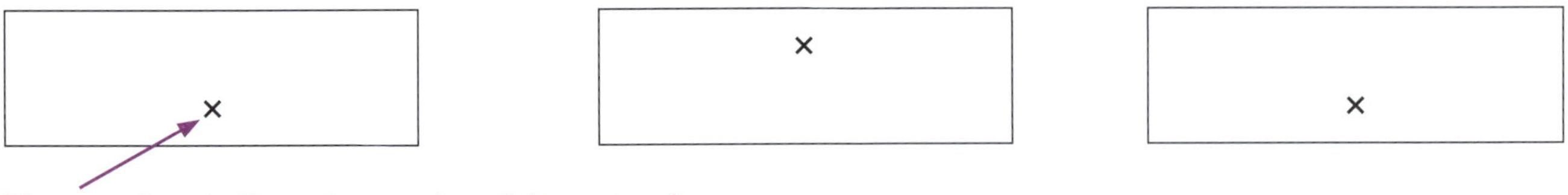

Rotated 360°, the rectangle looks exactly the same.

The cross is to indicate the rotation of the rectangle.

A rectangle therefore has rotational symmetry of order 2 because it looks the same twice within a 360° rotation.

All shapes have rotational symmetry of at least order 1 as all shapes will look the same once rotated 360°.

What is the order of rotational symmetry of each of these shapes?

1. (square) _____

2. (semicircle shape) _____

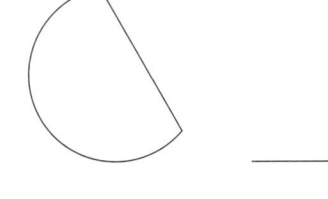

3. (parallelogram) _____

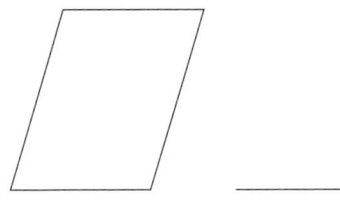

4. (octagon) _____

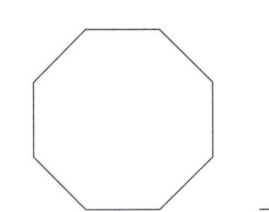

> Regular shapes have the same order of rotation as number of sides.

5. Shade one more square on the diagram so that the new shape has rotational symmetry of order 2.

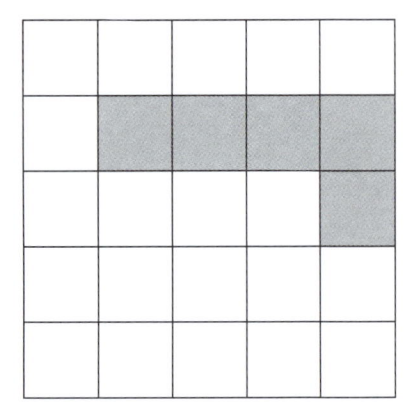

6. Shade two more squares on the diagram so that the new shape has rotational symmetry of order 4.

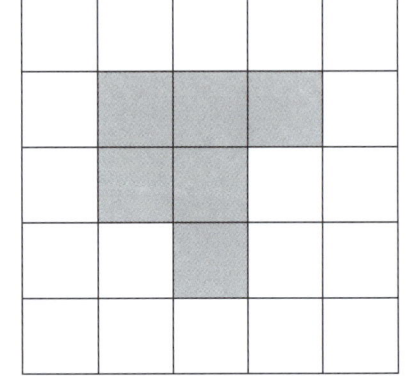

116 Schofield & Sims

Properties of 3D shapes

3D shapes are solid. 3D is an abbreviation of 3-dimensional. Remember, a dimension is something that can be measured. 3D shapes have three dimensions that can be measured: a length, a width and a height (or depth).

3D shapes are made up of faces, **edges** and **vertices**.

The faces are the 2D shapes that make up each part of the 3D shape.

The edges are where the sides of the faces meet.

The vertices are the points where three or more edges meet. A single point is called a vertex.

There are two main types of 3D shape: pyramids and prisms.

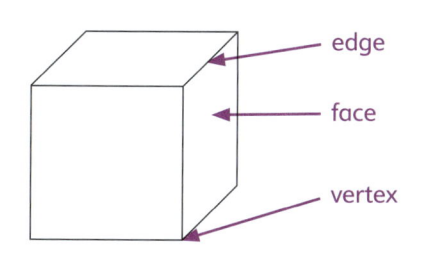

Pyramids

Pyramids rise to a point. It you cut them at any point up their height, the shape of the face will stay the same but will be a different size.

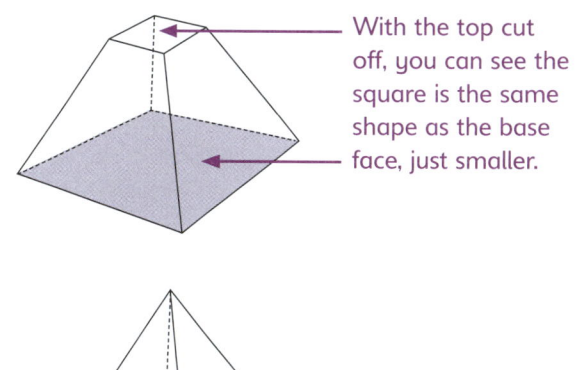

The number of triangular faces a pyramid has depends on how many sides the base face has. This number is always the same unless the pyramid is a tetrahedron. For example, a square-based pyramid has four triangular faces. The shape of the base gives the pyramid its name.

- Triangle-based pyramids (also known as tetrahedrons) have a triangle base.
- Square-based pyramids have a square base.
- Pentagonal pyramids have a pentagon base.
- Hexagonal pyramids have a hexagon base, and so on.

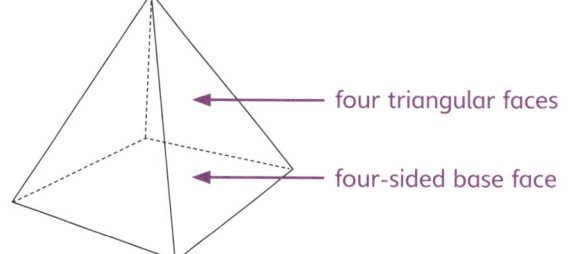

Prisms

Prisms stay the same size throughout their length. Wherever it is cut, the face will be the same shape and size.

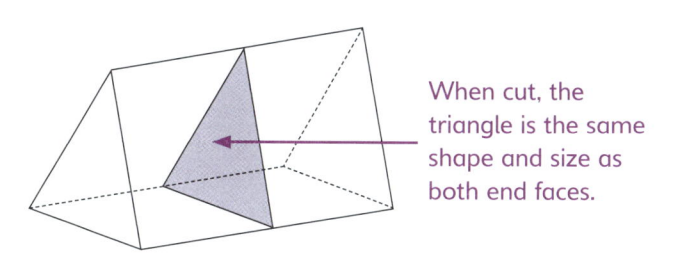

They have identical faces at each end and these give the prism its name. Depending on how many sides the end faces have, that number of rectangular faces will join the two end faces. For example, a triangular prism has three rectangular faces.

- Triangular prisms have triangles at each end.
- Pentagonal prisms have pentagons at each end.
- Hexagonal prisms have hexagons at each end, and so on.
- Cubes (or square prisms) have square faces.
- Cuboids are also known as square prisms if they have square ends and as rectangular prisms if they have rectangular ends.

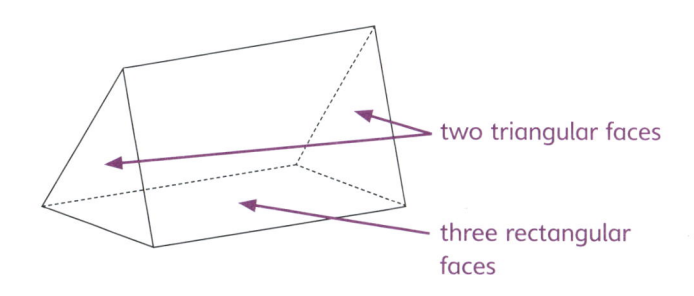

Properties of 3D shapes

Cylinders, cones and spheres are also common 3D shapes but are not classified as either pyramids or prisms. They are unusual because they have curved faces. See below and on page 119 for the properties of these 3D shapes.

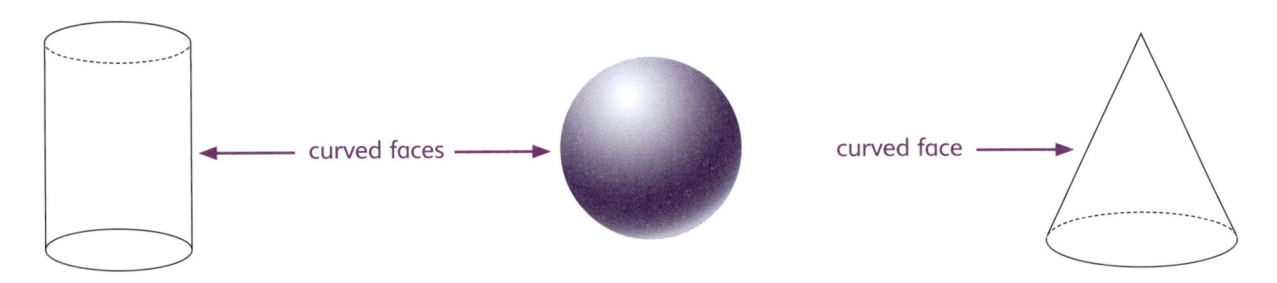

← curved faces → curved face →

> **!** Prisms and pyraminds are **polyhedrons** which means that all their faces are flat. A cylinder is not a prism even though it stays the same shape and size throughout its length because it has a curved face.

It is important to be able to recognise 3D shapes and be able to work out the number of faces, edges and vertices in a 3D shape. These will always be based on the shape that makes either the base of the pyramid or the end faces of a prism.

A square-based pyramid

Because the base face is a square, it will have four triangular faces, making a total of five faces. The four sides of the square base shape will create four edges, one with each triangle. The four triangles will then join each other along four edges, which makes a total of eight edges. The edges will meet at each of the four corners of the square base and at the tip of the point, making a total of five vertices.

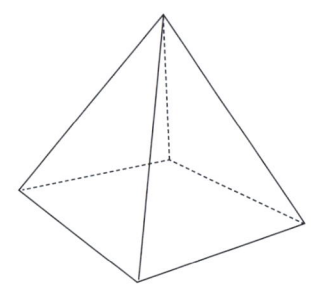

> **TIP** All pyramids have the same number of faces as vertices.

A triangular prism

Because the two end faces are triangles, they will be joined by three rectangular faces, making a total of five faces.

The three sides of one triangular face will create three edges, one with each rectangle, as will the triangular face at the other end. The three rectangles will then join each other along three edges, making a total of nine edges. The edges will meet at each of the corners of the triangular ends, three at one end and three at the other, making a total of six vertices.

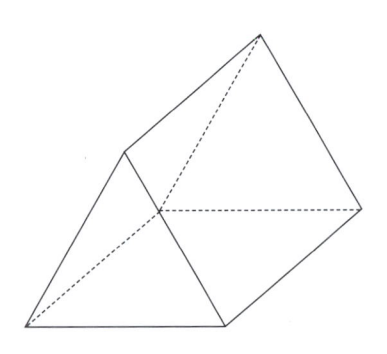

A cone

A cone has two faces. It has one circular face and one curved face that tapers to a point. It has one edge where the curved and flat face meet and one vertex.

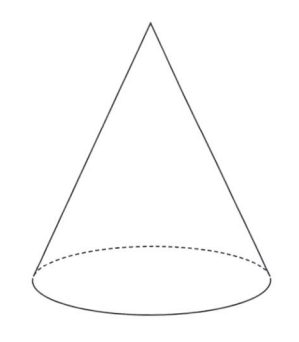

Schofield & Sims

Properties of 3D shapes

A cylinder

A cylinder only has three faces as the curved face joining the two circular ends counts as one face. There are two edges where the two circular end faces join the central curved face and there are no vertices, as these two edges do not meet.

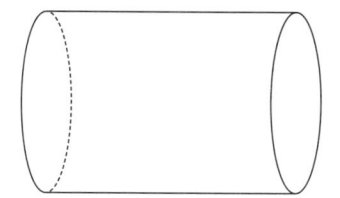

A sphere

A sphere has only one face. There are no edges (as you need two faces to join to make an edge) and no vertices (as there are no edges)!

A sphere that appears to be cut in half is called a hemisphere.

Complete the table. Name each shape, then work out the number of faces, edges and vertices.

	Shape	Name of shape	Number of faces	Number of edges	Number of vertices
1.					
2.					
3.					
4.					
5.					
6.					

11+ Maths Study and Practice Book

Nets of 3D shapes

3D shapes can be made using **nets**. A net is a flat pattern which can be folded to make the 3D shape. The shapes that make up the net become the faces of the 3D shape.

To identify the net of a 3D shape, you need to think about the faces that make up each 3D shape. You also need to imagine how the edges will fold and how the faces will join.

A cuboid is made up of three pairs of rectangular faces that are opposite each other in the cuboid.

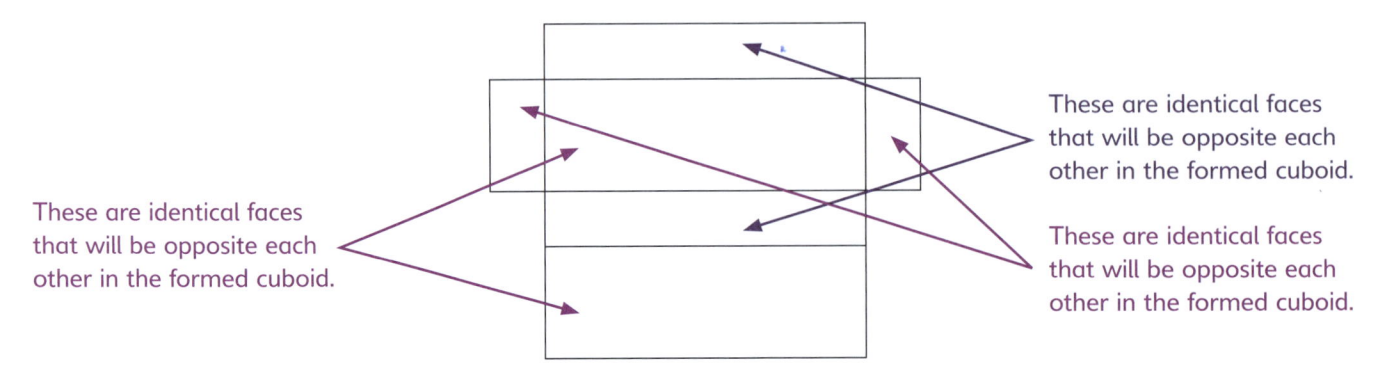

These are identical faces that will be opposite each other in the formed cuboid.

These are identical faces that will be opposite each other in the formed cuboid.

These are identical faces that will be opposite each other in the formed cuboid.

There is usually more than one net that you can use to make a 3D shape. Here are just a few nets that will create cubes.

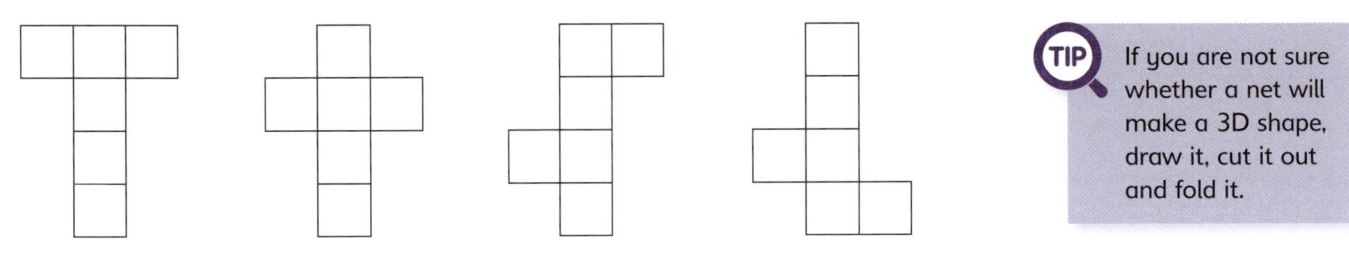

TIP If you are not sure whether a net will make a 3D shape, draw it, cut it out and fold it.

Now answer the following questions.

1. Circle the letter under the net that is not of a square-based pyramid.

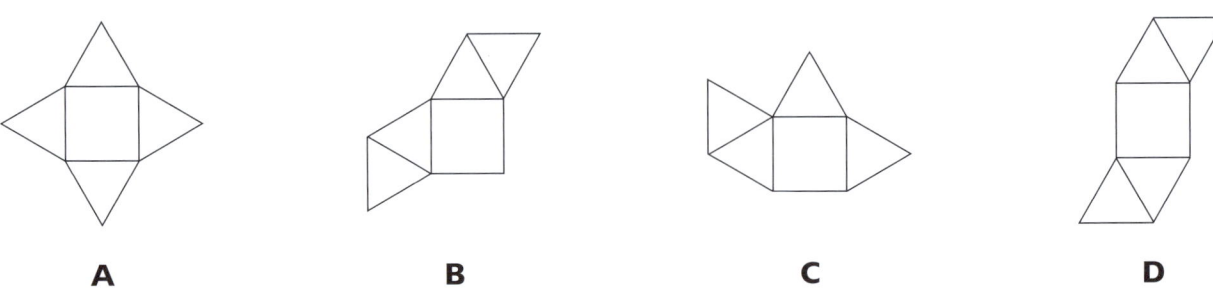

A   B   C   D

2. Draw in the final face to make this a net of a cube.

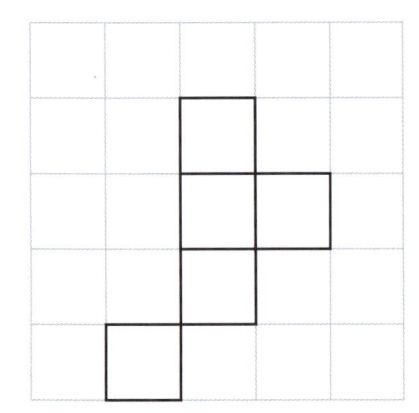

3. I am thinking of a net. It is made up of a rectangle and 2 circles. Which 3D shape am I thinking of?

_____

4. I am thinking of a net. It is made up of 5 triangles and a pentagon. Which 3D shape am I thinking of?

_____

Rotations of 3D shapes

Sometimes, you will be asked to imagine what 3D shapes look like when they are rotated.

When 3D shapes are rotated, it can be tricky to identify the correct rotation. This is because, unlike 2D shapes, which can only be rotated clockwise and anticlockwise, 3D shapes can also be rotated forwards and backwards, and around left and right.

The easiest way to work out what the rotated shape will look like is to imagine the 3D shape as separate blocks and look carefully at how they are attached.

Which of the 3D shapes on the right is a rotation of the 3D shape on the left?

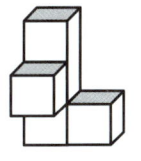

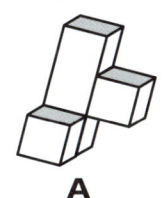

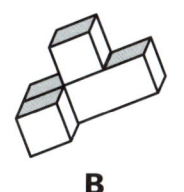

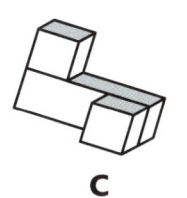

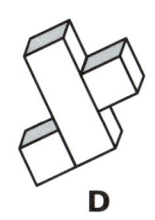

A   B   C   D

While the cubes are at the end and half-way up, the one half-way up is connected to the right of the end cube, rather than the left, so **A** cannot be a rotation of the original 3D shape.

The cube half-way up the cuboid is connected to the left of the cube at the end of the cuboid, therefore **B** is a rotation of the original 3D shape.

There is no cube half-way up, so **C** cannot be a rotation of the original 3D shape.

The cubes are not on adjacent faces of the cuboid, so **D** cannot be a rotation of the original 3D shape.

You can see that the shape on the left consists of one long cuboid and two cubes. One cube is at one end of the cuboid and the other is half-way up the cuboid on the adjoining face to the left, so the answer must be **B**.

Answer: B

Which of the 3D shapes on the right is a rotation of the 3D shape on the left? Circle the correct letter.

1. A   B   C   D

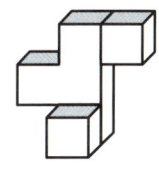

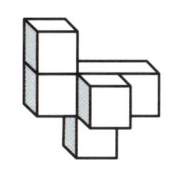

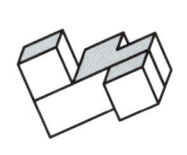

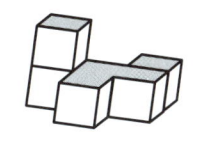

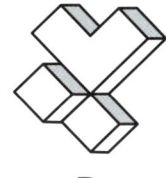

2. A   B   C   D

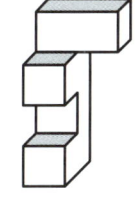

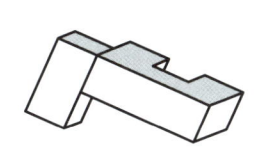

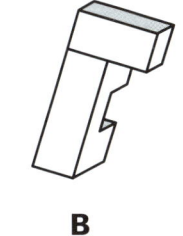

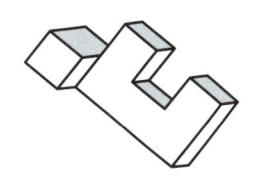

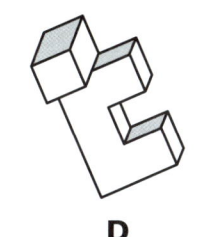

3. A   B   C   D

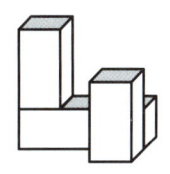

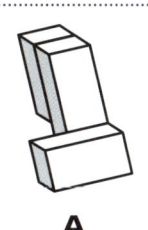

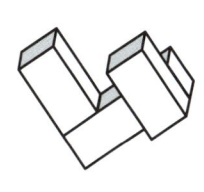

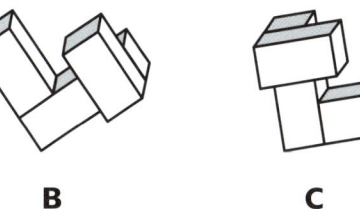

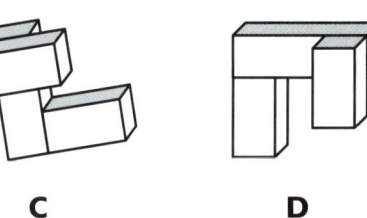

11+ Maths Study and Practice Book

Coordinates

Coordinates show the points on a grid. They are always made up of two numbers. The first number shows the point's position on the *x*-axis (the horizontal line), and the second number shows the point's position on the *y*-axis (the vertical line). Coordinates are always written in brackets, such as (1, 4) or (−6, 2).

What are the coordinates for points A and B?

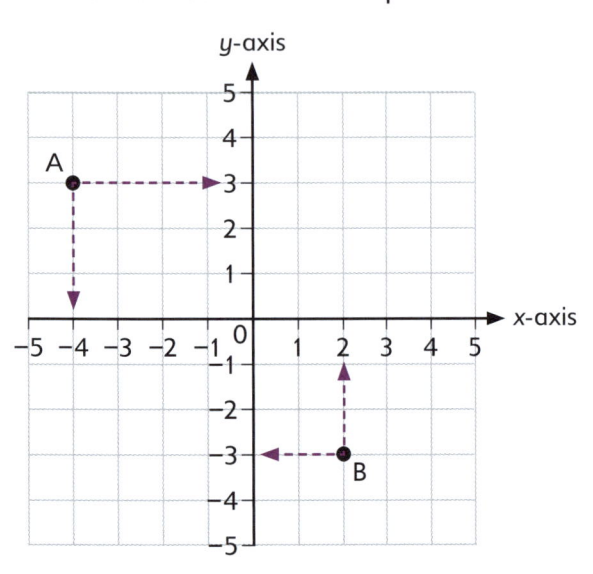

Remember, the *x*-axis coordinate always comes first. By dropping down from point A to the *x*-axis, you can see that it is in line with −4.

By going across to the *y*-axis from point A, you can see that it is in line with 3. So the coordinates for point A are (−4, 3).

By going up from point B to the *x*-axis, you can see that it is in line with 2.

By going across to the *y*-axis from point B, you can see that it is in line with −3. So the coordinates for point B are (2, −3).

Answer: (−4, 3) and (2, −3)

TIP As x comes before y in the alphabet, so the *x*-axis coordinate comes before the *y*-axis coordinate.

Sometimes, the axes will not be labelled but the points on the grid may be. You will then be asked to work out the coordinates for one of the points.

What are the coordinates for point C?

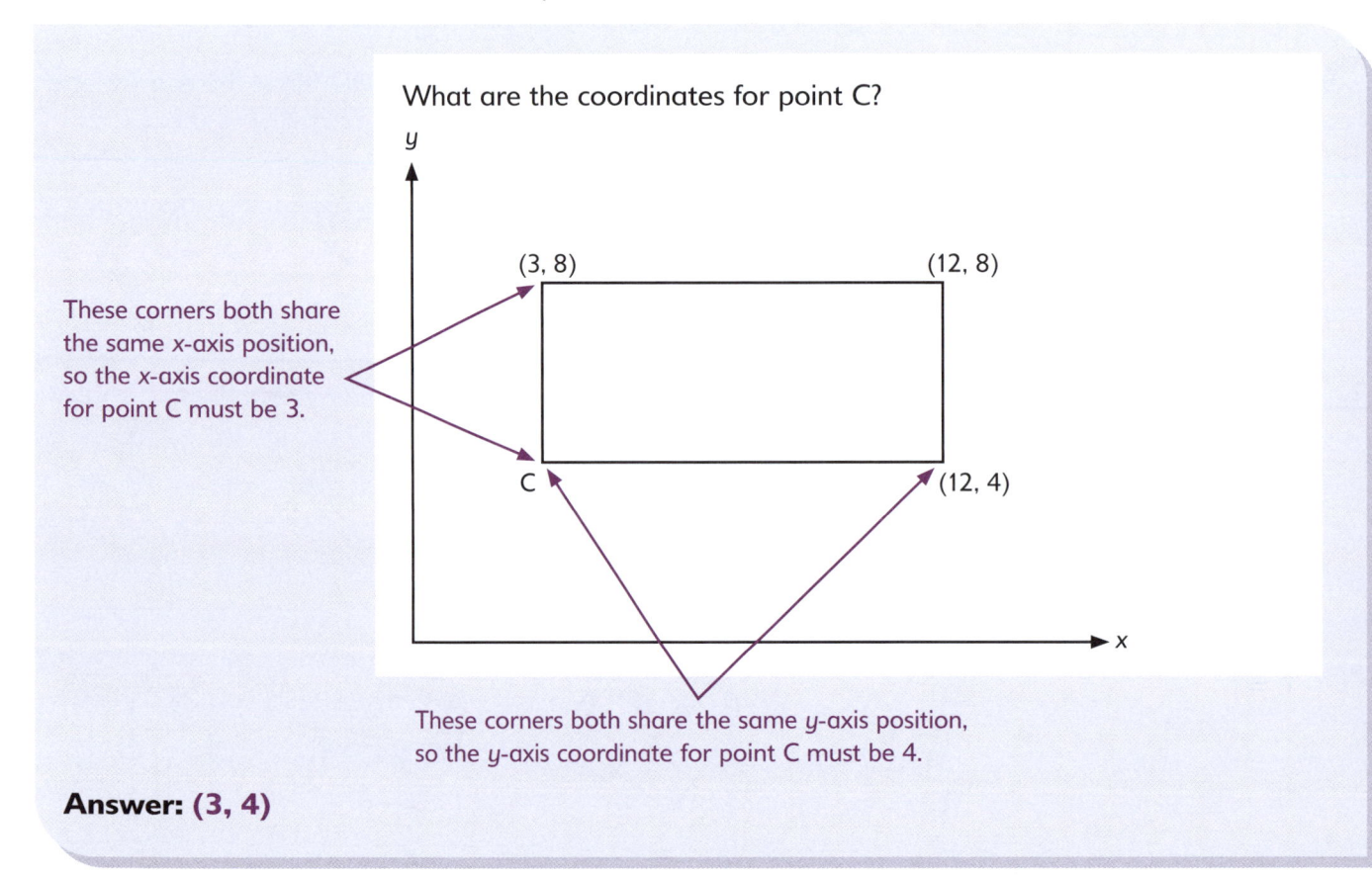

These corners both share the same *x*-axis position, so the *x*-axis coordinate for point C must be 3.

These corners both share the same *y*-axis position, so the *y*-axis coordinate for point C must be 4.

Answer: (3, 4)

Coordinates

✎ Write the coordinates for each corner of the square.

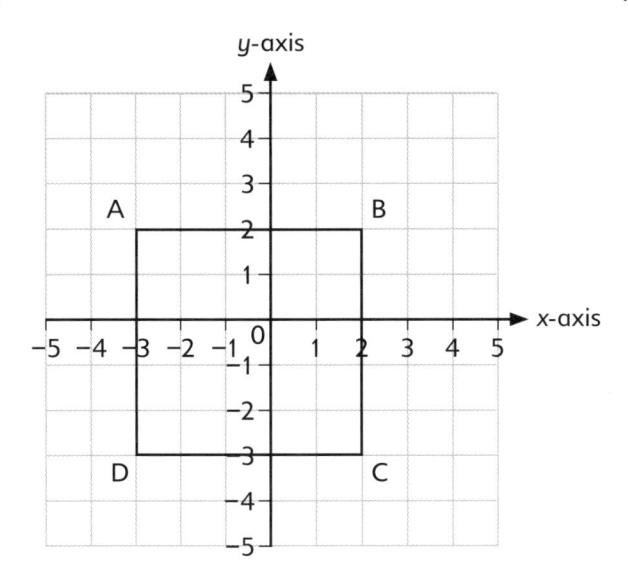

1. A = _____

2. B = _____

3. C = _____

4. D = _____

Work out the coordinates for point A and point B.

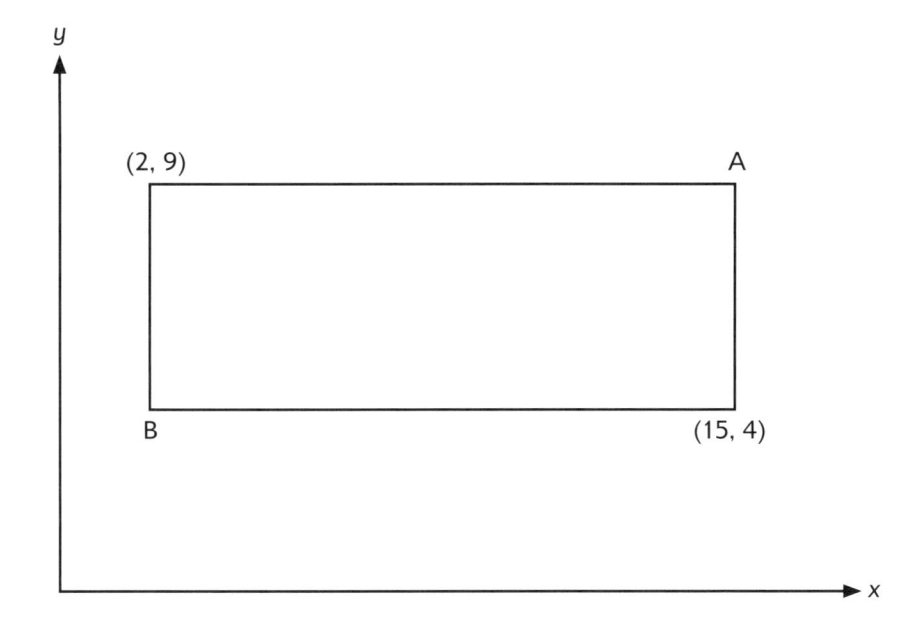

5. A = _____

6. B = _____

11+ Maths Study and Practice Book

Reflections

Shapes are reflected in a line called a mirror line. The reflection will be a mirror image of the original and all parts of it will be the same distance from the mirror line as the original. The original shape (**object**) and its reflection (**image**) are identical even though they are flipped around. We say that the shapes are congruent.

Draw the reflection of the shape in the mirror line.

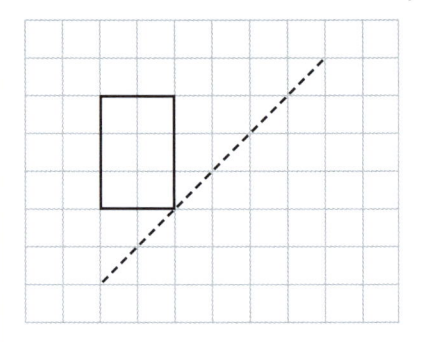

You need to look at each corner of the shape and work out where it would be on the other side of the mirror line.

! Each corner and its reflection will be the same perpendicular distance from the mirror line.

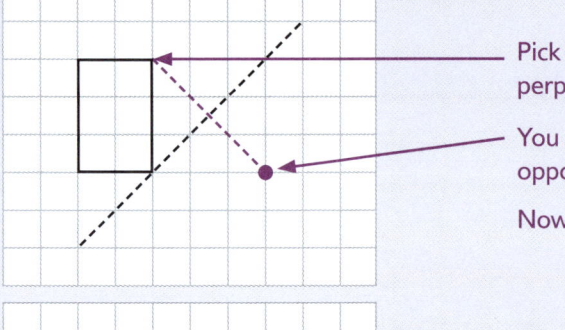

Pick your first corner. It does not matter which you pick. Move perpendicular to the mirror line and count the squares you cross.

You need to cross $1\frac{1}{2}$ squares, so carry on $1\frac{1}{2}$ squares on the opposite side of the mirror line and mark the position.

Now move around the shape to the next corner.

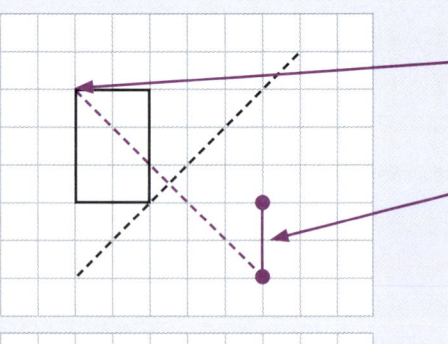

The next corner is $2\frac{1}{2}$ squares to the mirror line, so carry on $2\frac{1}{2}$ squares on the opposite side of the mirror line and mark the position.

Join the two marks.

Now move around the shape to the next corner.

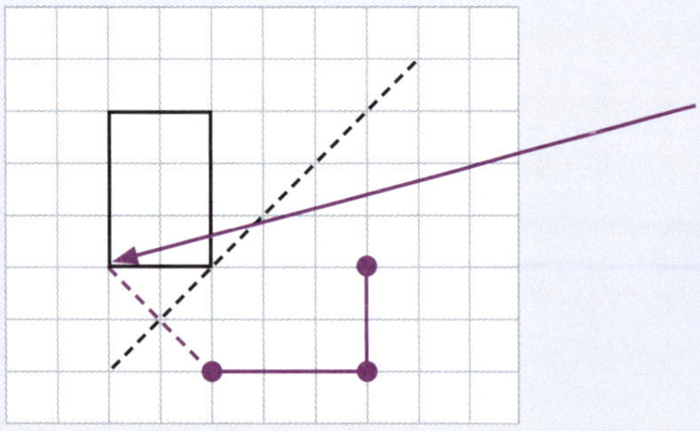

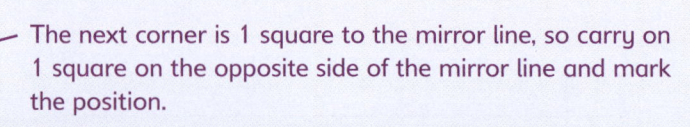

The next corner is 1 square to the mirror line, so carry on 1 square on the opposite side of the mirror line and mark the position.

Join the two marks.

Now move around the shape to the next corner.

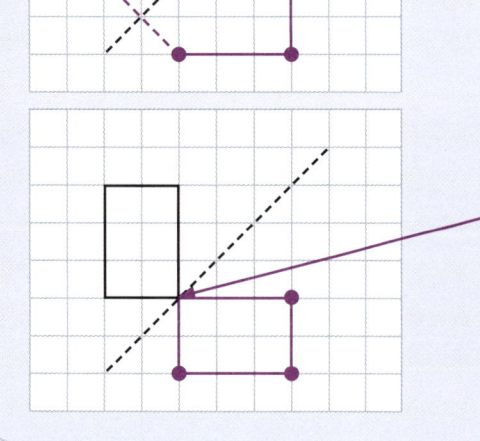

The final corner is actually on the line, so the reflected corner will be in the same place.

You can now finish joining up all the corners. You have drawn a perfect reflection.

Reflections

When working out how a shape will be reflected, make sure you work your way logically around the shape from one corner to the next, marking the reflected corners and joining the points as you go. If you wait until the end to join all the points, you may not join them in the right order.

Draw the reflection of each shape in the mirror line.

1.

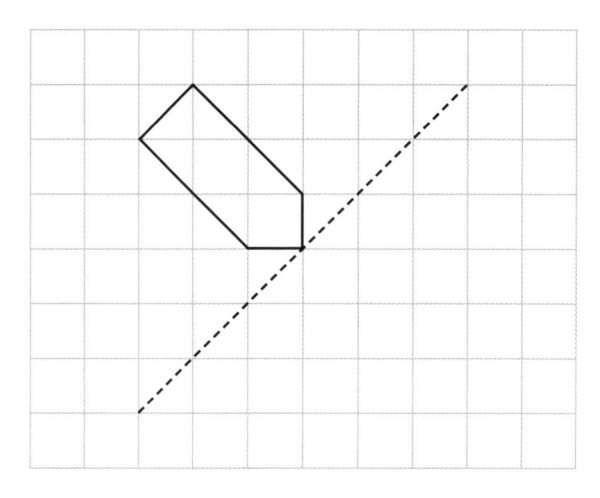

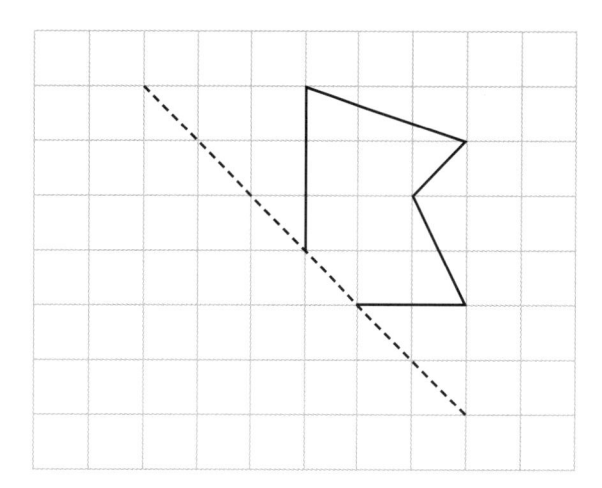

2.

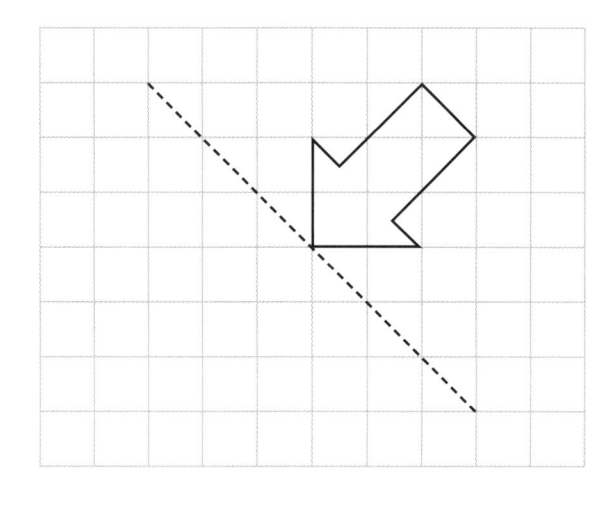

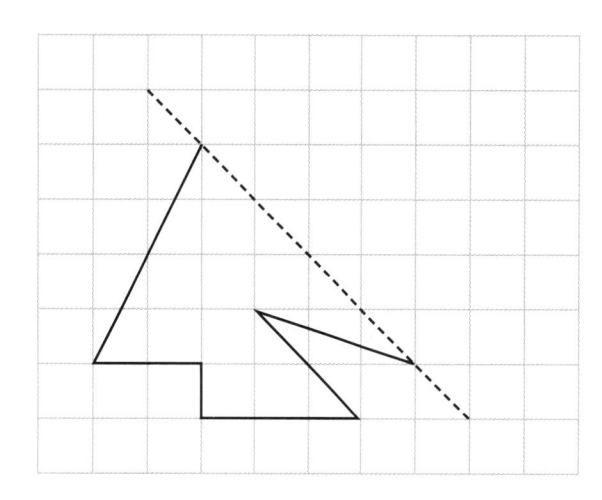

3.

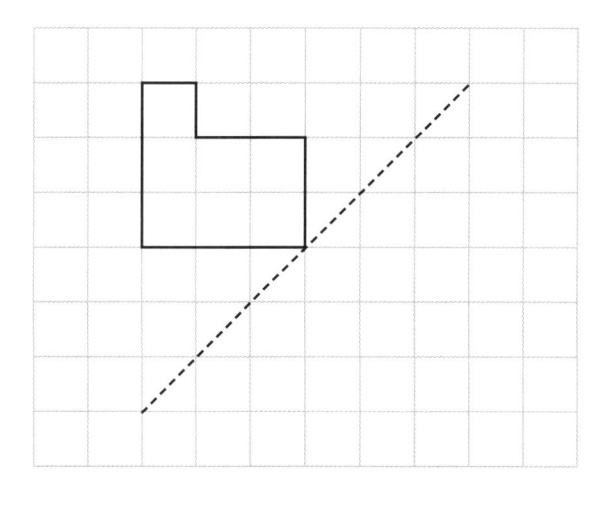

4.

5.

6.

11+ Maths Study and Practice Book

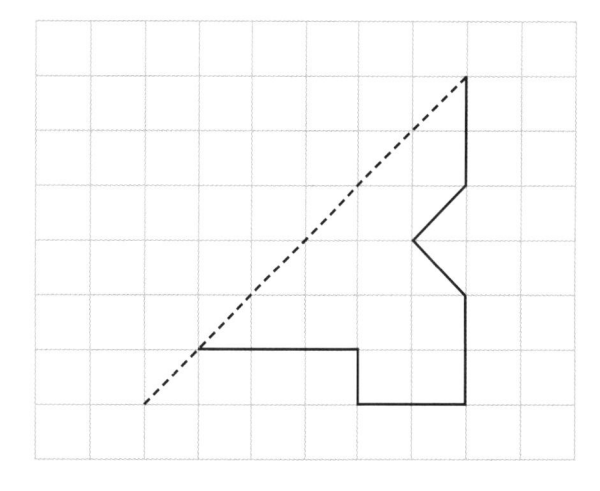

Translations

When an object is **translated** it is simply slid up or down and right or left. The object itself will stay looking exactly the same – it just moves position. The new shape is known as the image.

Shape A has been translated 4 spaces to the right and 2 spaces down to create shape B.

Translations may be written in words, for example 2 right, 3 up, or they could just be written in letters, for example R2, U3. R = right, L = left, U = up and D = down.

You will often be asked to describe the position of the image. You need to give the coordinates for all the corners. Unless specified, it does not matter in which order you write the coordinates.

Shape B has coordinates (5, 2), (7, 2), (7, 5), (5, 5).

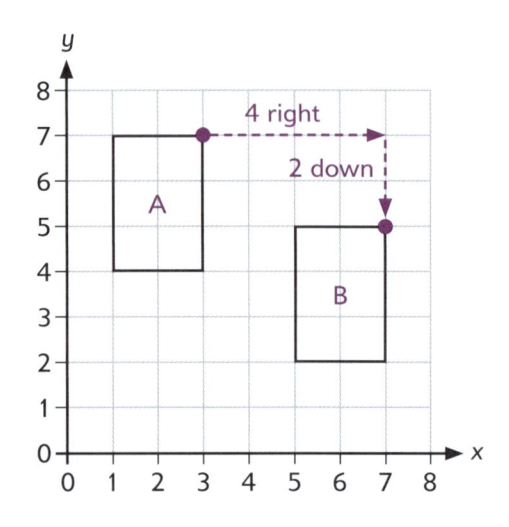

TIP Pick one corner and work out where that corner will be on the translated shape. Draw the translated shape from that one corner. Alternatively, translate each corner in turn, joining them up as you go.

Look at the grid.

1. Translate the shape L2, D3 and label the image A.

2. Write the coordinates for image A.

   _____

3. Now translate image A U1, R4 and label the image B.

4. Write the coordinates for image B.

   _____

Look at the grid.

5. Write the translation to move E to F.

   _____

6. Write the translation to move E to G.

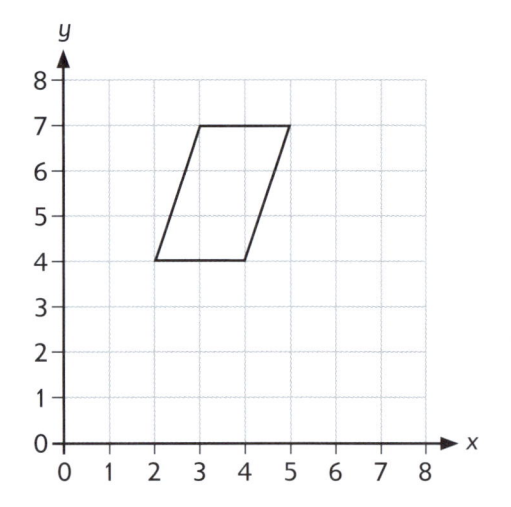

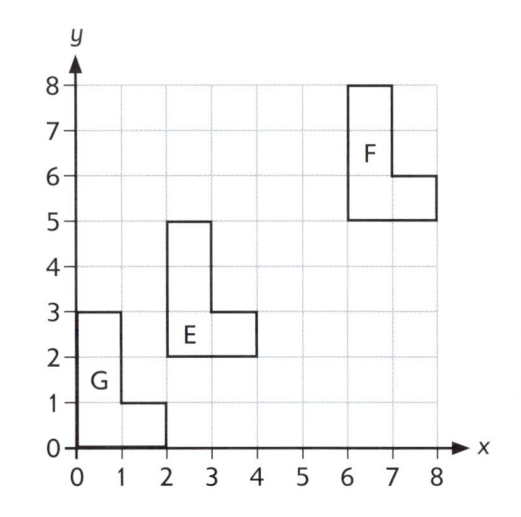

   _____

Geometry practice page 1

Now test your skills with these practice pages. If you get stuck, go back to pages 106 to 126 for some reminders.

Parallel and perpendicular lines

Are these statements true or false?

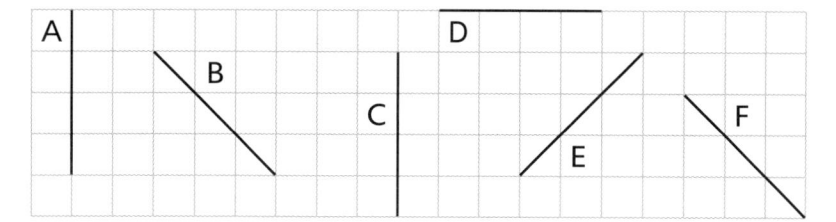

1. Lines A and B are perpendicular. _____
2. Lines B and E are perpendicular. _____
3. Lines A and C are parallel. _____
4. Lines E and F are parallel. _____
5. Draw arrows to show the pairs of parallel lines. 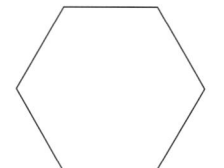
6. Draw squares to show where the perpendicular lines meet.

Angles

7. Circle the letter of the shape that has 2 internal right angles and 4 obtuse internal angles.

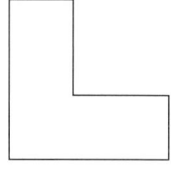

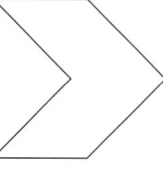

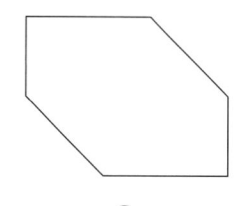

    A   B   C

8. On a compass, what is the size of the smallest angle between NE and NW? _____

9. Ellie is facing west. She turns 135° clockwise. In which direction is she now facing? _____

Measure these angles.

10. _____ 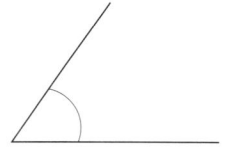
11. _____

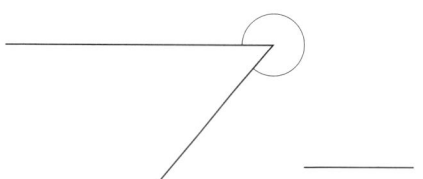

Calculate the angles labelled with letters.

12. Triangle with angles 51°, 59°, and a.

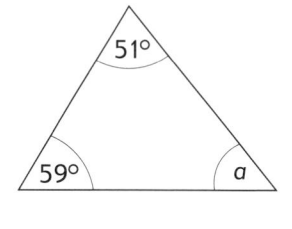

    $a = $ _____

13. Angles 137°, j, and 78°, k on parallel lines.

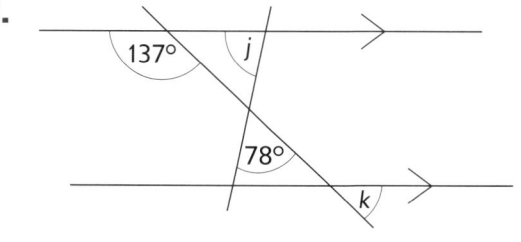

    $j = $ _____ $k = $ _____

11+ Maths Study and Practice Book

Geometry practice page 2

Directions of turn

Describe the direction and size of turn for each pair of shapes.

1. _____

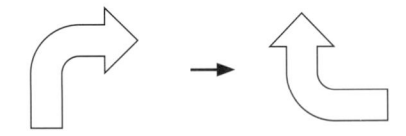

2. _____

3. _____

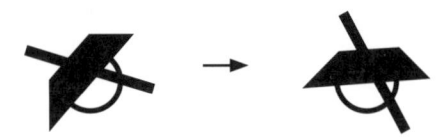

4. I'm facing N. I turn 90° clockwise and then 180° anticlockwise. In which direction am I now facing?

   _____

Properties of 2D shapes

5. I have four equal sides and two pairs of equal angles. What am I? _____

6. I have three sides and none of them are the same. What am I? _____

What is the name of each shape?

7. _____

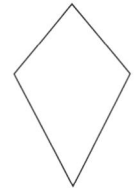

8. _____

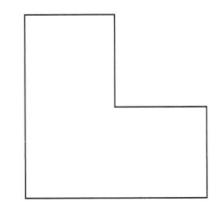

9. _____

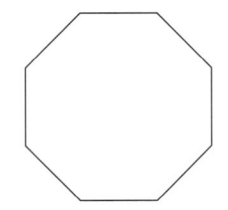

10. What is the total number of degrees in a hexagon? _____

Regular shapes

11. Circle the letters under the regular shapes.

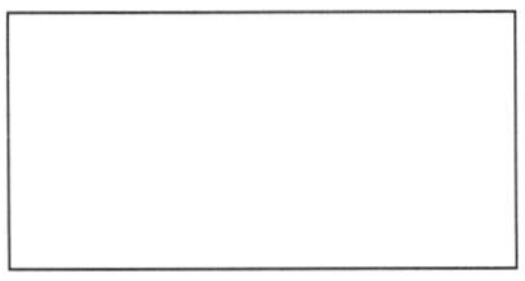

    A 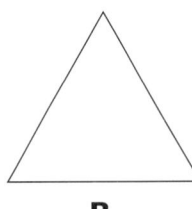   B 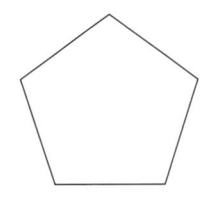   C 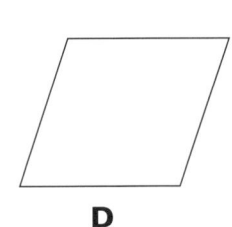   D

12. How many lines of symmetry are there in a regular hexagon? _____

13. What is the order of rotational symmetry of a regular octagon? _____

14. What is the perimeter of this regular decagon?

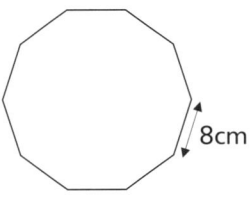

    _____   8cm

Geometry practice page 3

Circles

1. The diameter of a circle is 16cm. What is the radius? _____
2. The diameter of a circle is 45mm. What is the radius? _____
3. The radius of a circle is 12cm. What is the diameter? _____
4. The radius of a circle is 5m. What is the diameter? _____
5. Using the formula $2\pi r$ ($\pi = 3.14$), work out the circumference of a circle with a radius of 7cm. _____
6. Using the formula πr^2 ($\pi = 3.14$), work out the area of a circle with a diameter of 20cm. _____

Symmetry

How many lines of symmetry do each of these shapes have?

7. 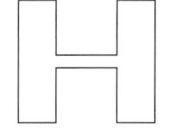 (H shape) _____
8.  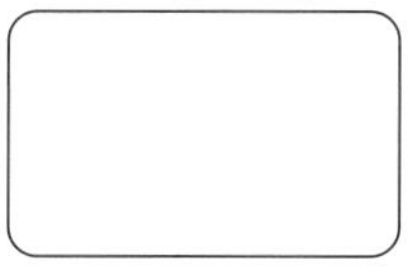 (rounded rectangle) _____
9. 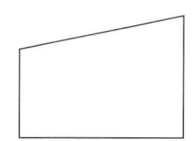 (trapezium) _____
10.  (Pac-Man shape) _____

Draw the lines of symmetry on these shapes.

11. 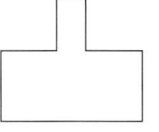 (T shape)
12. (square)

Rotational symmetry

What is the order of rotational symmetry of each of these shapes?

13. 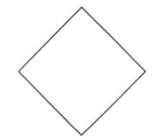 (rhombus) _____
14. 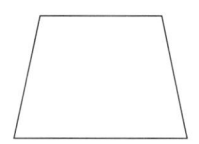 (trapezium) _____
15. 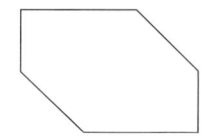 (pentagon) _____
16. 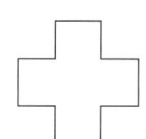 (plus/cross) _____
17. 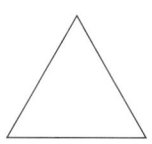 (triangle) _____

18. 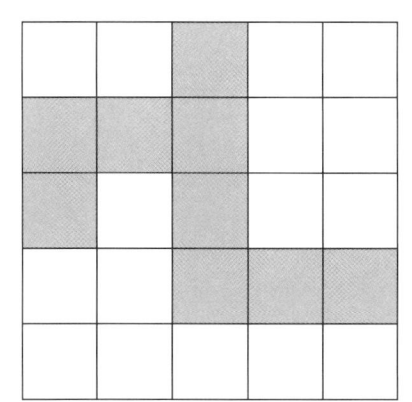 Shade two more squares on the diagram so that the new shape has rotational symmetry of order 2.

Geometry practice page 4

Properties of 3D shapes

Complete the table. Name each shape, then work out the number of faces, edges and vertices.

Shape	Name of shape	Number of faces	Number of edges	Number of vertices
1. (cylinder) 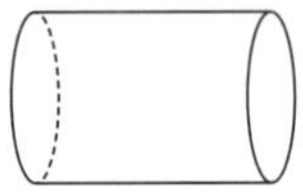				
2. (hexagonal pyramid) 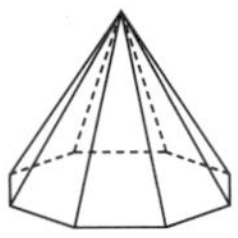				

3. I have six rectangular faces and two hexagonal faces. What am I? _____

4. I have four triangular faces. What am I? _____

Nets of 3D shapes

What will these nets become?

5. _____

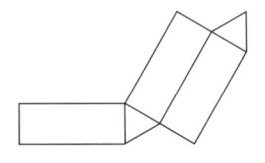

6. _____

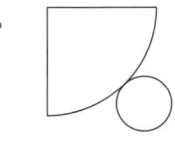

7. Circle the letter of the shape that is not the net of a cube.

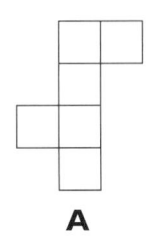

A 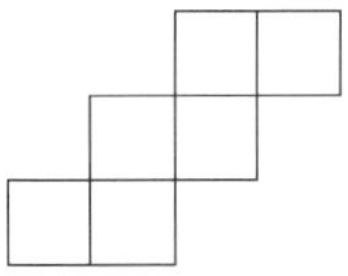   B 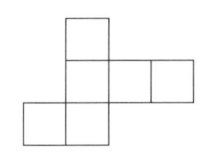   C 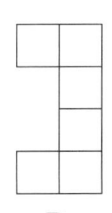   D

Rotations of 3D shapes

Which of the 3D shapes on the right is a rotation of the 3D shape on the left? Circle the correct letter.

8. 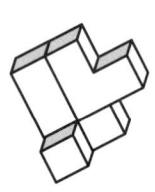   A 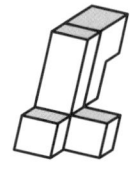   B 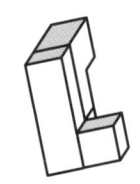   C 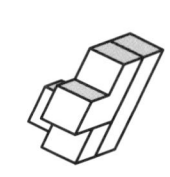   D

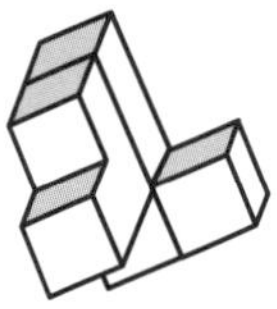

9. 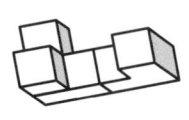   A 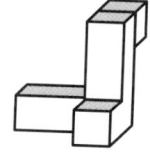   B 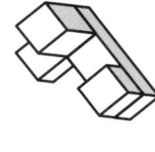   C 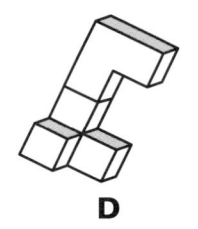   D

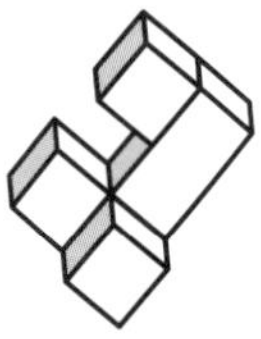

Geometry practice page 5

Coordinates

Write the coordinates for each corner of the hexagon.

1. A = _____
2. B = _____
3. C = _____
4. D = _____
5. E = _____
6. F = _____

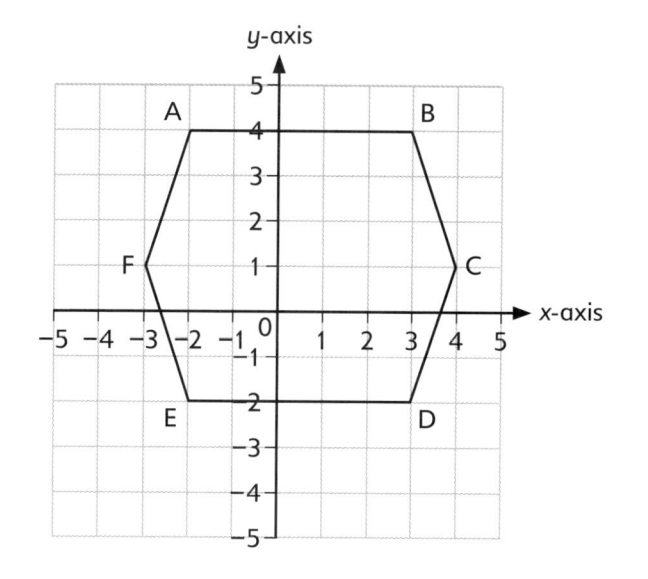

Reflections

Draw the reflection of each shape in the mirror line.

7.

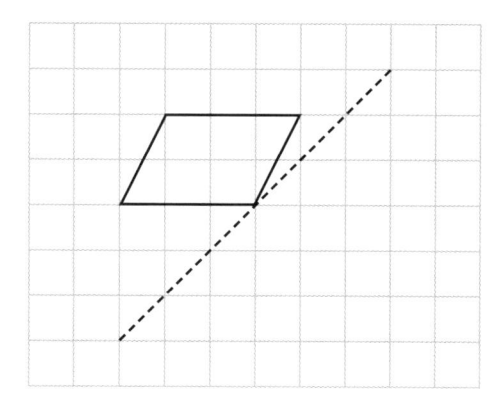

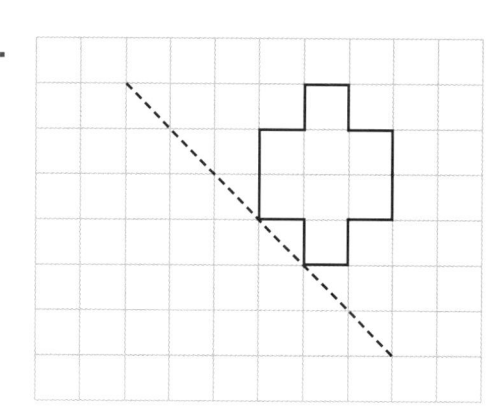

8.

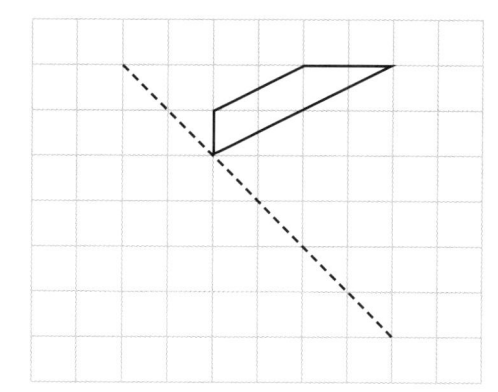

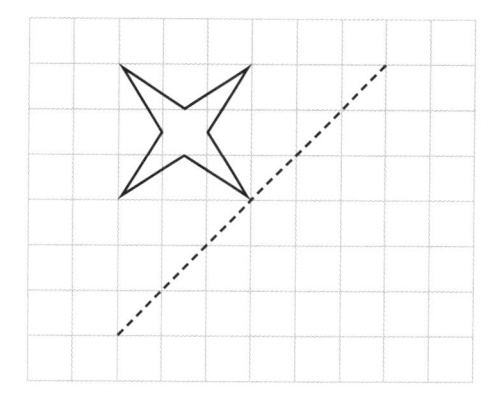

9.

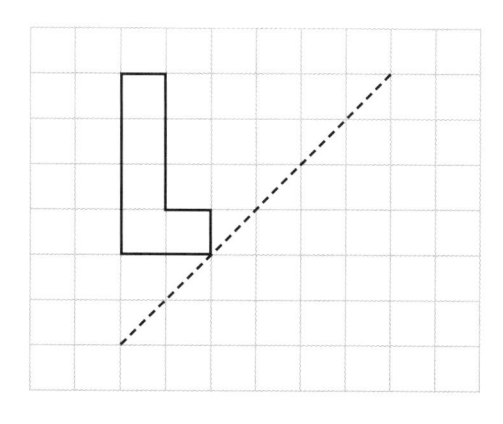

10.

11.

12.

11+ Maths Study and Practice Book

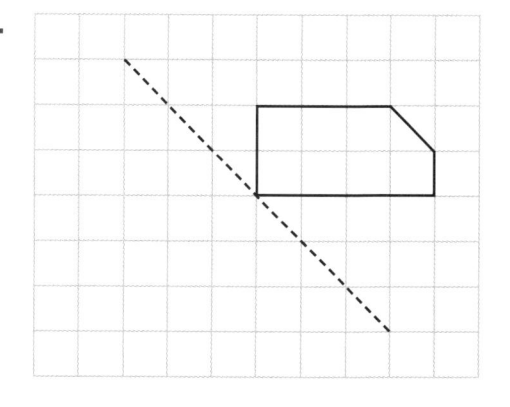

Geometry practice page 6

Translations

Look at the grid.

1. Translate the shape R4, D4 and label the image A.

2. Write the coordinates for image A.

   _____

3. Now translate image A U2, L3 and label it image B.

4. Write the coordinates for image B.

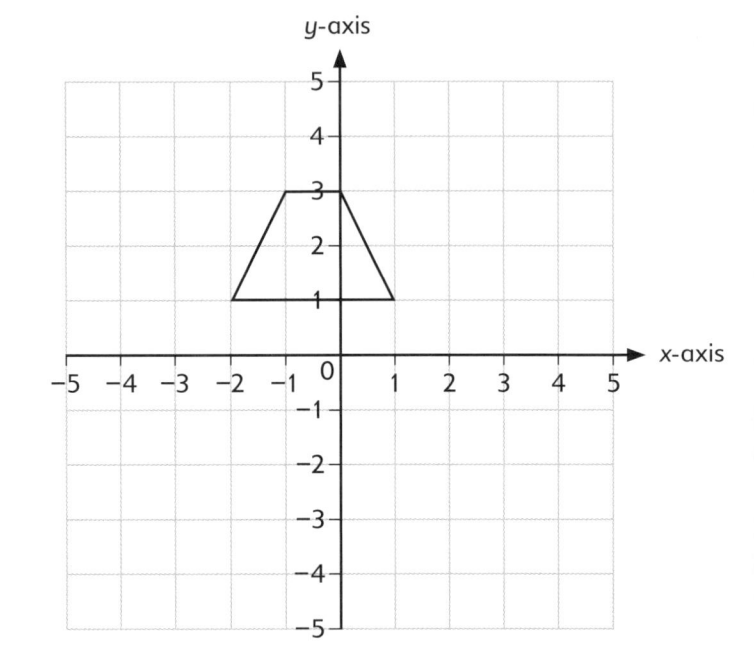

   _____

Look at the grid.

5. Translate the shape L6, U1 and label the image A.

6. Write the coordinates for image A.

   _____

7. Now translate image A U1, R4 and label it image B.

8. Write the coordinates for image B.

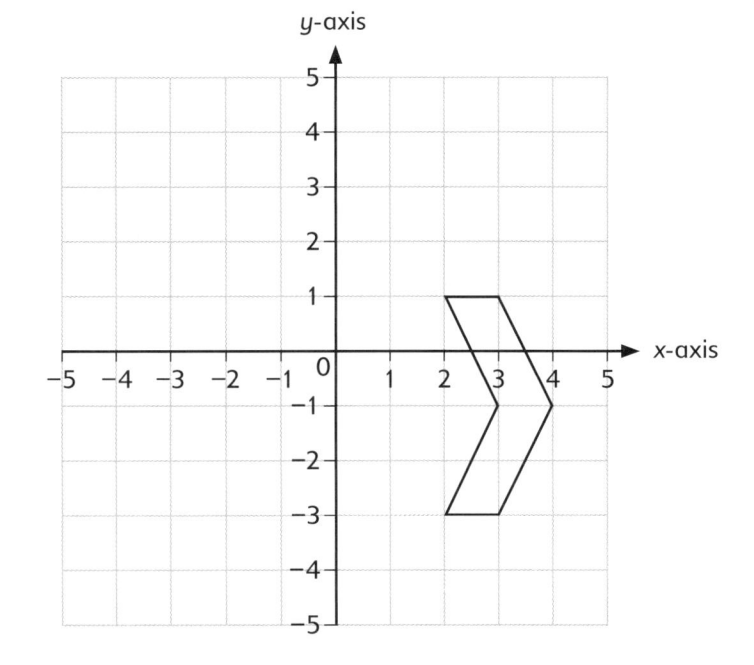

   _____

Tables

Tables are used to display data. They make the data easier to look at and analyse, especially when there is a lot of it. You need to understand how to answer questions about data displayed in tables, and how to complete tables with missing data.

Complete the table below showing the number of people that went to a cinema over the course of one week.

	Mon–Fri	Weekend	Total
Men	368		782
Women	518	953	
Boys	89	403	
Girls		419	
Total	1056		

In order to fill in the empty boxes in the table, you need to look at the information that is given.

If 368 men went to the cinema Mon–Fri and in total 782 go, then 782 − 368 = 414, so **414** men went to the cinema at the weekend.

You can work out the total number of women going to the cinema by adding the totals from Mon–Fri and the weekend. 518 + 953 = 1471, so **1471** women went in total.

You can work out the total number of boys going to the cinema by adding the totals from Mon–Fri and the weekend. 89 + 403 = 492, so **492** boys went in total.

Having worked out the number of girls that went to the cinema Mon–Fri, you can add this to the weekend number to find the total. 81 + 419 = 500, so **500** girls in total went to the cinema.

We cannot work out the number of girls who went to the cinema based on the total number of girls, as we are not given that number. However, we are given the total number of people who attended Mon–Fri, so we can use that to work out the number of girls. 368 + 518 + 89 = 975. 1056 − 975 = 81, so **81** girls went to the cinema Mon–Fri.

Having already worked out that 414 men went to the cinema at the weekend, you can now add all of the weekend numbers to find the weekend total. 414 + 953 + 403 + 419 = **2189**.

To find the total number of people who attended the cinema over the week, either add the Mon–Fri and weekend totals, or the totals for men, women, boys and girls. The latter involves adding 4 numbers, so it will be easier to add the Mon–Fri and weekend totals. 1056 + 2189 = 3245, so in total **3245** people attended the cinema that week.

1. Complete the table below showing the number of children in a school.

Year group	Girls	Boys	Total
3	42		88
4		39	80
5	46	43	
6		50	
Total	167		345

Pictograms

Pictograms use pictures or symbols to show numbers of things or how often something happens. It is important to look carefully at the key to see exactly what each picture or symbol represents.

Some children chose their favourite flavours of ice cream. The results were displayed in a pictogram.

Ice cream flavour	Number of children
Vanilla	🍦🍦🍦🍦🍦
Chocolate	🍦🍦🍦🍦🍦(half)
Strawberry	🍦🍦(half)
Mint choc chip	🍦🍦
Pistachio	🍦(half)

Key: 🍦 = 2 children

How many more children preferred chocolate to mint choc chip?

There are $4\frac{1}{2}$ ice cream pictures for chocolate, which totals 9 children. There are 2 ice cream pictures for mint choc chip, which totals 4 children. The difference between 9 and 4 is 5.

The key shows that each picture is worth 2 children. If there is half an ice cream, that is worth 1 child.

Answer: 5

Jamie spent an hour counting the birds in his garden. He made a pictogram of his results.

Type of bird	Number of birds
Robin	♡(half)
Pigeon	♡♡♡♡(half)
Magpie	♡♡♡
Blue tit	(half)

Key: ♡ = 2 birds

1. How many pigeons did he count? _____
2. How many more magpies did he spot than blue tits? _____
3. How many birds did he spot altogether? _____

Yuli sorted her animal pasta into the different animal shapes. She presented her results in a pictogram.

Animal shape	Number of pieces
Lion	⬠⬠⬠⬠(part)
Crocodile	⬠⬠⬠
Giraffe	⬠⬠⬠(part)
Monkey	⬠⬠⬠⬠(part)
Hippo	⬠⬠⬠(part)

Key: ⬠ = 5 pieces

4. How many monkeys did she find? _____
5. How many more lions were there than hippos? _____
6. How many pieces of pasta did Yuli count altogether? _____

Tally charts and frequency tables

Tally charts are used to collect data quickly and efficiently. Using marks to represent numbers is much faster than writing them out in words or figures. A single vertical line represents one and when five is reached, the fifth line is used to cross the previous four: |||| Using tallies is a much quicker way of counting data. This data can then be used to create graphs and charts.

Tallies are usually written in tables with a frequency column at the end which totals the tallies.

Complete the tally chart showing the number of cars in a car park.

Colour car	Tally	Frequency
Silver	|||| |||| |||| ||	17
Grey	|||| |||| |||	13
Black	|||| |||| |||| ||||	20
White	|||| |||| ||||	14
Blue	|||	3
Red	|||| ||	7

It is quick and easy to count in fives and then add on any extra ones.

Look at this data that shows the pieces of fruit in a restaurant's fruit bowl.

| O A P K K O B A A P N O O B A K A |
| A K K P P N N B B K O O A N N N |
| O K P A P K P B B P A B B O O K A |
| A A P N N P K A A O K O B N K N A |
| P P A K N O K O O B B A P N K K K |

O = orange
A = apple
P = pear
B = banana
N = nectarine
K = kiwi

1. Use the data to complete the tally chart and frequency table.

Fruit	Tally	Frequency
Orange	|||| |||| ||||	14
Apple	|||| |||| |||| ||	17
Pear	|||| |||| |||	13
Banana	|||| ||||		11
Nectarine	|||| |||| ||	12
Kiwi	|||| |||| |||| ||	17

2. How many pieces of fruit were there altogether? __84__

3. How many more apples were there than bananas? __6__

Bar charts

Bar charts represent data using horizontal or vertical bars of certain lengths. The labels on the axes explain what each bar represents.

This bar chart shows the favourite colours of a group of children. The vertical axis shows the colours and the horizontal axis shows the number of children. Without even having to look at the numbers, you can see straight away that blue is the most popular colour and yellow is the least popular colour. By looking at the horizontal axis, you can find out exactly how many children like each colour, and you can work out how many children were asked their favourite colour by adding all the totals together. You can then answer questions based on the data.

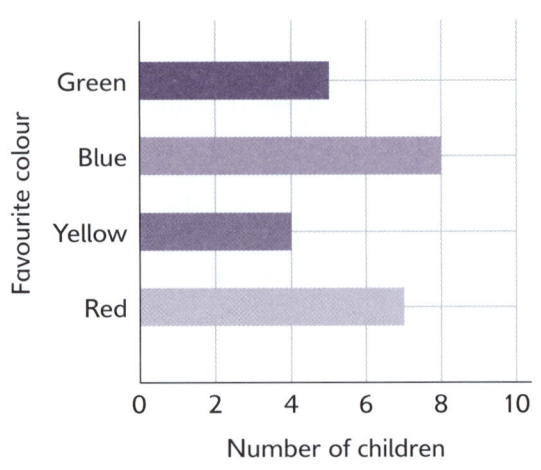

TIP You must always check the scale on the numbered axis to see by how much the numbers are going up. In this example, the scale goes up by 2 each time.

How many more children liked blue than green?

8 children liked blue and 5 liked green. 8 − 5 = 3
Answer: 3

How many children were surveyed altogether?

5 children chose green, 8 blue, 4 yellow and 7 red. 5 + 8 + 4 + 7 = 24
Answer: 24

This bar chart shows the exam results from Emma's end of year exams.

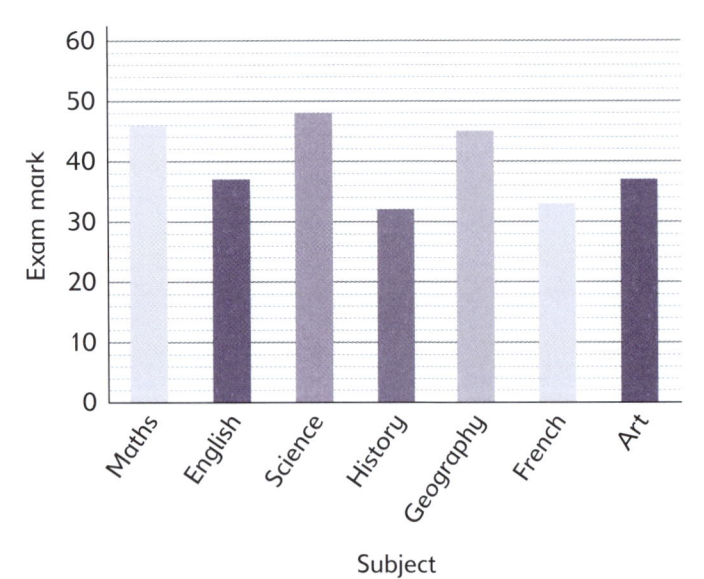

1. In which subject did Emma earn most marks?

    _____

2. In which two subjects did Emma score the same mark?

    _____

    _____

3. How many more marks did Emma earn in geography than in history?

    _____

Line graphs

Line graphs show two sets of data and how they relate to each other. They give you a visual representation of how one thing changes as the other thing changes. Line graphs normally include a measurement of time.

The individual pieces of data are plotted on the graph using the measurements on each axis, and then the points are joined to create a single line.

This line graph shows the average temperature each month over a year.

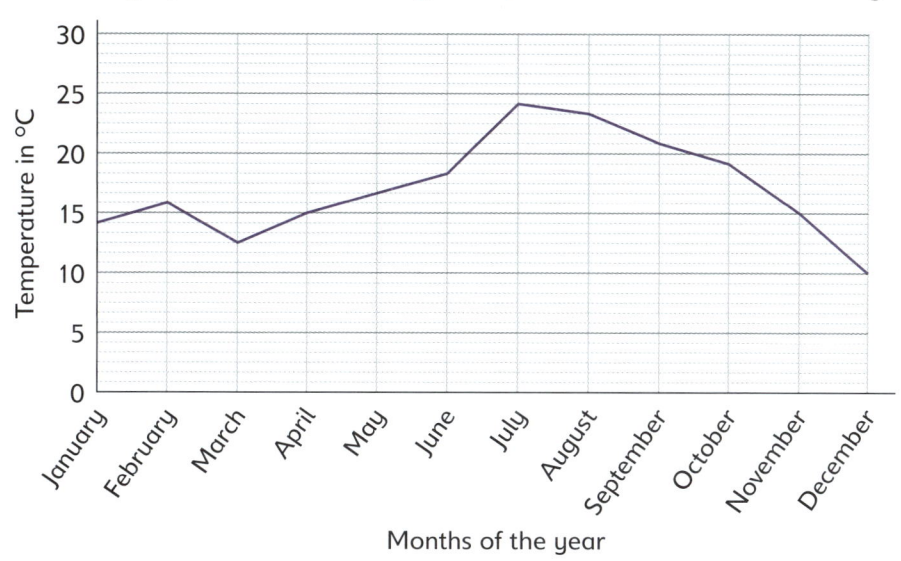

Which are the hottest and coldest months?

The line peaks in July and dips to its lowest point in December.

Answer: July is the hottest month and December is the coldest.

Between which two months is there the biggest increase in temperature?

You can see that the biggest increase in temperature from one month to another is between June and July because it has the steepest line going up.

Answer: June and July

In which month does the temperature reach 24°C?

Find 24°C on the y-axis. Follow the line horizontally until you come to the line graph. Look down from that point to the x-axis.

Answer: July

This line graph shows Daniel's journey to his grandparent's house.

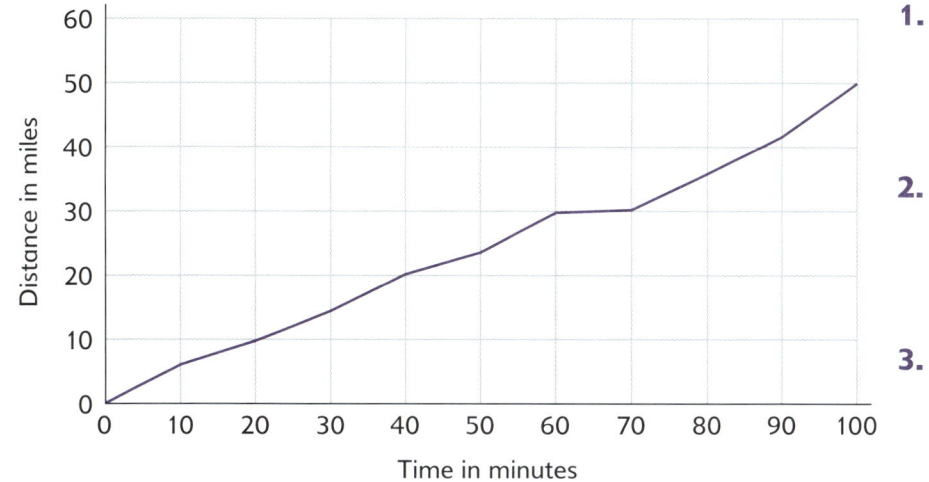

1. How far had he travelled after the first 20 minutes?

   _____

2. How far away do Daniel's grandparents live?

   _____

3. What happened after 1 hour?

   _____

   _____

11+ Maths Study and Practice Book

Pie charts

Pie charts are useful for showing proportions. Each section (or sector) of the pie chart represents a proportion of the whole.

Sometimes, you will be given information about what each section is worth, either as actual amounts, fractions or percentages. Other times you will need to measure or estimate the angle of each section in order to work out what each section is worth.

A netball team played 20 matches in a season. The pie chart shows the results of those matches.

How many matches were **i)** won, **ii)** lost, **iii)** drawn?

Netball matches

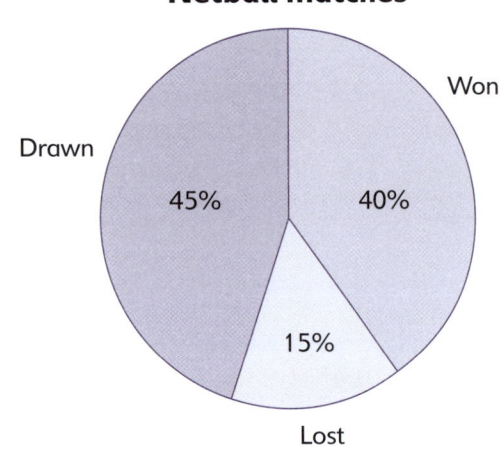

(Pie chart: Drawn 45%, Won 40%, Lost 15%)

Each section has been given a percentage.

i) Out of 20 matches, 40% were won.
   40% of 20 = 8
   Answer: 8

ii) Out of 20 matches, 15% were lost.
    15% of 20 = 3
    Answer: 3

iii) Out of 20 matches, 45% were drawn.
     45% of 20 = 9
     Answer: 9

Grayson collected data relating to the number of pets each child in his class had. If there are 32 children in Grayson's class how many children had **i)** 0 pets, **ii)** 1 pet, **iii)** 2 pets and **iv)** 3 pets?

Pets

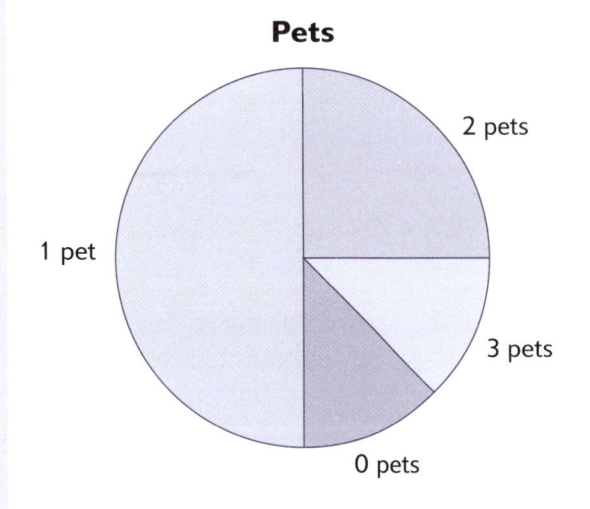

(Pie chart showing sections: 1 pet, 2 pets, 3 pets, 0 pets)

Each section is a clear fraction.

i) The section for 0 pets is $\frac{1}{8}$. $\frac{1}{8}$ of 32 = 4
   Answer: 4

ii) The section for 1 pet is $\frac{1}{2}$. $\frac{1}{2}$ of 32 = 16
    Answer: 16

iii) The section for 2 pets is $\frac{1}{4}$. $\frac{1}{4}$ of 32 = 8
     Answer: 8

iv) The section for 3 pets is $\frac{1}{8}$. $\frac{1}{8}$ of 32 = 4
    Answer: 4

Pie charts

The pie chart below shows the favourite shops of the 120 children in Year 6.

1. How many children prefer clothes shops?
2. How many more children prefer toy shops to book shops?

Favourite shop

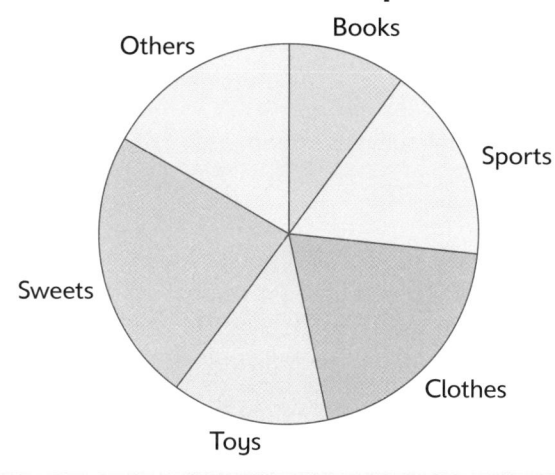

Measure the angle of each section. As there are 360° in a circle, each section is a fraction of 360.

1. The section for clothes measures 72°. As a fraction of the entire circle, that is $\frac{72}{360} = \frac{1}{5}$. $\frac{1}{5}$ of 120 children = 24

   Answer: 24

2. The section for toys measures 48°. As a fraction of the entire circle, that is $\frac{48}{360} = \frac{2}{15}$. $\frac{2}{15}$ of 120 children = 16, so 16 children prefer toy shops. The section for books measures 36°. As a fraction of the entire circle, that is $\frac{36}{360} = \frac{1}{10}$. $\frac{1}{10}$ of 120 children = 12, so 12 children prefer book shops. You then need to subtract 12 from 16.

   Answer: 4

Lauren asked 64 of her friends what their favourite flavour of crisp was. She then created this pie chart.

Crisps

1. How many preferred salt and vinegar flavoured crisps? _____
2. How many preferred roast chicken flavoured crisps? _____
3. How many more children preferred cheese and onion flavoured crisps to pickled onion flavoured crisps? _____

This pie chart shows the holiday destination of 60 families.

Holiday destinations

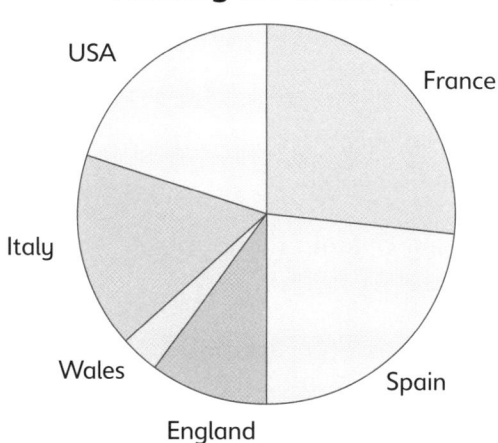

4. How many families holidayed in France? _____
5. How many more families holidayed in Spain than in England? _____
6. How many families went to Wales and Italy altogether? _____

11+ Maths Study and Practice Book

Venn diagrams

Venn diagrams sort data and present it in a way that allows you to see connections. The area where the circles overlap contains data that relates to both groups.

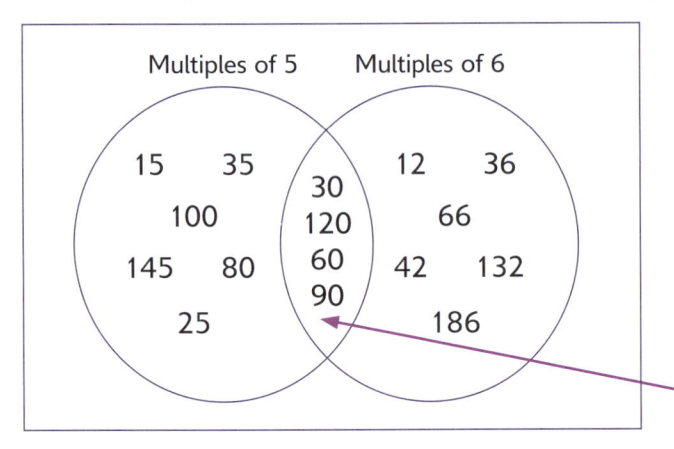

This Venn diagram is displaying multiples of both 5 and 6.

The left-hand oval shows multiples of 5. The right-hand oval shows multiples of 6.

Where the two ovals cross over, the numbers are multiples of both 5 and 6.

These numbers are multiples of both 5 and 6.

Venn diagrams also allow you to see information that may not fit with the data.

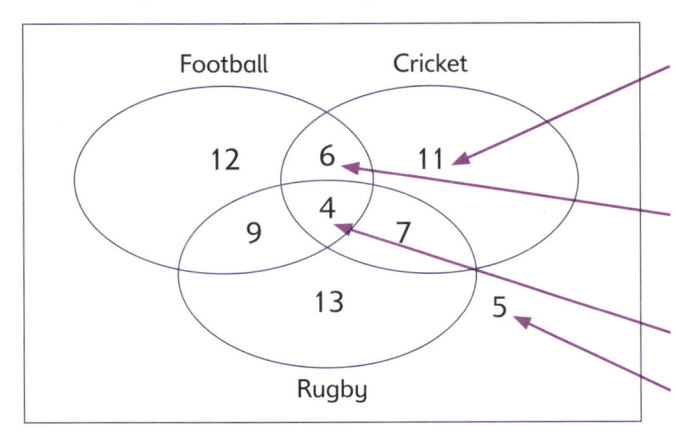

The numbers in the centre of the ovals show those children who only play that sport. For example, 11 children only play cricket.

Where two ovals cross over, it shows the number of children who play both those sports. For example, 6 children play both football and cricket.

The space in the centre where all three ovals cross over shows the number of children who play all three sports. So, 4 children play all three sports.

The 5 on the outside indicates how many children don't play any of those three sports.

This Venn diagram shows the holiday destinations of a group of children.

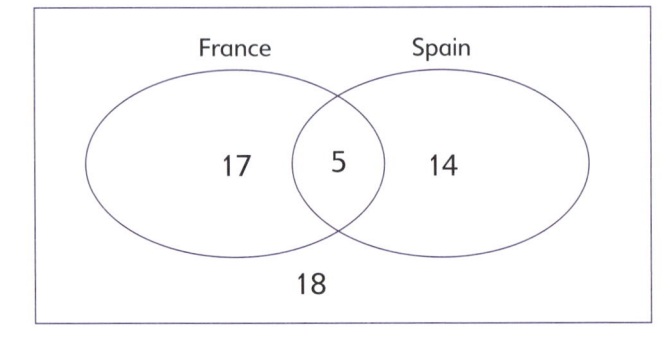

1. How many children have only been to France? _____
2. How many children have been to both France and Spain? _____
3. How many children have been to neither country? _____
4. How many children are there altogether? _____

This Venn diagram shows the pets owned by a group of children.

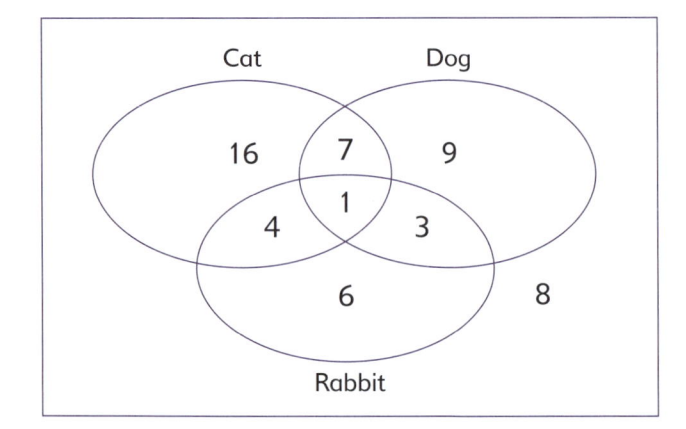

5. How many children have both a dog and a rabbit _____
6. How many children have a cat, a dog and a rabbit? _____
7. How many children do not have a pet? _____
8. How many children were asked about their pets? _____

Mean, mode, median and range

Mean, **mode** and **median** are different ways of describing the **average** or most typical value within a group of numbers. The **range** is the difference between the smallest and largest number within a group. Each is found in a different way and so may give different values for the same group of numbers.

Mean

The mean is commonly known as the 'average'. The mean is found by adding together all the numbers in a group and dividing them by the total number of items.

Find the mean of this set of numbers.

3, 5, 8, 4, 3, 6, 7, 3, 6

3 + 5 + 8 + 4 + 3 + 6 + 7 + 3 + 6 = 45

45 ÷ 9 = 5

Answer: 5

Mode

The mode is the number that appears most often in the group.

Find the mode of this set of numbers.

3, 5, 8, 4, 3, 6, 7, 3, 6

The most common number is 3 because it appears three times.

Answer: 3

Median

If all the numbers are arranged in order from smallest to largest, the median is the number in the centre of the group. If there is an even number of numbers, the median is half-way between the two central numbers.

Find the median of this set of numbers.

3, 5, 8, 4, 3, 6, 7, 3, 6

Write in order of size: 3, 3, 3, 4, (5), 6, 6, 7, 8

5 is the middle number.

Answer: 5

> **TIP** 'Mode' and 'most' both begin with the same sound: m-o-w. 'Mean' is mean because it makes you do both addition and division sums. 'Median' sounds like 'medium', which comes in the middle of small and large. You are looking for the middle number.

Range

The range is the difference between the smallest and largest number. To find the difference between two numbers, you must do a subtraction calculation.

Find the range of this set of numbers.

3, 5, 8, 4, 3, 6, 7, 3, 6

The range is 8 − 3.

Answer: 5

Mean, mode, median and range

Sometimes, you might be asked to work through these processes the other way. For example, you might be given the mean and then be asked to identify a value.

> The average of 3 numbers is 12. If one of the numbers is 8 and one is 16, what must the 3rd number be?

If you know the mean is 12, then by multiplying that by 3 you can find out the total of the three numbers (remember that to find the mean you add the numbers together and divide by the number of items, so we have to do the opposite when working backwards).

3 × 12 = 36, so the total of the three numbers is 36.

The total of the first two numbers is 8 + 16 = 24, so the third value must be 12 because 36 − 24 = 12.

Answer: 12

You might also be asked to find a new value if the mean is changed.

> The average number of goals scored by a football team over 5 matches is 4. After their 6th match the average increases to 5. How many goals were scored in the 6th match?

TIP Remember, if the word average is used, you need to work out the mean.

Sometimes, you won't know all the individual values – just the average – but you can still work out the answer. You can't work out the exact number of goals the football team scored in each of the first five matches, only that the total was 20.

Once again you need to think backwards. If the average after five matches was 4 goals, that must mean that in total they scored 20 goals because 5 × 4 = 20. If the average after six matches is 5 goals then their new total must be 30 because 6 × 5 = 30. The difference in goals is 10, so they must have scored 10 goals in the sixth match.

Answer: 10

Now answer the following questions.

1. Find the mean, mode, median and range of this set of numbers: 17   13   19   13   18

   mean: _____   mode: _____   median: _____   range: _____

2. The highest temperature at a seaside town was recorded each day over a week as follows: 26°C, 27°C, 29°C, 29°C, 28°C, 24°C and 26°C. What was the average daily maximum temperature for the week? _____

3. For her birthday, Megan received money from 5 relatives. The average amount was £8. Her sister then gave her some money taking the average to £9. How much money did her sister give her? _____

Probability

The **probability** of something is how likely it is to happen.
Probability is usually recorded in one of two ways: with words or with fractions.

Recording probability with words

The following words can all be used to describe the probability of something happening: impossible, unlikely, even chance, likely and certain. They are quite general statements rather than being specific.

Impossible	Unlikely	Even chance	Likely	Certain
It will never happen.	It could happen, but probably won't.	It might happen, or it might not.	It will probably happen.	It will definitely happen.

It will be 1 o'clock at some point today. ← This is certain – at 1 a.m. and 1 p.m.

A dog will grow wings and fly tomorrow. ← This is impossible – dogs cannot grow wings!

Someone in your family will win £1 000 000. ← This is unlikely. It might happen – somebody has to win – but it is very unlikely.

The next baby born will be a girl. ← There is an even chance of this. It will either be a boy or a girl.

You will see the sun today. ← This is likely, but it might be cloudy all day, in which case you won't see it.

Recording probability with fractions

Other probability scenarios can be quantified (measured accurately). If something is certain to happen, its probability is 1. If something is certain not to happen, its probability is 0. If something is neither certain to happen, nor certain not to happen, then its probability can be expressed as a fraction.

For example, imagine you are rolling a dice.

There are 6 numbers you could roll, so the probability of rolling a 3 is a 1 in 6 chance = $\frac{1}{6}$.

The probability of rolling an even number is a 3 in 6 chance (2, 4 and 6) = $\frac{3}{6} = \frac{1}{2}$.

The probability of rolling a number between 1 and 6 is a 6 in 6 chance = $\frac{6}{6} = 1$.

The probability of throwing a 7 is a 0 in 6 chance = $\frac{0}{6} = 0$.

> ! Always write the fraction in its lowest terms.

Now answer the following questions. Give the answers to questions 1 to 3 in words and the answers to questions 4 to 6 as fractions.

1. What is the probability that you will walk on the Moon tomorrow? _____
2. What is the probability that October will come after September? _____
3. What is the probability that you will see a rainbow tomorrow? _____
4. What is the probability that a flipped coin will land on heads? _____
5. What is the probability that you will pick an ace from a pack of cards? _____
6. What is the probability that someone you meet has a birthday in May? _____

Statistics practice page 1

Now test your skills with these practice pages. If you get stuck, go back to pages 133 to 143 for some reminders.

Tables

1. Complete the table showing the animals that visited the vets over four days.

Day	Dog	Cat	Rabbit	Hamster	Total
Monday	54	37	12	19	
Tuesday	46		7	12	104
Wednesday		26	11	6	89
Thursday	61			11	100
Total		121	39		

Pictograms

Rayna asked the children in her class what their favourite parties were. She made a pictogram of the results.

Type of party	Number of votes
Football	🎈🎈🎈🎈🎈🎈½
Swimming	🎈🎈🎈
Crafts party	🎈🎈🎈🎈🎈½
Cinema	🎈🎈🎈🎈
Sleepover	🎈🎈½

🎈 = 2 votes

2. How many children voted for a crafts party? _____
3. How many children preferred a sporty party? _____
4. How many more children voted for the cinema than the sleepover? _____
5. How many children did Rayna ask altogether? _____

Amara drew a pictogram to show the number of doughnuts sold each day.

Day	Number of doughnuts
Monday	🍩🍩🍩🍩🍩🍩🍩½
Tuesday	🍩🍩🍩🍩🍩½
Wednesday	🍩🍩🍩🍩
Thursday	🍩🍩🍩½
Friday	🍩🍩🍩🍩🍩🍩🍩🍩
Saturday	🍩🍩🍩🍩🍩🍩½
Sunday	🍩🍩🍩🍩½

🍩 = 4 doughnuts

6. How many doughnuts were sold on Tuesday? _____
7. How many more doughnuts were sold on Friday than on Thursday? _____
8. How many doughnuts were sold over the weekend? _____
9. How many doughnuts were sold altogether? _____

Statistics practice page 2

Tally charts and frequency tables

Look at this data that shows how many siblings each child in a class has.

1	0	2	0	3	2	1	2	3	4	0	1	5	0	2	2
3	1	1	4	2	2	1	6	0	5	0	2	3	1	2	1

1. Use the data to complete the tally chart and frequency table.

Number	Tally	Frequency
0		
1		
2		
3		
4		
5		
6		

2. Which is the least common number of siblings?

_____

3. How many children have three or more siblings?

_____

Look at this data that shows the colours of sweets Jamila pulled out of a bag.

R	Y	B	G	R	R	O	B	G	P	G	Y	Y	O	P
G	B	B	O	O	P	Y	R	B	G	B	P	G	O	R
R	Y	G	B	G	Y	B	R	O	P	Y	P	B	G	Y	Y
O	P	R	R	B	Y	R	B	B	B	Y	P	P	O	B
Y	R	O	O	G	G	R	Y	O	P	P	G	R	G	P

R = red
Y = yellow
B = blue
G = green
P = purple
O = orange

4. Use the data to complete the tally chart and frequency table.

Colour	Tally	Frequency
Red		
Yellow		
Blue		
Green		
Purple		
Orange		

5. Which was the most common colour of sweet?

_____

6. How many sweets did Jamila count altogether?

_____

11+ Maths Study and Practice Book

Statistics practice page 3

Bar charts

Nasim asked the children in his class what their favourite types of television show were. He presented the data in a bar chart.

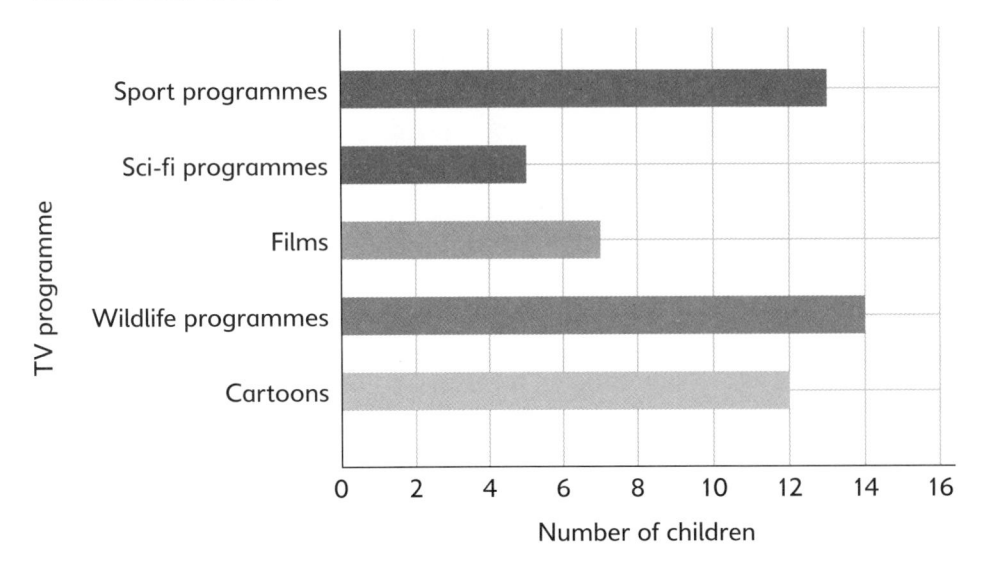

1. How many children liked sports programmes? _____
2. How many fewer children liked sci-fi programmes compared to cartoons? _____
3. What is the most popular type of programme? _____
4. How many children did Nasim ask altogether? _____

Stella helped her parents do jobs around the house to earn some money. She recorded how much she earned in a bar chart.

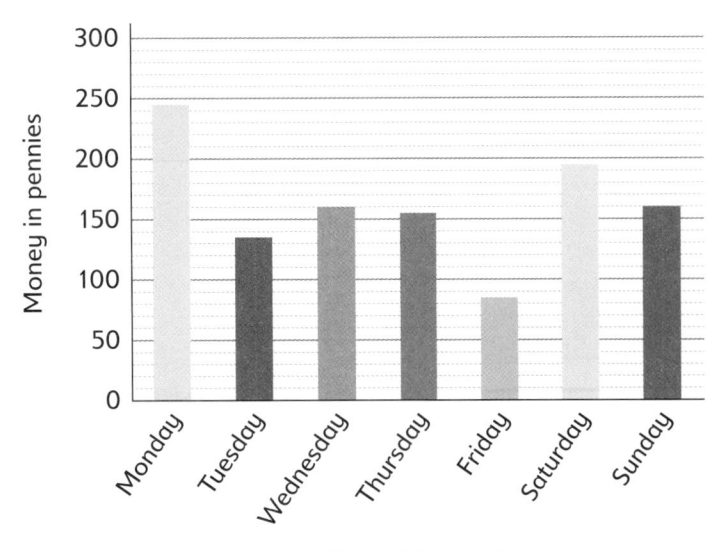

5. On which day did she earn the most money? _____
6. On which two days did she earn the same money? _____
7. What is the difference between the most and least money that she earned? _____
8. How much money did she earn altogether? _____

Statistics practice page 4

Line graphs

Manny counted how many skips he could complete in six minutes. He presented the results in the line graph below.

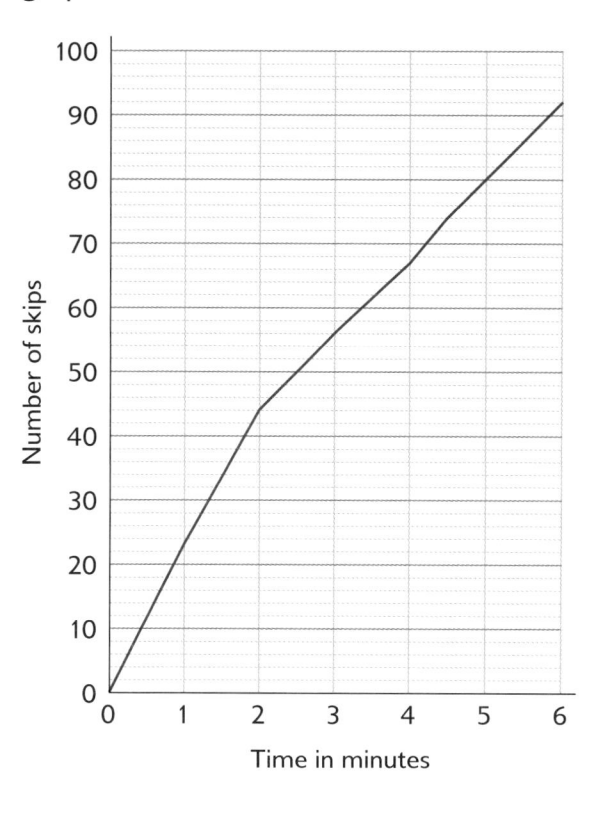

1. How many skips did Manny complete after the first minute? _____

2. How many fewer skips did he complete in the second minute compared to the first minute? _____

3. How many skips had he completed after $4\frac{1}{2}$ minutes? _____

4. How many skips did he complete altogether? _____

Juliet measured how much rain fell over a period of eight hours. She presented the data in a line graph.

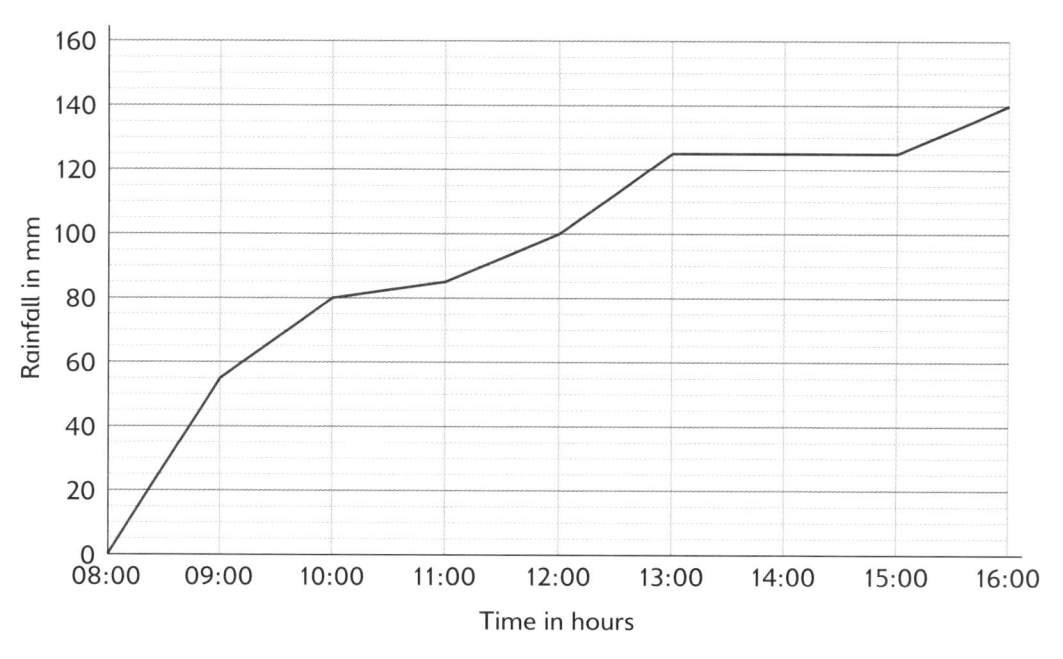

5. Between which two hours did the most rain fall? _____

6. For how long did it not rain? _____

7. How much rain fell between 3.00 p.m. and 4.00 p.m.? _____

8. How much rain had fallen by 11.00 a.m.? _____

Statistics practice page 5

Pie charts

Tamara asked her 24 classmates how they travelled to school. She presented the results in a pie chart.

Hayley used a pie chart to record the weight of the ingredients in her chocolate cake. They totalled 720g.

Travel to school

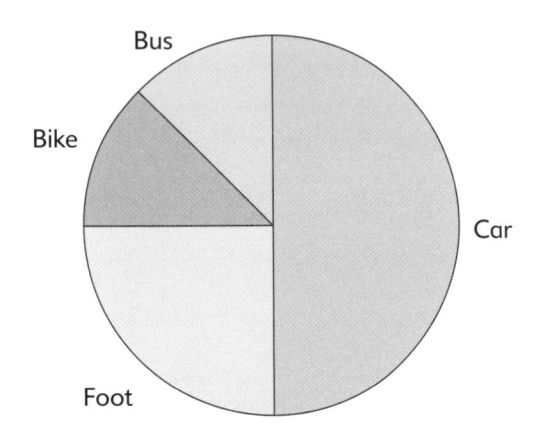

Weight of ingredients

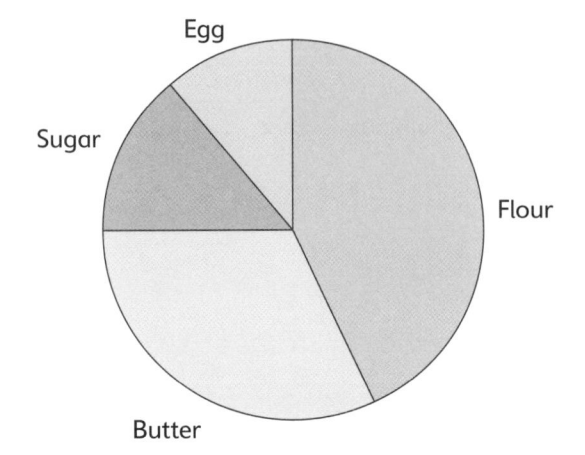

1. How many children were driven to school by car? _____

2. What fraction of those asked cycled to school? _____

3. What was the weight of the flour in the recipe?

   _____

4. What was the weight of the butter in the recipe?

   _____

Venn diagrams

This Venn diagram shows some of the clubs that children at a school attend.

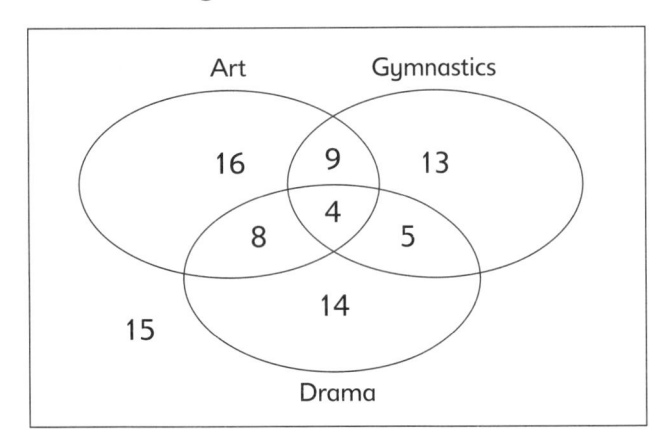

5. How many children went to the art club? _____

6. How many children went to both gymnastics and drama? _____

7. How many children didn't attend any of the clubs? _____

8. How many children attended all three clubs? _____

Statistics practice page 6

Mean, mode, median and range

In a maths exam, 6 friends scored 83, 92, 74, 83, 81 and 79.

1. What is the mean score? _____

2. What is the mode score? _____

3. What is the median score? _____

4. What is the range of scores? _____

5. One friend has his paper re-marked and his score goes up from 81 to 84. What is the new mean score? _____

Meg and her 4 friends do a sponsored swim. Together they swim 372 lengths.

6. What is the average number of lengths swum? _____

7. Meg's friend Hannah joins in at the last minute and manages to swim 81 lengths. What is the new average? _____

In a netball competition the average number of goals scored between 8 children is 9.

8. When Rosie has her go the average increases to 10. How many goals did Rosie score? _____

Probability

Use the terms impossible, unlikely, even chance, likely and certain to describe these situations.

9. I will grow wings tomorrow. _____

10. The next car you see will be bright pink. _____

11. A tossed coin will land on tails. _____

Give your answers to the following questions as fractions.

12. There are 15 beads in a bag: 6 blue, 5 yellow and 4 red. What is the probability of picking out a blue bead? _____

13. An extra red bead is added to the bag. What is the probability of picking a red bead now? _____

14. Assam has collected 20 prizes for a raffle. If he sells 360 tickets, what is the probability that your ticket will win a prize? _____

15. You spin a spinner labelled 1 to 10. What is the probability that the spinner will land on a multiple of 3? _____

16. You ask a friend to think of a two-digit number. What is the probability that it will be a multiple of 5? _____

Parents' notes

This book is divided into six sections, representing six key areas tested in 11+ maths exams:

- number and place value
- calculations, algebra and number sequences
- fractions, decimals and percentages
- measurement
- geometry
- statistics.

Each section contains explanations of maths questions, as well as sets of practice questions. This book can therefore be worked through in its entirety, or you may select particular sections for your child to focus on.

If your child is sitting an 11+ exam set by CEM, you might find that a part of their exam is described as numerical reasoning. Numerical reasoning questions can be straightforward mathematical calculations or word problems that they will need to use logic to solve, both of which they will be familiar with from their maths lessons. The examples and explanations in this book provide complete practice in the skills your child needs for a numerical reasoning exam.

Administering the Practice test

- When your child is confident answering each question type, they should sit the Practice test. This should be done in exam conditions, with an adult timing and marking the test.
- Before beginning the test, make sure your child has a pencil, an eraser, a ruler, a protractor and several sheets of rough paper. Also ensure that your child is able to see a clock or a watch.
- Advise your child to read each question carefully.
- Answers need to be written clearly on the answer line. If the child needs to do any calculations, these should be done on a separate piece of paper.
- Encourage your child to check their answers if they have time at the end of the test. This will also allow them to make sure that they haven't accidentally missed out any questions.
- The Practice test is divided into topics to allow you to identify any areas that your child has not yet understood.
- There is a time limit of 1 hour 30 minutes. When your child has finished the test, you should mark it using the answers section of this book. There are 100 marks available in total.
- The table below will help you to plan the next steps. However, these are suggestions only. Please use your own judgement as you decide how best to proceed.

Score	Time taken	Target met?	Action
1–79	Any	Not yet	Work through the explanation sections of this book again, ensuring that all topics are understood. If your child struggled with particular topics on the Practice test, focus on those sections.
80–100	Over the target – child took too long	Not yet	Use the appropriate age level **11+ Maths Rapid Tests** to improve speed.
80–100	On target – child took suggested time or less	Yes	Move on to **11+ Maths Rapid Tests** or **Progress Papers** to continue developing speed, accuracy and skill.

For further guidance on 11+ maths exams, download the free **Parents' Guide to the 11+** from the **Schofield & Sims** website. This provides an overview of the exams and contains useful advice on organising your child's revision, as well as how to help them prepare for the day of the exam.

Practice test

Test time: 1 hour 30 min

Number and place value

1. Write this number in words.

   3 408 264

   _____

2. Write these words as a number.

   nine million and twelve _____

3. Write these numbers in ascending order.

   7 123 835   7 124 635   7 123 935   7 132 823   7 122 245

   _____

4. Round 93 528 to the nearest 1000. _____

5. −34 − 16 = _____

6. Write the factors of 32 in ascending order.

   _____

7. Which two different prime numbers can be added together to make 25? _____

8. Write 96 as a product of its prime factors.

   _____

9. Circle the numbers that are divisible by 4, 6 and 9.

   324   672   450   936   281   644   684

Write these Roman numerals as numbers.

10. DCCCLXVII _____

11. MMMDCLXXIV _____

/14

Calculations, algebra and number sequences

12. 35 673 + 29 498 = _____

13. 9000 − 6578 = _____

14. 0.0067 × 1000 = _____

15. 3627 × 46 = _____

16. 2250 ÷ 18 = _____

Practice test

17. Delia is making cupcakes for a charity bake sale.

She can fit 8 cupcakes on each plate. She makes 236 cupcakes altogether.

    i)   If she fills each plate, how many plates will she need? _____

    ii)   How many cupcakes will be left over? _____

18. $3 + 6 (2 \times 4^2) =$ _____

19. The total of three consecutive numbers is 162.
What are the three numbers? _____

20. Which two prime numbers multiply to make 159? _____

21. 17   32   [×5   +27]   ___ ___

22. c stands for a whole number.

c + 6 is greater than 50. c − 9 is less than 40.

Find all the numbers that c could be. _____

23. In each of the sequences below, there is a rule for finding the next term.
Find the next two terms in each sequence and explain the rule.

    i)   15, 6, −3, −12, _____ , _____

           The rule is: _____

    ii) 6.3, 7.5, 8.7, 9.9, _____ , _____

           The rule is: _____

/23

Fractions, decimals and percentages

24. On a flight to New York, $\frac{2}{3}$ of the passengers were adults.

If there were 97 children on the flight, how many
passengers were there altogether? _____

25. Circle the two equivalent fractions.

$\frac{8}{12}$ $\frac{15}{50}$ $\frac{4}{9}$ $\frac{6}{9}$ $\frac{11}{22}$ $\frac{14}{18}$ $\frac{1}{4}$

Practice test

Convert these mixed numbers into improper fractions.

26. $6\frac{1}{8}$ _____

27. $7\frac{3}{5}$ _____

Convert these improper fractions into mixed numbers.

28. $\frac{23}{5}$ _____

29. $\frac{38}{9}$ _____

30. $\frac{3}{8} + \frac{2}{5} =$ _____

31. $\frac{2}{3} \times \frac{1}{6} =$ _____

32. Ronna was sorting the non-fiction books on her bookshelf.

    55% were about animals, 10% were about famous people and the remaining 21 were about types of vehicle.

    How many non-fiction books did Ronna have? _____

33. In a bag of 30 marbles, 20% are green, $\frac{1}{3}$ are blue and the rest are red. How many marbles are red? _____

34. Alice is twice as old as Frank who is 3 times older than George. Their ages add up to 90.

    How old is each person?

    Alice is _____ years old.

    Frank is _____ years old.

    George is _____ years old.

    /17

Measurement

35. There are approximately 2.2 pounds in a kilogram.

    Laila sells oranges at 20p per pound.

    Naomi sells oranges at 42p per kilogram.

    Who sells the cheaper oranges? _____

36. Priyanka checks the map to see how far it is from her house to her aunt's house.

    The distance on the map measures 4.5cm. When Priyanka checks the scale, it says 1:400 000.

    How far is it to Priyanka's aunt's house? _____

Practice test

37. Dexter walked 15 minutes to the football pitch near his friend's house, played football for an hour and a half, sat on the bench eating ice cream for 10 minutes and then ran home in 5 minutes. If he returned home at 14:20, what time did he leave home? _____

38. Elijah cycled at 24 mph for 30 minutes, then slowed down to 18mph for the next 40 minutes. How far did he travel in total? _____

The following table shows the temperature in four cities on January 1st.

City	Temperature °C
Edinburgh	4
Brisbane	25
Moscow	−8
Marrakesh	12

39. What is the difference in temperature between Marrakesh and Moscow? _____

40. Which two cities have a difference of 21°C? _____

41. Tom needs to buy fertiliser for his lawn.

Each bag contains enough fertiliser to cover an area of 10m².

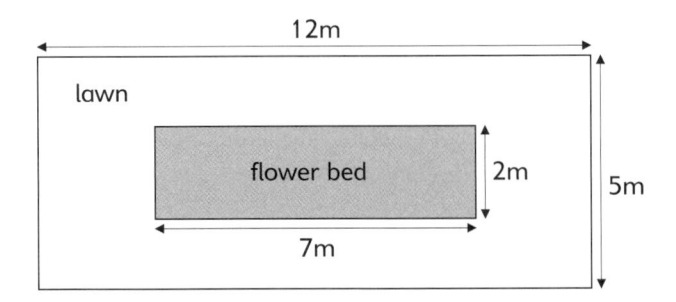

(Lawn: 12m × 5m, with a flower bed of 7m × 2m inside)

How many bags of fertiliser will Tom need to buy? _____

42. An isosceles triangle has a perimeter of 14cm.

One of its sides is 6cm. What could the length of each of the other two sides be?

Give **two** possible answers.

_____ and _____

_____ and _____

/19

Practice test

Geometry

43. Draw arrows to show the pairs of parallel lines.

44. I am facing SE. I turn 90° anticlockwise, then 135° clockwise and finally 180° anticlockwise.

In which direction am I now facing? _____

45. The following 8 circles fit into a rectangle.

If the diameter of each circle is 4.5cm, what is the length of the rectangle?

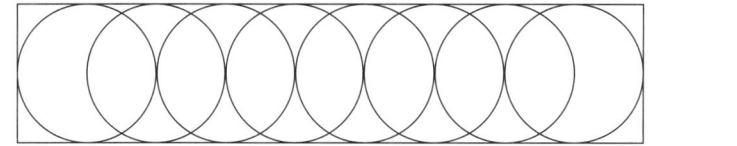

_____

46. What is the order of rotational symmetry of this shape?

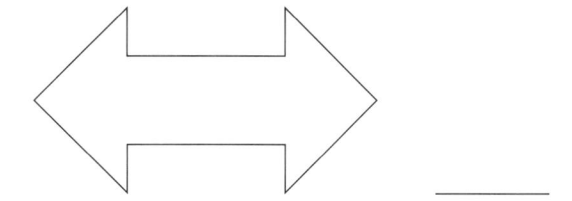

_____

47. Shade two more squares on the diagram so that the new shape has rotational symmetry of order 4.

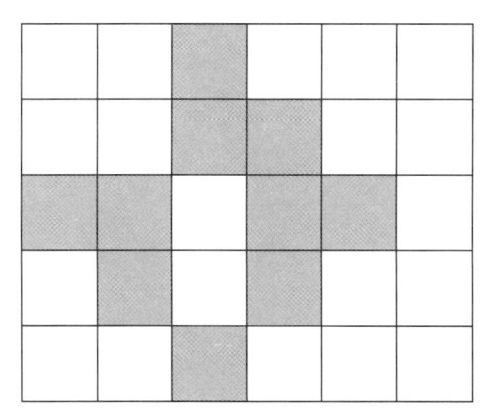

48. How many vertices are there in a square based pyramid? _____

11+ Maths Study and Practice Book

Practice test

49. A, B, C and D are vertices of a parallelogram.

Points A and B are shown on the grid.

Point C is at (5, 2).

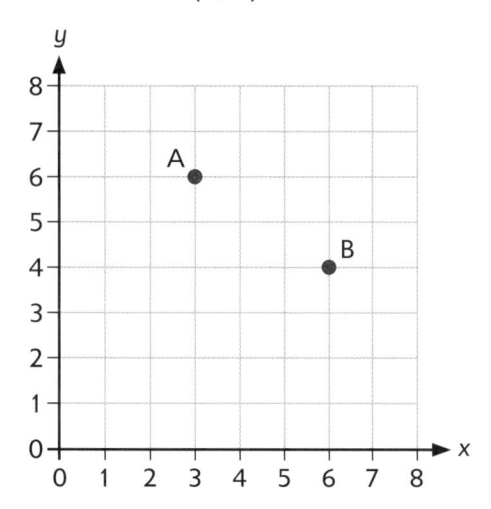

Work out the coordinates for point D. D = _____

50. Draw the reflection of the following shape in the mirror line.

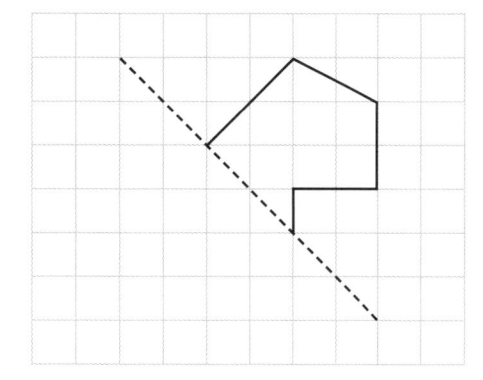

/13

Statistics

51. These bar charts show data about four children, Sal, Marco, Naana and Chanel.

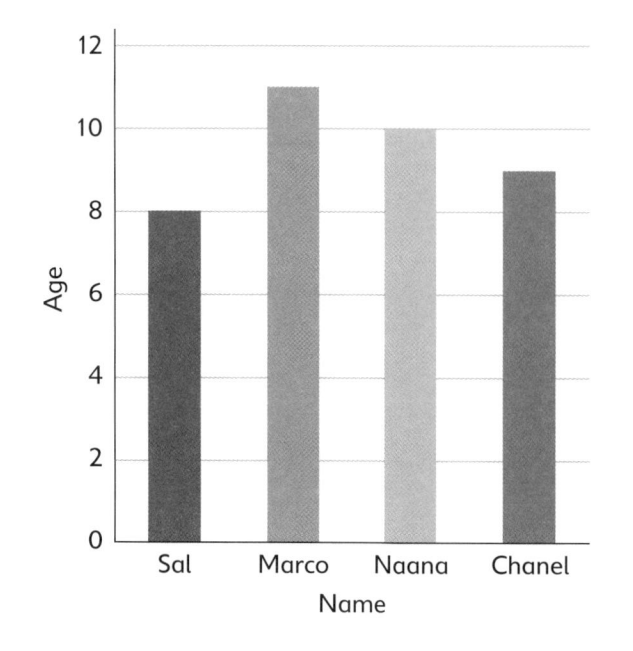

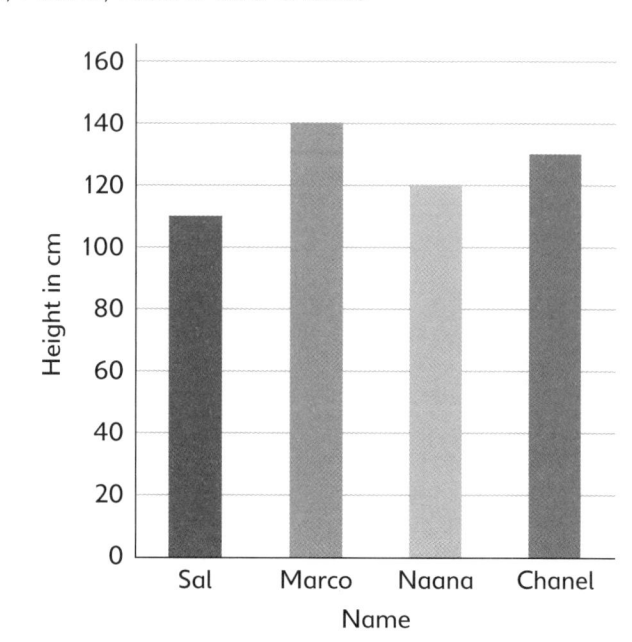

Practice test

Use the data to complete the Venn diagram with the children's names.

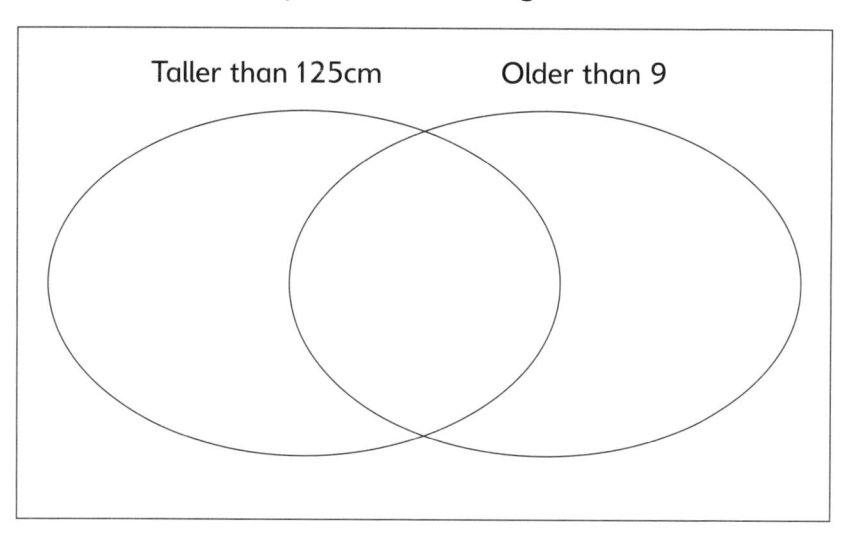

Taller than 125cm   Older than 9

Ella asked 60 of her friends what their favourite school lunches were.

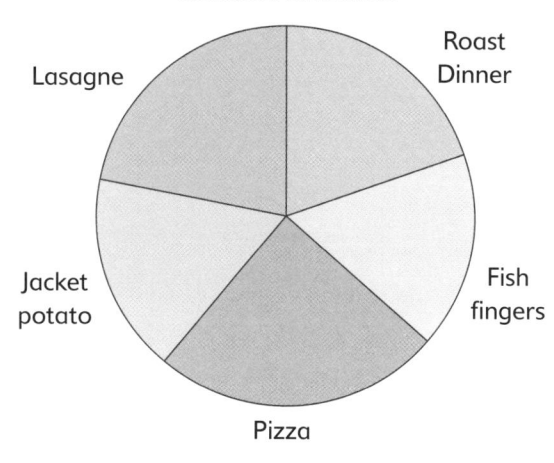

School lunches

Lasagne, Roast Dinner, Fish fingers, Pizza, Jacket potato

52. How many children preferred roast dinner? _____

53. How many children preferred jacket potato? _____

54. Over 5 cricket matches, Asif scored an average of 68 runs.

    After his 6th match, his average score increased to 71 runs.

    How many runs must he have scored in his 6th match? _____

55. A bag contains 5 red counters, 3 blue counters and 4 green counters. What is the probability of picking out a blue counter? _____

/14

Total score:	/100	Time taken:	

Answers

Number and place value

Place value (page 6)

1. seventy-eight thousand, nine hundred and thirteen
2. one point eight two five
3. 18.342
4. 138 047 599
5. 50
6. 30 000

Ordering and comparing numbers (pages 7–8)

1. 89 894 (the 8 and 9 at the beginning of the numbers are both the same, the hundreds number in 89 894 is smaller)
2. 652 122   562 876   234 895   56 290   23 869
3. false (175 423 is the bigger number)
4. 6 837 942 > 6 837 892 > 6 738 813 < 6 952 824
5. 67 362 < 348 235 < 412 789 < 2 683 683 < 5 789 267
6. ≥ 5km (he ran at least 5km)

Rounding (page 9)

1. 13 000 (7 rounds up)
2. 4.8 (6 rounds up)
3. 200 000 (3 rounds down)
4. 13.81 (2 rounds down)
5. 385.43 (2 rounds up)
6. 52.6 (5 rounds up)

Estimating (page 10)

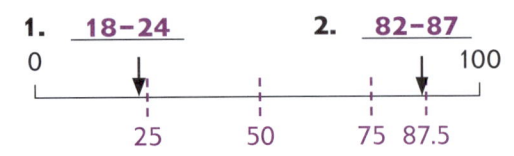

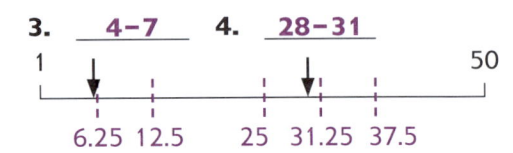

1. 18–24
2. 82–87
3. 4–7
4. 28–31
5. 420 (270 + 150 = 420)
6. 610 (790 − 180 = 610)

Negative numbers (page 11)

1. −5
2. −11
3. −4°C
4. −£8
5. −5, −8
6. −7, −3

Factors (page 13)

1. 1, 2, 3, 4, 6, 12
2. 1, 2, 3, 4, 6, 9, 12, 18, 36
3. 1, 2, 3, 6, 9, 18, 27, 54
4. 1, 2, 4, 5, 8, 10, 16, 20, 40, 80
5. 3 (factors of 15: 1, **3**, 5, 15; factors of 21: 1, **3**, 7, 21)
6. 14 (factors of 28: 1, 2, 4, 7, **14**, 28; factors of 42: 1, 2, 3, 6, 7, **14**, 21, 42)

Multiples (page 14)

1. 56, 35, 14, 49
2. 72, 36, 48, 24
3. 18, 54, 63, 108
4. 24 (multiples of 3: 3, 6, 9, 12, 15, 18, 21, **24**; multiples of 8: 8, 16, **24**)
5. 12 (multiples of 4: 4, 8, **12**; multiples of 12: **12**)
6. 8 (multiples of 4: 4, **8**; multiples of 8: **8**)
7. 536

Divisibility rules (page 16)

1. 456, 132
2. 135, 345
3. 1120
4.

	2	3	4	5	6	7	8	9	10
624	✓	✓	✓		✓		✓		
1530	✓	✓		✓	✓			✓	✓
2205		✓		✓		✓		✓	
572	✓		✓						

5. 317 (317 − 7 = 310)
6. 760 (760 − 4 = 756, 7 + 5 + 6 = 18, 1 + 8 = 9)

Prime numbers and prime factors (pages 17–18)

1. prime
2. not prime (divisible by 2 as it is even)
3. not prime (divisible by 3 and 9 as the digits add up to 9)
4. not prime (divisible by 5 as it ends in 5)
5. prime
6. 37
7. 2 × 2 × 2 × 3
8. 7 × 7

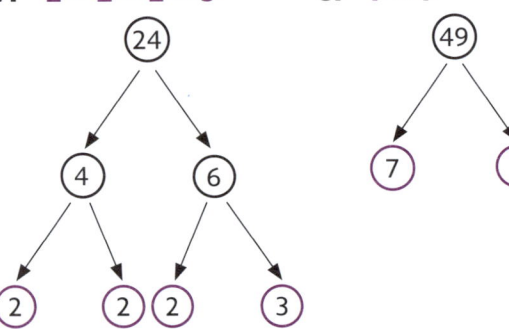

158

Answers

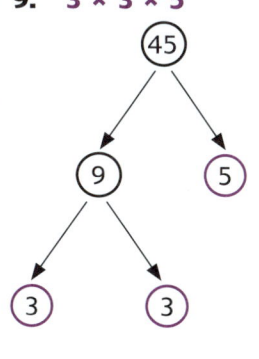

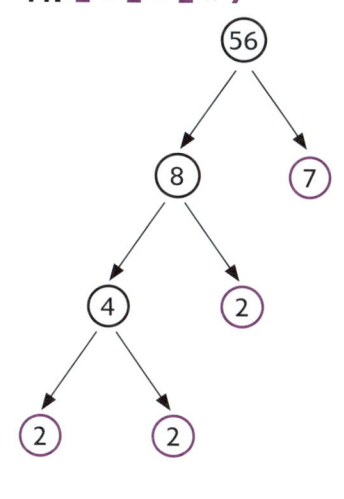

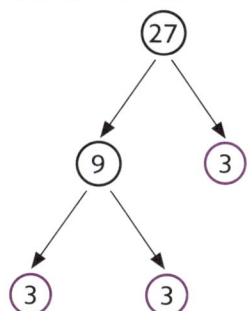

9. 3 × 3 × 5

   45 → 9, 5
   9 → 3, 3

10. 3 × 3 × 3

    27 → 9, 3
    9 → 3, 3

11. 2 × 2 × 2 × 7

    56 → 8, 7
    8 → 4, 2
    4 → 2, 2

12. 2 × 19

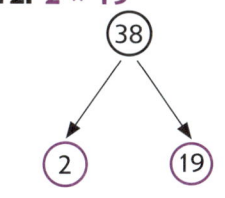

    38 → 2, 19

Square and cube numbers (page 19)

1. 27
2. 49 + 25
3. 14
4. 9
5. 2
6. 8^2
7. 64
8. 133
9. 26
10. 343
11. 6
12. 5^3

Roman numerals (page 20)

1. 427 (CD = 400, XX = 20, VII = 7)
2. 1396 (M = 1000, CCC = 300, XC = 90, VI = 6)
3. 6128 ($\overline{VI}$ = 6000, C = 100, XX = 20, VIII = 8)
4. DLXXXI (D = 500, LXXX = 80, I = 1)
5. MMDCCCXXXII (MM = 2000, DCCC = 800, XXX = 30, II = 2)
6. $\overline{IX}$CDLXVI ($\overline{IX}$ = 9000, CD = 400, LX = 60, VI = 6)

Number and place value practice page 1
(page 21)

1. six hundred and forty-five thousand, one hundred and three
2. one million, three hundred and sixty-two thousand and eighty-six
3. 42 872
4. 2 358 604
5. 60 000
6. 400 000
7. 367 158 < 367 518
8. 8 174 479 > 8 147 479
9. 4 672 456 458 235 452 782 56 263 45 278
10. 4 728 578 4 782 567 4 728 758 (4 782 657)
11. 2 145 673 > 214 657 < 412 756 < 2 415 673 < 4 215 637
12. ≤ 4 metres
13. 55 000
14. 123 000
15. 540 000
16. 970 000
17. 780 (460 + 320 = 780)
18. 100 000 (2000 × 50 = 100 000)

Number and place value practice page 2
(page 22)

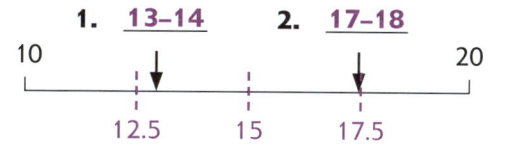

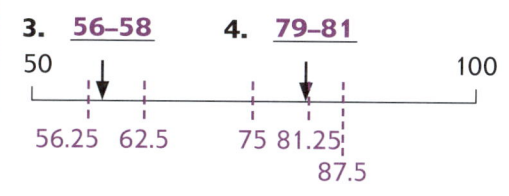

1. 13–14
2. 17–18

   10 ─── 12.5 ─── 15 ─── 17.5 ─── 20

3. 56–58
4. 79–81

   50 ─── 56.25 62.5 ─── 75 81.25 87.5 ─── 100

5. 280 (60 + 70 + 40 + 110 = 280)
6. 3400 (1400 + 800 + 1200 = 3400)
7. −6
8. −24
9. −74
10. 3
11. −8
12. −5°C (2°C − 7°C = −5°C)
13. 1, 2, 3, 4, 6, 8, 12, 24
14. 1, 2, 3, 4, 6, 8, 9, 12, 18, 24, 36, 72
15. 1, 7, 49
16. 1, 2, 3, 4, 6, 7, 12, 14, 21, 28, 42, 84
17. 4 (factors of 12: 1, 2, 3, **4**, 6, 12; factors of 28: 1, 2, **4**, 7, 14, 28)
18. 3 (factors of 15: 1, **3**, 5, 15; factors of 27: 1, **3**, 9, 27)
19. 24 (factors of 24: 1, 2, 3, 4, 6, 8, 12, **24**; factors of 72: 1, 2, 3, 4, 6, 8, 9, 12, 18, **24**, 36, 72)
20. 18 (factors of 18: 1, 2, 3, 6, 9, **18**; factors of 108: 1, 2, 3, 4, 6, 9, 12, **18**, 27, 36, 54, 108)

Number and place value practice page 3
(page 23)

1. 33, 88, 99, 121
2. 50, 100, 175, 325
3. 18 (multiples of 6: 6, 12, **18**; multiples of 9: 9, **18**)
4. 42 (multiples of 3: 3, 6, 9, 12, 15, 18, 21, 24, 27, 30, 33, 36, 39, **42**; multiples of 14: 14, 28, **42**)
5. 54
6. 300 (look for multiples of 4 with a 0 on the end)
7. true (56 is divisible by 8)

11+ Maths Study and Practice Book

Answers

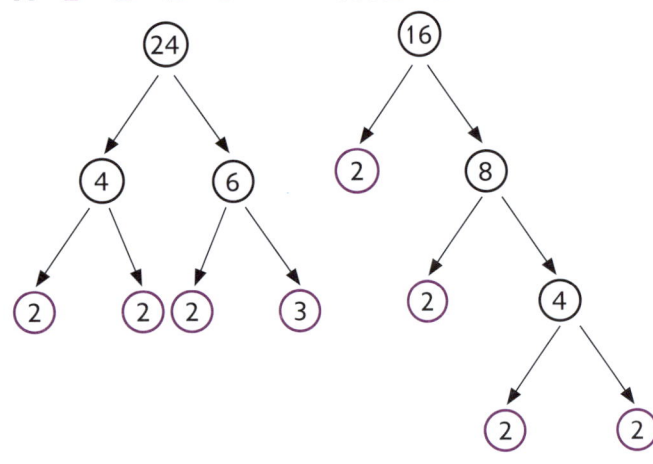

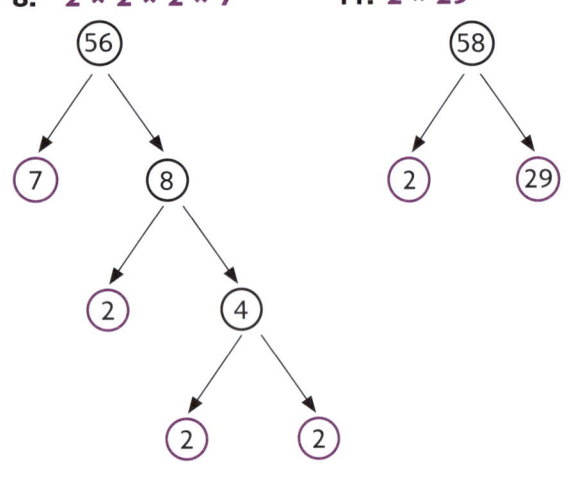

Number and place value practice page 3
(page 23) continued

8. **false** (2 + 6 + 3 + 1 = 12, 1 + 2 = 3)
9. **false** (it is odd, so can't be divisible by 6)
10. **234, 252**   11. **240**   12. **105**   13. **252**

Number and place value practice page 4
(page 24)

1. **2, 3, 5, 7, 11, 13**   3. **67**   5. **59**
2. **63**   4. **37**   6. **73**
7. **2 × 2 × 2 × 3**
8. **2 × 2 × 2 × 7**
9. **2 × 37**
10. **2 × 2 × 2 × 2**
11. **2 × 29**
12. **2 × 2 × 2 × 3 × 5**

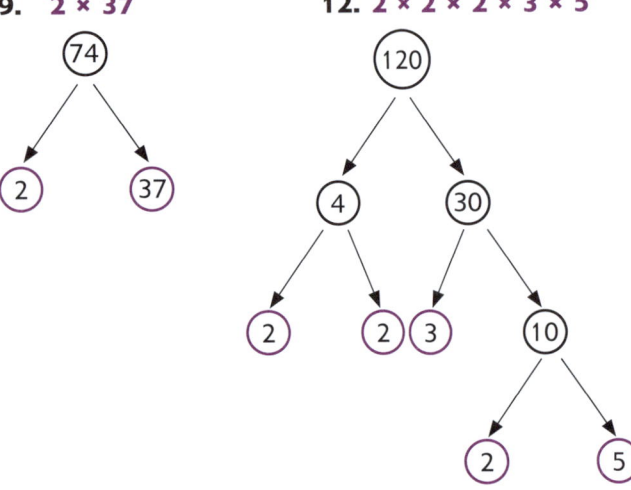

13. **25** (5 × 5 = 25)
14. **121** (11 × 11 = 121)
15. **73** (3 × 3 = 9, 8 × 8 = 64, 9 + 64 = 73)
16. **9** (81 ÷ 9 = 9)
17. **27** (3 × 3 × 3 = 27)
18. **125** (5 × 5 × 5 = 125)
19. **267** (CC = 200, LX = 60, VII = 7)
20. **761** (DCC = 700, LX = 60, I = 1)
21. **12 345** (X̄II = 12 000, CCC = 300, XL = 40, V = 5)
22. **LIX** (L = 50, IX = 9)
23. **CXCIII** (C = 100, XC = 90, III = 3)
24. **DLXVII** (D = 500, LX = 60, VII = 7)

Calculations, algebra and number sequences

Addition (page 27)

1. **53** (near double: 26 + 26 = 52, so 26 + 27 = 53)
2. **85** (add 30 − 1: 56 + 30 = 86, 86 − 1 = 85)
3. **635**

    ```
      3 7 9
    + 2 5 6
    ─────────
      6 3 5
        1 1
    ```

4. **18 819**

    ```
      1 7 3 8 3
    +   1 4 3 6
    ───────────
      1 8 8 1 9
              1
    ```

5. **55 512**

    ```
      4 8 7 3 4
      6 5 4 3
    +     2 3 5
    ───────────
      5 5 5 1 2
      1 1 1 1
    ```

6. **£8946**

    ```
      3 7 6 8
    + 5 1 7 8
    ─────────
      8 9 4 6
        1 1
    ```

Subtraction (page 29)

1. **38** (subtract 20 + 2: 56 − 20 = 36, 36 + 2 = 38)
2. **153** (mental partitioning: 376 − 200 = 176, 176 − 20 = 156, 156 − 3 = 153)
3. **6** (counting on)
4. **2815**

    ```
        4
      5 ⁷7 ²2 ¹3
    − 2 9 0 8
    ─────────
      2 8 1 5
    ```

5. **4219**

    ```
        8 9 9
      9 ¹0 ¹0 ¹1
    − 4 7 8 2
    ─────────
      4 2 1 9
    ```

6. **2969**

    ```
        5
      6 ¹3 8 6
    − 2 8 5 3
    ─────────
      3 5 3 3
    ```

    ```
        2 14 12
      3 5 3 ¹3
    −     5 6 4
    ─────────
      2 9 6 9
    ```

7. **£28** (£54 − £10 − £20 = £24, £24 + £3 + £1 = £28)

Answers

Multiplying and dividing by 10, 100 and 1000 (page 30)

1. 450
2. 600
3. 0.012
4. 100
5. £14.20 (142 ÷ 10 = 14.2)
6. 1200 litres (1.2 × 1000 = 1200)

Multiplication (page 32)

1. 72 (mental calculation)
2. 512

   ```
       3 2
   ×   1 6
   ─────────
     3 2 0   (×10)
   + 1 9₁2   (×6)
   ─────────
     5 1 2
       1
   ```

3. 132 (mental calculation)
4. £750 (mental calculation: 25 × 3 = 75, 75 × 10 = 750)
5. £5662

   ```
       2 9 8
   ×     1 9
   ─────────
     2 9 8 0   (×10)
   + 2 6₈8₇2   (×9)
   ─────────
     5 6 6 2
       1 1
   ```

6. 1302

   ```
       4 2
   ×   3 1
   ─────────
     1 2 6 0   (×30)
   +     4 2   (×1)
   ─────────
     1 3 0 2
         1
   ```

Division and remainders (pages 34–35)

1. 6
2. 43

   ```
        0 4 3
   5 )2 ²1 ¹5
   ```

3. 50 (you know 35 ÷ 7 = 5, so 350 ÷ 7 = 50)
4. 25

   ```
        0 2 5
   5 )1 ¹2 ²5
   ```

5. 124

   ```
        1 2 4
   7 )8 ¹6 ²8
   ```

6. 24

   ```
          0 2 4
   15 )3 ³6 ⁶0
   ```

7. 19r.3, $19\frac{3}{5}$, 19.6

   ```
        1 9 r.3           1 9 ³⁄₅           1 9 . 6
   5 )9 ⁴8            5 )9 ⁴8           5 )9 ⁴8.³0
   ```

8. 72r.1, $72\frac{1}{2}$, 72.5

   ```
        7 2 r.1           7 2 ¹⁄₂           7 2 . 5
   2 )1 ¹4 5          2 )1 ¹4 5         2 )1 ¹4 5.¹0
   ```

9. 23r.7, $23\frac{7}{10}$, 23.7

   ```
          2 3 r.7           2 3 ⁷⁄₁₀          2 3 . 7
   10 )2 ²3 ³7       10 )2 ²3 ³7       10 )2 ²3 ³7.⁷0
   ```

10. 76 (458 ÷ 6 = 76r.2; only 76 boxes can be filled – the remaining 2 eggs would not fill another box)
11. 43 (297 ÷ 7 = 42r.3; 42 boxes will not be enough, so she will need to buy 43)
12. 4 (1000 ÷ 12 = 83r.4)

Order of operations (page 37)

1. 29 ((7 + (3 × 6)) + 2^2 so 7 + 18 + 4 = 29)
2. 27 (6 × 4 + 9 ÷ 3 so 24 + 3 = 27)
3. 32 (((4 + 4)² ÷ 2 so 64 ÷ 2 = 32)
4. 49 (8 ÷ 2 + 15 × 3 so 4 + 45 = 49)
5. 6 (18 − 3 × 4 so 18 − 12 = 6)
6. 53 (2^3 × 7 − 6 + 3 so 56 − 6 = 50, 50 + 3 = 53)

Word problems (page 38)

1. 504 (4 shelves have 112 books and 1 shelf has 56: 112 × 4 = 448, 448 + 56 = 504)
2. 51 (work backwards: 295 + 11 = 306, 306 ÷ 6 = 51)
3. 1116 (12 classes with 31 children: 12 × 31 = 372 children, 3 pencils each = 372 × 3 = 1116)
4. 1280 (18 + 12 + 2 = 32 boxes altogether, 32 × 40 = 1280)
5. 90 (457 − 231 = 226, 226 − 136 = 90)
6. £19 502 (2314 ÷ 48 = 48r.10, so 49 coaches are needed. 49 × £398 = £19 502)

Function machines (page 39)

1. 72 (12 + 12 = 24, 24 × 3 = 72)
   105 (23 + 12 = 35, 35 × 3 = 105)
2. −17 (2 × 4 = 8, 8 − 25 = −17)
   7 (8 × 4 = 32, 32 − 25 = 7)
3. 90 (−3 + 13 = 10, 10 × 9 = 90)
   9 (−12 + 13 = 1, 1 × 9 = 9)
4. 60 (37 − 7 = 30, 30 × 2 = 60)
   88 (51 − 7 = 44, 44 × 2 = 88)
5. 35 (95 ÷ 5 = 19, 19 + 16 = 35)
   22 (30 ÷ 5 = 6, 6 + 16 = 22)
6. 12 (8 × 6 = 48, 48 ÷ 4 = 12)
   21 (14 × 6 = 84, 84 ÷ 4 = 21)

Algebra (page 40)

1. 12 (3 × 7 − (3 + 6) so 21 − 9 = 12)
2. 18 (3^2 + (6 ÷ 3) + 7 so 9 + 2 + 7 = 18)
3. 9 ($\frac{6 \times 7}{7}$ + 3 so 6 + 3 = 9)
4. 5 (+4 to both sides: 3a + 10 = 5a, −3a from both sides: 10 = 2a, therefore a = 5)
5. 3 (+2 to both sides: 4c = 3c + 3, −3c from both sides: c = 3)
6. £100 (P = 35 + (8 × 5) + 25 = 35 + 40 + 25 = £100)

Answers

Number sequences (page 41)

1. **27, 48** (+7)
2. **22, 10** (−7, −6, −5, −4, −3, −2)
3. **8, 125** (cube numbers)
4. **12, 20** (alternating rule: +5 and +3)
5. **27, 49** (+2, +4, +6, +8, +10, +12)
6. **3, −121** (−2, −4, −8, −16, −32, −64)

Finding the nth term (page 43)

1. i) **5n − 1** (the pattern is +5, so it becomes 5n, then −1)
   ii) **49** (5 × 10 = 50, 50 − 1 = 49)
2. i) **4n + 7** (the pattern is +4, so it becomes 4n, then + 7)
   ii) **107** (4 × 25 = 100, 100 + 7 = 107)
3. i) **9n − 8** (the pattern is +9, so it becomes 9n, then − 8)
   ii) **118** (9 × 14 = 126, 126 − 8 = 118)
4. i) **7n − 4** (the pattern is +7, so it becomes 7n, then − 4)
   ii) **696** (7 × 100 = 700, 700 − 4 = 696)
5. **49** (three lines are added each time, so the number sequence is 4, 7, 10, 13. The pattern is +3, so it becomes 3n, then +1. 16 × 3 = 48, 48 + 1 = 49)
6. **204** (two white squares are added each time, so the number sequence is 8, 10, 12, 14. The pattern is +2, so it becomes 2n, then +6. 99 × 2 = 198, 198 + 6 = 204)

Calculations, algebra and number sequences practice page 1 (page 44)

1. **131** (add 60 − 1, so 72 + 60 = 132, 132 − 1 = 131)
2. **340** (mental partitioning: 215 + 100 = 315, 315 + 20 = 335, 335 + 5 = 340)
3. **6643**
   ```
     3 7 3 5
   + 2 9 0 8
   ─────────
     6 6 4 3
         1 1
   ```
4. **141 806**
   ```
     7 4 5 9 1
   + 6 7 2 1 5
   ───────────
   1 4 1 8 0 6
       1 1   1
   ```
5. **236** (25 + 37 + 63 + 111 = 236)
6. **2202** (562 + 1289 + 351 = 2202)
7. **52** (99 − 40 = 59, 59 − 7 = 52)
8. **449** (700 − 250 = 450, 450 − 1 = 449)
9. **2654**
   ```
     4 ⁶7̶ ¹¹2̶ ¹1
   − 2 0 6 7
   ─────────
     2 6 5 4
   ```
10. **2533** (counting on: 2467 + 33 = 2500, 2500 + 2500 = 5000, therefore 2467 + 2533 = 5000)
11. **48** (126 − 78 = 48)
12. **148** (1534 − 1386 = 148)
13. **370**
14. **0.456**
15. **20.6**
16. **0.0528**
17. **1000** (0.036 × 1000 = 36)
18. **3108 grams** (or **3.108 kg**) (31.08 × 100 = 3108)

Calculations, algebra and number sequences practice page 2 (page 45)

1. **630** (7 × 9 = 63, so 70 × 9 = 630)
2. **96** (double 24 = 48, double 48 = 96)
3. **360** (double 45 = 90, double 90 = 180, double 180 = 360)
4. **1054**
   ```
         6 2
   ×     1 7
   ─────────
         6 2 0  (×10)
   +     4 3₁4  (×7)
   ─────────
       1 0 5 4
             1
   ```
5. **2898**
   ```
         1 2 6
   ×       2 3
   ─────────
       2 5₁2 0  (×20)
   +     3 7₁8  (×3)
   ─────────
       2 8 9 8
   ```
6. **160** (32 × 10 = 320, half of 320 = 160)
7. **30** (24 ÷ 8 = 3, so 240 ÷ 8 = 30)
8. **6** (36 ÷ 6 = 6, so 360 ÷ 60 = 6)
9. **87** ('bus stop method')
10. **422** ('bus stop method')
11. **30** (36 ÷ 12 = 3, so 360 ÷ 12 = 30)
12. **76** ('bus stop method')
13. **19r.1, $19\frac{1}{5}$, 19.2**
14. **37r.4, $37\frac{4}{10}$** (or $37\frac{2}{5}$), **37.4**
15. **265r.1, $265\frac{1}{2}$, 265.5**
16. **213r.2, $213\frac{2}{5}$, 213.4**
17. **3** (1475 ÷ 4 = 368r.3)
18. **50** (297 ÷ 6 = 49r.3, so the remaining 3 passengers will need to go in another taxi, making it 50 taxis needed)
19. **79** ($4 \times (3 \times 6)^{18} + 7$ so 72 + 7 = 79)
20. **7** ($4 + 9 - 3 \times 2^{6}$ so 4 + 9 − 6 = 7)
21. **54** ($(15 \times 2^2 - 6)^{4} \div 2$ so 60 − 6 = 54)
22. **104** ($((9 + 2)^2)^{11} - 7$ so $11^2 - 17$, $121^{121} - 17 = 104$)
23. **20** ($(12 \times 3 \div 2)^{36} + (3 - 1)^{2}$ so 36 ÷ 2 + 2, 18 + 2 = 20)
24. **13** ($(5^2)^{25} - 4 \times 3^{12}$ so 25 − 12 = 13)

Answers

Calculations, algebra and number sequences practice page 3 (page 46)

1. **180** (15 × 12 = 180)
2. **15 per crate, 7 left over** (397 ÷ 26 = 15r.7)
3. **16 289** (2327 × 7 = 16 289)
4. **£161 515** (£307 129 − £145 614 = £161 515)
5. **358** (164 + 97 + 97 = 358)
6. **63** (12 + 12 = 24, 24 + 39 = 63)
7. **100** (16 + 4 = 20, 20 × 5 = 100)
   140 (24 + 4 = 28, 28 × 5 = 140)
8. **8** (18 − 14 = 4, 4 × 2 = 8)
   44 (36 − 14 = 22, 22 × 2 = 44)
9. **10** (15 × 2 = 30, 30 ÷ 3 = 10)
   24 (36 × 2 = 72, 72 ÷ 3 = 24)
10. **41** (4 × 12 = 48, 48 − 7 = 41)
    173 (15 × 12 = 180, 180 − 7 = 173)
11. **6** (19 + 4 = 23, 23 − 17 = 6)
    29 (42 + 4 = 46, 46 − 17 = 29)
12. **70** (23 − 9 = 14, 14 × 5 = 70)
    40 (17 − 9 = 8, 8 × 5 = 40)
13. **39** (3 × 9 = 27, 27 + 12 = 39)
14. **63** (9 ÷ 3 = 3, 5 × 12 = 60, 3 + 60 = 63)
15. **12** (5 × 3 = 15, 15 − 12 = 3, 3 + 9 = 12)
16. **249** (12^2 = 144, 12 × 9 = 108, 144 − 3 = 141, 141 + 108 = 249)
17. **4** (−3, so 5a = 3a + 8, then −3a, so 2a = 8, therefore a = 4)
18. **7** (+12, so 6b + 21 = 9b, then −6b, so 21 = 3b, therefore b = 7)

Calculations, algebra and number sequences practice page 4 (page 47)

1. **23, 27** (+4)
2. **26, 23** (−8, −7, −6, −5, −4, −3)
3. **96, 192** (×2)
4. **16, 9** (squared numbers going backwards)
5. **8, 20** (alternating pattern: +5 and ×2)
6. **3, 21** (adding previous 2 numbers)
7. i) **3n + 1** (the pattern is +3, so it becomes 3n, then +1)
   ii) **301** (3 × 100 = 300, 300 + 1 = 301)
8. i) **7n + 2** (the pattern is +7, so it becomes 7n, then +2)
   ii) **268** (7 × 38 = 266, 266 + 2 = 268)
9. i) **2n + 17** (the pattern is +2, so it becomes 2n, then +17)
   ii) **151** (2 × 67 = 134, 134 + 17 = 151)
10. i) **6n + 7** (the pattern is +6, so it becomes 6n, then +7)
    ii) **595** (6 × 98 = 588, 588 + 7 = 595)
11. **B**
12. **397** (the pattern is increasing by 4 each time, so 4n, then +1, so the formula is 4n + 1, 4 × 99 = 396, 396 + 1 = 397)

Fractions, decimals and percentages

Fractions of shapes (page 48)

1. $\frac{2}{5}$
2. $\frac{3}{4}$
3. $\frac{3}{6}$ (or $\frac{1}{2}$)
4. $\frac{5}{16}$
5. $\frac{2}{8}$ (or $\frac{1}{4}$) 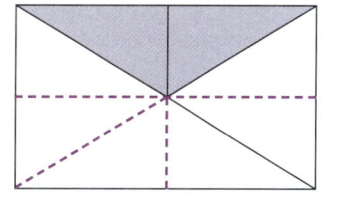
6. $\frac{2}{16}$ (or $\frac{1}{8}$)

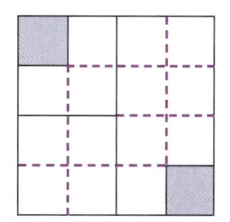

Fractions of quantities (page 50)

1. **25** (30 ÷ 6 = 5, 5 × 5 = 25)
2. **10 minutes** (45 ÷ 9 = 5, 5 × 2 = 10)
3. **4m** (she had $\frac{1}{3}$ left, 12 ÷ 3 = 4)
4. **42kg** (72 ÷ 12 = 6, 6 × 7 = 42)
5. **27** (if $\frac{5}{8}$ = 45, then $\frac{1}{8}$ = 9 (45 ÷ 5 = 9), so $\frac{3}{8}$ = 27 (9 × 3 = 27))
6. **£240** (£360 ÷ 3 = £120, £360 − £120 = £240)

Equivalent fractions (page 51)

1. **9** (×3)
2. **5** (÷3)
3. **4** (÷4)
4. **20** (×2)
5. $\frac{1}{2}$ $\frac{5}{10}$
6. $\frac{8}{12}$ $\frac{4}{6}$

Improper fractions and mixed numbers (page 52)

1. $2\frac{4}{5}$
2. $2\frac{1}{4}$
3. $\frac{25}{6}$
4. $\frac{51}{8}$
5. **50**
6. **504**

Answers

Simplifying fractions (page 53)

1. $\frac{6}{7}$ (÷4)   3. $\frac{1}{4}$ (÷17)   5. $\frac{3}{4}$ (÷14)
2. $\frac{5}{9}$ (÷5)   4. $\frac{12}{19}$ (cannot be simplified)   6. $\frac{5}{14}$ (÷9)

Ordering fractions (page 55)

1. $\frac{1}{2}$ $\frac{2}{3}$ $\frac{6}{8}$ $\frac{5}{6}$ $\frac{11}{12}$ (common denominator = 24)
2. $2\frac{3}{4}$ $3\frac{1}{4}$ $3\frac{4}{7}$ $3\frac{5}{8}$ $3\frac{9}{14}$ (common denominator for mixed numbers beginning 3 = 56)
3. $\frac{1}{4}$ $\frac{1}{3}$ $\frac{1}{2}$ $\frac{5}{9}$ $\frac{4}{6}$ (common denominator = 36)
4. $\frac{9}{10}$ $\frac{3}{4}$ $\frac{16}{25}$ $\frac{3}{5}$ $\frac{7}{20}$ (common denominator = 100)
5. $6\frac{5}{6}$ $6\frac{1}{2}$ $5\frac{7}{10}$ $5\frac{2}{3}$ $5\frac{3}{5}$ (common denominator for mixed numbers beginning 6 = 6, common denominator for mixed numbers beginning 5 = 15)
6. $12\frac{1}{10}$ $10\frac{11}{12}$ $10\frac{7}{9}$ $10\frac{2}{11}$ $10\frac{1}{6}$ (common denominator for mixed numbers beginning 10 = 396)

Adding and subtracting fractions (page 57)

1. $\frac{13}{21}$ ($\frac{2}{7} = \frac{18}{63}$, $\frac{3}{9} = \frac{21}{63}$, $\frac{18}{63} + \frac{21}{63} = \frac{39}{63}$; both the numerator and denominator can be divided by 3, so $\frac{39}{63} = \frac{13}{21}$)
2. $\frac{3}{10}$ ($\frac{4}{8} = \frac{20}{40}$, $\frac{1}{5} = \frac{8}{40}$, $\frac{20}{40} - \frac{8}{40} = \frac{12}{40}$; both the numerator and denominator can be divided by 4, so $\frac{12}{40} = \frac{3}{10}$)
3. $1\frac{11}{15}$ ($\frac{5}{6} = \frac{25}{30}$, $\frac{9}{10} = \frac{27}{30}$, $\frac{25}{30} + \frac{27}{30} = \frac{52}{30}$; divide the numerator by the denominator: 52 ÷ 30 = 1r.22, so $\frac{52}{30} = 1\frac{22}{30}$. This can be simplified as both the numerator and denominator can be divided by 2, so $1\frac{22}{30} = 1\frac{11}{15}$)
4. $\frac{17}{30}$ ($2\frac{2}{5} = \frac{12}{5}$, $1\frac{10}{12} = \frac{22}{12}$; common denominator = 60: $\frac{12}{5} = \frac{144}{60}$, $\frac{22}{12} = \frac{110}{60}$, $\frac{144}{60} - \frac{110}{60} = \frac{34}{60}$; both the numerator and denominator can be divided by 2, so $\frac{34}{60} = \frac{17}{30}$)
5. $8\frac{1}{8}$ (5 + 2 = 7; common denominator = 8: $\frac{1}{2} = \frac{4}{8}$, $\frac{4}{8} + \frac{5}{8} = \frac{9}{8}$; divide the numerator by the denominator: 9 ÷ 8 = 1r.1, so $\frac{9}{8} = 1\frac{1}{8}$; 7 + $1\frac{1}{8}$ = $8\frac{1}{8}$)
6. $1\frac{13}{36}$ ($4\frac{1}{4} = \frac{17}{4}$, $2\frac{8}{9} = \frac{26}{9}$; common denominator = 36: $\frac{17}{4} = \frac{153}{36}$; $\frac{26}{9} = \frac{104}{36}$; $\frac{153}{36} - \frac{104}{36} = \frac{49}{36}$; divide the numerator by the denominator: 49 ÷ 36 = 1r.13, so $\frac{49}{36} = 1\frac{13}{36}$)

Multiplying and dividing fractions (page 58)

1. $\frac{15}{28}$ ($\frac{3}{4} \times \frac{5}{7} = \frac{15}{28}$)
2. $\frac{2}{27}$ ($\frac{1}{9} \times \frac{4}{6} = \frac{4}{54} = \frac{2}{27}$; both numerator and denominator divided by 2)
3. $\frac{8}{25}$ ($\frac{2}{5} \times \frac{8}{10} = \frac{16}{50} = \frac{8}{25}$; both numerator and denominator divided by 2)
4. $2\frac{2}{3}$ ($\frac{6}{9} \times \frac{4}{1} = \frac{24}{9} = 2\frac{6}{9} = 2\frac{2}{3}$; both numerator and denominator divided by 3)
5. $2\frac{1}{4}$ ($\frac{9}{14} \times \frac{7}{2} = \frac{63}{28} = 2\frac{7}{28} = 2\frac{1}{4}$; both numerator and denominator divided by 7)
6. 4 ($\frac{2}{3} \times \frac{6}{1} = \frac{12}{3} = 4$)

Fraction sequences (page 59)

1. $1\frac{1}{4}$ $1\frac{1}{2}$ (+ $\frac{1}{4}$)   4. $1\frac{3}{16}$ $1\frac{1}{8}$ (− $\frac{1}{16}$)
2. $3\frac{2}{3}$ $3\frac{1}{3}$ (− $\frac{1}{3}$)   5. $\frac{1}{4}$ $1\frac{1}{4}$ (+ $\frac{1}{2}$)
3. $\frac{1}{2}$ $\frac{3}{5}$ (+ $\frac{1}{10}$)   6. $5\frac{2}{3}$ $5\frac{1}{6}$ (− $\frac{1}{6}$)

Decimal fractions (page 60)

1. 1.25 (each increment is worth $\frac{1}{4}$ or 0.25)
2. 0.44 (each increment is worth 0.01)
3. $\frac{3}{100}$ 4. $\frac{1}{10}$ 5. $6\frac{39}{50}$ 6. $17\frac{891}{1000}$

Ordering decimals (page 61)

1. 0.6   6.304   6.34   6.341   6.43
2. 0.1   1.011   1.1   1.101   1.111
3. 1.23   1.3   10.23   12.03   12.3
4. 90.7   9.701   9.7   9.17   9.07
5. 8.1   1.851   1.815   1.58   1.18
6. 37.4   34.73   34.7   34.3   34.07

Rounding decimals (page 62)

1. 7.4   3. 5.2   5. 7.0
2. 14.67   4. 18.43   6. 21.13

Adding and subtracting decimals (page 63)

1. 5.2 (26 + 26 = 52, therefore 2.6 + 2.6 = 5.2)
2. 0.8 (37 − 29 = 8, therefore 3.7 − 2.9 = 0.8)

Answers

3. **7.743**
    ```
      4.7 8 3
    + 2.9 6 0
      ───────
      7.7 4 3
      1 1
    ```

5. **21.155**
    ```
      1 2.7 0 0
    + 0 8.4 5 5
      ─────────
      2 1.1 5 5
          1 1
    ```

4. **5.044**
    ```
      1 8.0 ⁹9 ¹0
    - 1 3.0 4 6
      ─────────
      0 5.0 4 4
    ```

6. **32.267**
    ```
      ⁵5 ⁹9 ¹0
      5 6.0 ⁱ1 ¹0
    - 2 3.7 4 3
      ─────────
      3 2.2 6 7
    ```

Multiplying and dividing decimals (pages 64–65)

1. **0.45** (9 × 5 = 45, 45 ÷ 100 = 0.45)
2. **7.2** (12 × 6 = 72, 72 ÷ 10 = 7.2)
3. **1.92** (24 × 8 = 192, 192 ÷ 100 = 1.92)
4. **92.4** (132 × 7 = 924, 924 ÷ 10 = 92.4)
5. **24.96** (156 × 16 = 2496, 2496 ÷ 100 = 24.96)
6. **39.552** (96 × 412 = 39552, 39552 ÷ 1000 = 39.552)
7. **0.5** (2.5 × 10 = 25, 25 ÷ 5 = 5, 5 ÷ 10 = 0.5)
8. **0.9** (8.1 × 10 = 81, 81 ÷ 9 = 9, 9 ÷ 10 = 0.9)
9. **60** (4.8 × 100 = 480, 0.08 × 100 = 8, 480 ÷ 8 = 60)
10. **30** (5.1 × 100 = 510, 0.17 × 100 = 17, 510 ÷ 17 = 30)
11. **3.2** (4.48 × 100 = 448, 1.4 × 100 = 140, 448 ÷ 140 = 3.2)
12. **46** (10.12 × 100 = 1012, 0.22 × 100 = 22, 1012 ÷ 22 = 46)
13. **10** (13.25 × 100 = 1325, 1.29 × 100 = 129, 1325 ÷ 129 = 10.27. Jacob can't buy part of a bag of oranges, so he buys 10 bags.)

Percentages (page 67)

1. **7** (10% of 20 = 2, so 30% = 6 and 5% = 1. 6 + 1 = 7)
2. **11.2** (10% of 56 = 5.6, so 20% = 11.2)
3. **49.6** (10% of 80 = 8, so 60% = 48 and 1% = 0.8, so 2% = 1.6. 48 + 1.6 = 49.6)
4. **36** (10% of 80 = 8, so 40% = 32 and 5% = 4. 32 + 4 = 36)
5. **42** (35% were left on the shelf; 10% of 120 = 12, so 30% = 36 and 5% = 6, 36 + 6 = 42)
6. **£27.20** (10% of £32 = £3.20, so 5% = £1.60, 15% = £4.80, £32 − £4.80 = £27.20)
7. **£526.50** (10% of 450 = 45, 5% = 22.5, 1% = 4.5, 2% = 9, so 17% of 450 = 45 + 22.5 + 9 = 76.5; £450 + £76.50 = £526.50)

Converting between fractions, decimals and percentages (page 68)

1.

Fractions	Decimals	Percentages
$\frac{7}{10}$	**0.7**	**70%**
$\frac{1}{5}$	**0.2**	**20%**
$\frac{4}{5}$	0.8	**80%**
$\frac{14}{25}$	0.56	**56%**
$\frac{9}{20}$	**0.45**	45%
$\frac{3}{100}$	0.03	3%

Word problems (page 69)

1. **120** (find equivalents: so $\frac{1}{3} = \frac{20}{60}$, $\frac{1}{5} = \frac{12}{60}$ and $\frac{1}{4} = \frac{15}{60}$. Altogether this makes $\frac{47}{60}$. This means that $\frac{13}{60}$ is left, which is what Amy kept. As we know Amy kept 26, then $\frac{13}{60} = \frac{26}{120}$, so she had to have 120 sweets to start with)

2. **182** (if $\frac{2}{7}$ were children, then $\frac{5}{7}$ were adults. This means that there were $\frac{3}{7}$ more adults than children as $\frac{5}{7} - \frac{2}{7} = \frac{3}{7}$. As there were 78 more adults, then $\frac{3}{7}$ = 78. If $\frac{3}{7}$ = 78, then $\frac{1}{7}$ = 26. If $\frac{1}{7}$ = 26, then the total must be 26 × 7 = 182)

3. **374** (if 15% have blue eyes, then 85% don't. If 15% = 66, then 5% = 22. 5% × 17 = 85%, so 22 × 17 = 374)

4. **£540** (if it has been reduced by 20%, then the remaining £432 = 80%. Divide this by 4 to find 20%: £432 ÷ 4 = £108. This is the reduction. Add it back on to find the original price: £432 + £108 = £540)

5. **4.2** (work backwards: 7.5 + 5.1 = 12.6, 12.6 ÷ 3 = 4.2)

6. **5.6** (13.44 ÷ 2.4 = 5.6)

7. **$\frac{4}{5}$** (20% is $\frac{1}{5}$. If $\frac{1}{5}$ were red, then $\frac{4}{5}$ were not red)

8. **15%** ($\frac{1}{2}$ = 50%, $\frac{1}{5}$ = 20%, so 50 + 15 + 20 = 85%, therefore 15% of his socks are black)

Ratio and proportion (page 71)

1. **77**

```
        Hannah      Maya
          6    :    11
    ×7 (                 ) ×7
         42    :    77
```

11+ Maths Study and Practice Book

Answers

Ratio and proportion (page 71) continued

2. **130** Red Blue
   ×26 (4 : 5 = 9) ×26
   104 : 130 = 234

3. **174** ($\frac{3}{4}$ are brown; $\frac{3}{4}$ of 232 = 174)

4. **72** Indira Sara Vicky
   ×12 (1 : 3 : 6 = 10) ×12
   12 : 36 : 72 = 120

5. **24** ($\frac{3}{7}$ are children so $\frac{4}{7}$ are adults. If there are 32 adults, then $\frac{4}{7}$ = 32, so $\frac{1}{7}$ = 8. If $\frac{3}{7}$ are children, then there are 24 children)

6. **180** Rashid Edward Cameron
   ×18 (6 : 3 : 1 = 10) ×18
   108 : 54 : 18 = 180

Fractions, decimals and percentages practice page 1 (page 72)

1. $\frac{2}{6} = \frac{1}{3}$
2. $\frac{3}{9} = \frac{1}{3}$
3. $\frac{2}{4} = \frac{1}{2}$
4. $\frac{2}{8} = \frac{1}{4}$
5. $\frac{1}{8}$
6. $\frac{2}{7}$
7. **7** (63 ÷ 9 = 7)
8. **84** (126 ÷ 3 = 42, 42 × 2 = 84)
9. **24** (if $\frac{2}{3}$ were brown, then $\frac{1}{3}$ were not; 72 ÷ 3 = 24)
10. **100** (if $\frac{2}{5}$ = 40, then $\frac{1}{5}$ = 20, then 5 × 20 = 100)
11. **18** (×6)
12. **1** (÷3)
13. **72** (×6)
14. **12** (÷6)
15. $\frac{9}{24}$ $\frac{6}{16}$
16. $\frac{2}{5}$ $\frac{14}{35}$
17. $2\frac{10}{12} = 2\frac{5}{6}$
18. $2\frac{1}{9}$
19. $4\frac{3}{5}$
20. $\frac{11}{4}$
21. $\frac{44}{7}$
22. $\frac{49}{9}$
23. $\frac{2}{5}$ (÷9)
24. $\frac{1}{4}$ (÷7)
25. $\frac{1}{4}$ (÷15)
26. $\frac{1}{3}$ (÷12)
27. $\frac{4}{11}$ (÷4)
28. $\frac{17}{54}$ (cannot be simplified)

Fractions, decimals and percentages practice page 2 (page 73)

1. $\frac{1}{10}$ $\frac{1}{8}$ $\frac{1}{7}$ $\frac{1}{4}$ $\frac{1}{3}$ (when all the fractions have 1 as a numerator, the larger the denominator, the smaller the fraction)

2. $\frac{1}{5}$ $\frac{2}{8}$ $\frac{7}{20}$ $\frac{3}{8}$ $\frac{3}{5}$ (common denominator = 40)

3. $\frac{2}{9}$ $\frac{3}{12}$ $\frac{5}{8}$ $\frac{3}{4}$ $\frac{5}{6}$ (common denominator = 72)

4. $4\frac{2}{9}$ $4\frac{1}{6}$ $2\frac{3}{4}$ $2\frac{4}{7}$ $2\frac{6}{14}$ (common denominator for mixed numbers beginning 4 = 18, common denominator for mixed numbers beginning 2 = 28)

5. $1\frac{5}{6}$ $1\frac{7}{12}$ $1\frac{1}{2}$ $1\frac{3}{8}$ $1\frac{1}{3}$ (common denominator = 24)

6. $\frac{27}{4}$ $\frac{13}{2}$ $\frac{32}{5}$ $\frac{27}{6}$ $\frac{13}{3}$ (turn the improper fractions into mixed numbers first, so $\frac{32}{5} = 6\frac{2}{5}$, $\frac{27}{4} = 6\frac{3}{4}$, $\frac{13}{3} = 4\frac{1}{3}$, $\frac{13}{2} = 6\frac{1}{2}$, $\frac{27}{6} = 4\frac{3}{6}$. Common denominator for mixed numbers beginning 6 = 20, common denominator for mixed numbers beginning 4 = 6)

7. $\frac{11}{15}$ ($\frac{1}{3} = \frac{5}{15}$, $\frac{2}{5} = \frac{6}{15}$, so $\frac{5}{15} + \frac{6}{15} = \frac{11}{15}$)

8. $\frac{9}{28}$ ($\frac{4}{7} = \frac{16}{28}$, $\frac{1}{4} = \frac{7}{28}$, so $\frac{16}{28} - \frac{7}{28} = \frac{9}{28}$)

9. $\frac{17}{18}$ ($\frac{1}{9} = \frac{2}{18}$, $\frac{5}{6} = \frac{15}{18}$, so $\frac{2}{18} + \frac{15}{18} = \frac{17}{18}$)

10. $\frac{11}{20}$ ($\frac{1}{4} = \frac{5}{20}$, $\frac{1}{5} = \frac{4}{20}$, $\frac{5}{20} + \frac{4}{20} = \frac{9}{20}$, so he spent $\frac{9}{20}$, therefore he saved $\frac{11}{20}$)

11. $\frac{7}{12}$ ($\frac{3}{4} = \frac{9}{12}$, $\frac{1}{6} = \frac{2}{12}$, so $\frac{9}{12} - \frac{2}{12} = \frac{7}{12}$)

12. $\frac{2}{15}$ (1 × 2 = 2, 3 × 5 = 15, so $\frac{2}{15}$)

13. $\frac{9}{28}$ (3 × 3 = 9, 4 × 7 = 28, so $\frac{9}{28}$)

14. $2\frac{2}{5}$ (4 × 9 = 36, 3 × 5 = 15, so $\frac{36}{15} = 2\frac{6}{15} = 2\frac{2}{5}$)

15. $1\frac{13}{15}$ (4 × 7 = 28, 5 × 3 = 15, so $\frac{28}{15} = 1\frac{13}{15}$)

16. $1\frac{7}{8}$ (5 × 3 = 15, 8 × 1 = 8, so $\frac{15}{8} = 1\frac{7}{8}$)

17. $3\frac{6}{7}$ (6 × 9 = 54, 1 × 14 = 14, so $\frac{54}{14} = 3\frac{12}{14} = 3\frac{6}{7}$)

18. $\frac{5}{8}$ $\frac{3}{4}$ (+$\frac{1}{8}$)

19. $\frac{1}{2}$ $\frac{3}{10}$ (−$\frac{1}{10}$)

20. $1\frac{2}{3}$ $3\frac{2}{3}$ (+$\frac{2}{3}$)

21. **6** $1\frac{1}{2}$ (fraction being subtracted increases by $\frac{1}{2}$)

22. **1.1** (each increment is 0.1)

Schofield & Sims

Answers

23. **1.35** (each increment is 0.05)
24. $\frac{3}{100}$
25. $\frac{9}{1000}$
26. $4\frac{24}{100} = 4\frac{6}{25}$
27. $7\frac{135}{1000} = 7\frac{27}{200}$

Fractions, decimals and percentages practice page 3 (page 74)

1. **0.44, 0.43, 0.34, 0.33, 0.04**
2. **0.65, 0.615, 0.561, 0.56, 0.506**
3. **0.79, 0.799, 0.97, 0.977, 0.979**
4. **1.234, 1.24, 1.342, 1.43, 1.432**
5. **19.8**
6. **1.04**
7. **4.2**
8. **30.0**
9. **5.50**
10. **23.6**
11. **274.786**

```
  1 5 2.8 4 6
+ 1 2 1.9 4 0
  ─────────────
  2 7 4.7 8 6
        1
```

12. **2.75**

```
      4 16
  1 5.7̶ 1̶
−  1 2.9 6
  ─────────
  0 2.7 5
```

13. **£15.78 million** (2.61 + 7.4 + 1.87 + 3.9 = £15.78)
14. **5.87 seconds** (19.47 − 13.6 = 5.87 sec)
15. **0.21** (7 × 3 = 21, 21 ÷ 100 = 0.21)
16. **1.08** (12 × 9 = 108, 108 ÷ 100 = 1.08)
17. **3.791** (223 × 17 = 3791, 3791 ÷ 1000 = 3.791)
18. **0.7** (49 ÷ 7 = 7, 7 ÷ 10 = 0.7)
19. **6** (36 ÷ 6 = 6)
20. **11** (121 ÷ 11 = 11)
21. **27** (10% of 90 = 9, so 30% of 90 = 27)
22. **3** (10% of 20 = 2, so 5% of 20 = 1, so 15% of 20 = 3)
23. **288** (if 60% are adults, 40% are children. 10% of 720 = 72, so 40% = 288)
24. **£33.60** (10% of £42 = £4.20, so 20% = £8.40. £42 − £8.40 = £33.60)
25. **£13 125** (10% of £12 500 = £1250, so 5% = £625. £12 500 + £625 = £13 125)

Fractions, decimals and percentages practice page 4 (page 75)

1. **8** (40% of 30 = 12, $\frac{1}{3}$ of 30 = 10, 12 + 10 = 22, 30 − 22 = 8)
2. **0.2   25% $\frac{9}{20}$ $\frac{1}{2}$ 55%   0.9** ($\frac{1}{2}$ = 50%, $\frac{9}{20} = \frac{45}{100}$ = 45%, 0.9 = 90%, 0.2 = 20%)
3. **20%   0.4   45% $\frac{2}{3}$ 0.7 $\frac{4}{5}$** (0.4 = 40%, $\frac{2}{3}$ = 66.6%, 0.7 = 70%, $\frac{4}{5}$ = 80%)
4. **65%** ($\frac{13}{20} = \frac{65}{100}$ = 65%)
5. **true** (0.6 = 60%, so 65% is greater than 0.6)
6. **false** ($\frac{1}{4}$ = 25%, so 20% is not greater than 25%)
7. **2600** (962 ÷ 37 = 26, so 1% = 26, 26 × 100 = 2600)
8. **£852** ($\frac{1}{3} + \frac{1}{4} = \frac{4}{12} + \frac{3}{12} = \frac{7}{12}$, which means $\frac{5}{12}$ of the money is made from groceries. If $\frac{5}{12}$ = 1065, then $\frac{1}{12}$ is 1065 ÷ 5 = 213. As newspapers are $\frac{4}{12}$ ($\frac{1}{3}$), then 213 × 4 = 852, so £852 is made from selling newspapers)
9. $\frac{1}{20}$ ($\frac{2}{5} = \frac{8}{20}, \frac{1}{4} = \frac{5}{20}, \frac{3}{10} = \frac{6}{20}$, so $\frac{8}{20} + \frac{5}{20} + \frac{6}{20} = \frac{19}{20}$, so $\frac{1}{20}$ left for forward rolls)
10. **40** (6 × 12 = 72. $\frac{4}{9}$ are eaten, so $\frac{5}{9}$ are left. $\frac{1}{9}$ of 72 = 8, so $\frac{5}{9}$ = 40)
11. **122.4cm** (10% of 180 = 18, 1% = 1.8, so 30% = 54, 2% = 3.6, so 32% = 57.6. If Zara is 57.6cm shorter, then 180 − 57.6 = 122.4cm)
12. **6.21 miles** (1.26 + 1.08 + 0.87 + 1.4 + 1.6 = 6.21 miles)
13. **45**

```
        P : B
     3 : 2   = 5   ⎫
    45 : 30 = 75   ⎭ ×15
```

14. **250g**

```
    12 cakes : 150g  ⎫ ÷3
     4 cakes :  50g  ⎬
    20 cakes : 250g  ⎭ ×5
```

15. **2.5l**

```
        L : S
      3 : 140g = 1l     ⎫ ÷2
    1.5 :  70g = 0.5l   ⎬
    7.5 : 350g = 2.5l   ⎭ ×5
```

16. **45**

```
        Q : M
    150 : 100   ⎫ ÷10
     15 :  10   ⎬
     45 :  30   ⎭ ×3
```

17. **6 hours** (the work would take 1 person 12 hours, so it would take 2 workers 6 hours)
18. **Jasper = 60, Faith = 20, Sunhil = 10**

```
       S : F : J
       1 : 2 : 6  = 9    ⎫ ×10
      10 :20 :60 = 90    ⎭
```

11+ Maths Study and Practice Book

Answers

Measurement

Length, mass and capacity (pages 77–78)

1. **2.804km**
2. **35mm**
3. **1.129l**
4. **7500ml**
5. **0.119kg**
6. **6250g**
7. **16** (0.2l = 200ml, 200ml + 250ml = 450ml. 4l = 4000ml. 4000ml ÷ 450ml = 8r.400, therefore she will be able to use 8 glasses and 8 mugs, so 16 containers altogether)
8. **3.439kg** (0.93kg = 930g, 0.74kg = 740g, 0.913kg = 913g, so the 4 heaviest are 930g + 913g + 816g + 780g = 3439g = 3.439kg)
9. **10.72km** (4.7km = 4700m. 6020m + 4700m = 10720m = 10.72km)
10. **775m** (0.51km = 510m, 0.627km = 627m, so 682m + 510m + 406m + 627m = 2225m. 3km = 3000m, so 3000m − 2225m = 775m)
11. **1960m** (4.7km = 4700m, 3.72km = 3720m. 4700m × 2 = 9400m, 3720m × 2 = 7440m. 9400m − 7440m = 1960m)
12. **100ml** (0.015l = 15ml, 15ml × 2 = 30ml a day. 30ml × 30 = 900ml. 1l = 1000ml. 1000ml − 900ml = 100ml left)

Imperial measures (page 79)

1. **6in**
2. **2.5l**
3. **25.6km**
4. **3.5gal**
5. **6000g**
6. **9lb**

Reading scales (page 81)

1. **35ml** (each increment is 10ml)
2. **2.5kg or $2\frac{1}{2}$kg** (each increment is 500g)
3. **7.75cm or $7\frac{3}{4}$cm** (each increment is 0.25cm)
4. **52°C** (each increment is 1°C)
5. **40kg** (each increment is 0.2kg)
6. **7.2l** (each increment is 200ml)
7. **45kg** (each increment is 10kg)
8. **40mph** (each increment is 10mph)

Scale (page 82)

1. **1:50 000** (2cm:1km = 2cm:100 000cm = 1cm:50 000cm, so the scale is 1:50 000)
2. **36m** (1cm:300cm = 12cm:3600cm, 3600cm = 36m)
3. **1:40 000** (5cm:2km = 5cm:200 000cm = 1cm:40 000cm = 1:40 000)
4. **4cm × 1cm** (the new rectangle is 4 times bigger, so the original rectangle will have been 4 times smaller; 16cm ÷ 4 = 4cm and 4cm ÷ 4 = 1cm)
5. **525cm²** (the new dimensions will be 35cm × 15cm; 35cm × 15cm = 525cm²)

Time (page 85)

1. **thirteen minutes to two or 01:47 or 1.47 a.m.**
2. **twenty-four minutes to eight or 19:36 or 7.36 p.m.**
3. **twenty-eight minutes past seven or 19:28 or 7.28 p.m.**
4. **1.49 p.m.** (3.24 p.m. − 1 hr = 2.24 p.m., 2.24 p.m. − 24 min = 2.00 p.m., 2.00 p.m. − 11 min = 1.49 p.m.)
5. **1.41 p.m.** (12.46 p.m. + 1 hr would be 1.46 p.m., then take off 5 min = 1.41 p.m.)
6. i) **42 min**

   +8 min, +34 min = 42 min
   10.52 → 11.00 → 11.34

   ii) **2 hr 9 min**

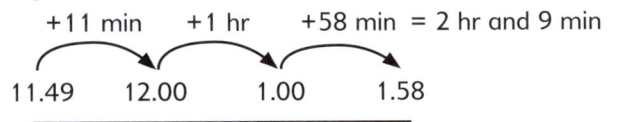

   +11 min, +1 hr, +58 min = 2 hr and 9 min
   11.49 → 12.00 → 1.00 → 1.58

   iii) **1 hr 13 min**

   +11 min, +1 hr, +2 min = 1 hr and 13 min
   11.49 → 12.00 → 1.00 → 1.02

Time zones (page 86)

1. **01:30** (Tokyo is 9 hours ahead. 16:30 + 9 hr = 01:30)
2. **14:50** (Delhi is 10.5 hours ahead of Lima. 04:20 + 10.5 hr = 14:50)
3. **06:15** (Los Angeles is 8 hours behind London. 14:15 − 8 hr = 06:15)
4. **19:30** (13:30 + 4 hr is 17:30, so the flight will land 17:30 London time. Athens is 2 hours ahead, so it will be 19:30 local time)
5. **13:15** (05:15 + 12 hr is 17:15, so the flight will land at 17:15 London time. Rio is 4 hours behind, so it will be 13:15 local time)
6. **11:00** (Sydney is 10 hours ahead of London, so 19:00 − 10 hr = 09:00. It would be 09:00 in London when the flight arrives in Sydney. If the flight took 22 hours, then 09:00 − 22 hr = 11:00. The flight will have left London at 11:00)

Days, weeks, months and years (page 88)

1. **26** (there are 52 weeks in 1 year, so half of that in half a year; 52 ÷ 2 = 26)
2. **96** (12 months in a year, so 12 × 8 = 96)
3. **13** (half a year is 26 weeks and a fortnight is 2 weeks, so 26 ÷ 2 = 13)

168 Schofield & Sims

Answers

4. **122** (31 days in March, 30 days in April, 31 days in May, 30 days in June; 31 + 30 + 31 + 30 = 122)
5. **27th May** (there are 42 days in 6 weeks)

   +15 days → +27 days
   15th April — 30th April — 27th May

6. **Thursday** (if 9th November is a Wednesday, so are 16th November, 23rd November, 30th November, 7th December, 14th December, 21st December, 28th December and 4th January; 5th January must therefore have been a Thursday)
7. **27th August** (subtract a week at a time until you have taken away 7 weeks: 8th October, 1st October, 24th September, 17th September, 10th September, 3rd September, 27th August)
8. **Sunday** (if 31st Jan was a Friday, so were 7th February, 14th February, 21st February and 28th February. 2020 was a leap year, so 29th February would be a Saturday and 1st March would be a Sunday)

Speed (page 90)

1. **51 minutes** (5km/h = 1km in 12 min. Therefore, 4km = 48 min (×4) and 0.25km = 3 min (÷4), so 4.25km = 51 min)
2. **3555 miles** (if 540 miles = 1 hr, then 540 × 6 = 3240, so 3240 miles in 6 hr. 1 hr ÷ 12 = 5 min, 540 ÷ 12 = 45 miles, so it can fly 45 miles in 5 min and therefore 315 miles in 35 min. 3240 + 315 = 3555 miles in 6 hr and 35 min)
3. **28km/h** (Darren cycled a total of 70km in 2 hr 30 min. 2 hr 30 min ÷ 5 = 30 min. 70 ÷ 5 = 14, so 14km in 30 min and 28km in 1 hr = 28km/h)
4. **Shelley by 2.4mph** (Shelley ran 9 miles in 50 min. Divide by 10 gives you 0.9 miles in 5 min. Multiply by 12 = 10.8 miles in 60 min, so 10.8mph. Abby ran 9.1 miles in 1 hr 5 min = 65 min. Divide by 13 gives you 0.7 miles in 5 min. Multiply by 12 = 8.4 miles in 60 min, so 8.4mph. 10.8 − 8.4 = 2.4, so Shelley was 2.4mph faster than Abby)
5. **She had stopped.** (the horizontal line shows that for 5 minutes, Leila didn't travel anywhere. Therefore, she had stopped)
6. **9km/h** (she travelled 4.5km in 30 min. Double this would be 9km in 60 min, therefore Leila ran an average of 9km/h)

Money (page 92)

1. **£1.03** (7.99 × 3. Round to 8 so 8 × 3 = 24, then adjust by taking off 3p. £24.00 − 3p = £23.97. £25.00 − £23.97 = £1.03)
2. **£2.82** (£2.45 + £1.99 + £3.09 + £1.79 = £9.32. If she only has £6.50, then £9.32 − £6.50 = £2.82)
3. **50p, 20p, 20p, 2p, 2p**
4. **3600 rupees** (40 × 90 = 3600)
5. **£9.50** (1235 ÷ 130 = 9.5)
6. **720 rupees** (90 × 8 = 720)

Temperature (page 93)

1. **37°C** (add 11°C to −11°C to get 0°C. Add another 26°C to get to 26°C. 11°C + 26°C = 37°C)
2. **35°C** (23°C + 12°C = 35°C)
3. **16°C** (7°C − 9°C = −2°C)
4. **18°C** (add 12°C to −12°C to get 0°C. Add another 6°C to get to 6°C. 12°C + 6°C = 18°C)
5. **8°C** (−17°C − 3°C = −20°C, −20°C − 5°C = −25°C. −3°C + −5°C = −8°C)
6. **44.6°F** (−1°C + 8°C = 7°C. 7°C × 1.8 + 32 = 44.6°F)

Perimeter and area (pages 95–98)

1. P = **56cm** (16 + 12 = 28, 28 × 2 = 56)
   A = **192cm²** (16 × 12 = 192)
2. P = **102m** (38 + 13 = 51, 51 × 2 = 102)
   A = **494m²** (38 × 13 = 494)
3. P = **54cm** (15 + 12 = 27, 27 × 2 = 54)
   A = **180cm²** (15 × 12 = 180)
4. L = **18m** (if the width is 8, 2 × 8 = 16. The perimeter minus the 2 widths = 36. This is the 2 lengths, so 36 ÷ 2 = 18)
   A = **144m²** (if L = 18, then 18 × 8 = 144)
5. W = **32mm** (768 ÷ 24 = 32)
   P = **112mm** (32 + 24 = 56, 56 × 2 = 112)
6. **16.5m²** (the total floor area is 5 × 3.5 = 17.5m². The bath area is 2 × 0.5 = 1m². The total floor area − the bath = 17.5 − 1 = 16.5m²)
7. P = **19cm**, A = **12cm²**
8. P = **21cm**, A = **13.5cm²**
9. P = **49cm**, A = **82.5cm²**
10. P = **40m**, A = **32m²**
11. P = **32mm**, A = **42mm²**
12. P = **81cm**, A = **261cm²**
13. P = **86cm**, A = **375cm²**
14. P = **76cm**, A = **327cm²**
15. P = **144mm**, A = **840mm²**
16. P = **82cm**, A = **336cm²**
17. P = **74cm**, A = **262cm²**
18. P = **46m**, A = **78m²**

Answers

Volume and surface area (page 99)

1. V = **96cm³** (8 × 3 × 4 = 96cm³)
   SA = **136cm²** (2 faces at 8cm × 3cm = 24cm², 2 faces at 8cm × 4cm = 32cm² and 2 faces at 3cm × 4cm = 12cm². Total surface area = 24 + 24 + 32 + 32 + 12 + 12 = 136cm²)

2. V = **144mm³** (6 × 6 × 4 = 144mm³)
   SA = **168mm²** (4 faces at 6mm × 4mm = 24mm² and 2 faces at 6mm × 6mm = 36mm². Total surface area = 24 + 24 + 24 + 24 + 36 + 36 = 168mm²)

3. V = **12cm³** (3 × 2 × 2 = 12cm³)
   SA = **32cm²** (4 faces at 3cm × 2cm = 6cm² and 2 faces at 2cm × 2cm = 4cm². Total surface area = 6 + 6 + 6 + 6 + 4 + 4 = 32cm²)

4. V = **525m³** (15 × 5 × 7 = 525m³)
   SA = **430m²** (2 faces at 15m × 5m = 75m², 2 faces at 15m × 7m = 105m² and 2 faces at 5m × 7m = 35m². Total surface area = 75 + 75 + 105 + 105 + 35 + 35 = 430m²)

Measurement practice page 1 (page 100)

1. **16 108g**
2. **34 010m**
3. **1200mm**
4. **0.37l**
5. **490ml**
6. **25** (1.25l = 1250ml, 1250 ÷ 50 = 25)
7. **3566km** (556km + 103km + 51km + 1073km = 1783km, 1783km × 2 = 3566km)
8. **280kg** (35kg × 8 = 280kg)
9. **180cm**
10. **210g**
11. **4.5l**
12. **18ft**
13. **12in**
14. **3.1m** (1ft ≈ 30cm, so 10ft ≈ 300cm. 1in ≈ 2.5cm, so 4in ≈ 10cm. 300 + 10 = 310cm = 3.1m)
15. **1250ml** (1pt ≈ 0.5l, so 2.5 × 0.5 = 1.25l = 1250ml)
16. **4st** (1st ≈ 6kg, 25kg ÷ 6 = 4r.1, so approximately 4st)

Measurement practice page 2 (page 101)

1. **18.25cm** (each increment is 0.25cm)
2. **170ml** (each increment is 20ml)
3. **28°C** (each increment is 1°C)
4. **7.25kg** (each increment is 0.5kg)
5. **1.5kg** (each small increment is 200g, 35.5kg − 34kg)
6. **26°C** (each increment is 2°C. The first thermometer shows −12°C, so add 12°C to get to 0°C. The second thermometer shows 14°C, so add another 14°C. 12°C + 14°C = 26°C)

Measurement practice page 3 (page 102)

1. **12.5km** (5cm × 250 000 = 1 250 000cm = 12 500m = 12.5km)
2. **1:5000** (5cm:250m = 5cm:25 000cm = 1cm:5000cm, so the scale is 1:5000)
3. **4cm** (if the scale is 1:325 000, then 1cm = 325 000cm, so 1cm = 3250m = 3.25km, so 2cm = 6.5km. Therefore 4cm = 13km)
4. **16.5km** (1cm = 275 000cm, so 1cm = 2750m, so 1cm = 2.75km. Therefore 6cm = 16.5km)
5. **30cm** (5cm × 6 = 30cm)
6. **441cm²** (7cm × 3 = 21cm. 21 × 21 = 441cm². You must scale up the length of the original square, not the area of the original square)
7. **22:22** (22:12 + 10 min = 22:22)
8. **4.16 p.m.** (16:41 − 25 min = 16:16 = 4.16 p.m.)
9. **1 hr 35 min**

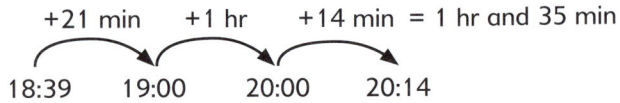

   18:39 +21 min→ 19:00 +1 hr→ 20:00 +14 min→ 20:14 = 1 hr and 35 min

10. **2 hr 35 min**

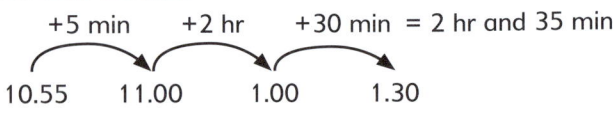

    10.55 +5 min→ 11.00 +2 hr→ 1.00 +30 min→ 1.30 = 2 hr and 35 min

11. **Louis** (when racing, the smallest time is the fastest)
12. **0.77 sec** (13.06 − 12.29 = 0.77 sec)

Measurement practice page 4 (page 103)

1. **15:30 (the day before)** (Honolulu is 22 hours behind Samoa)
2. **11:15** (San Diego is 8 hours behind London)
3. **2.15 a.m.** (New York is 10 hours behind Calcutta)
4. **12 hours**
5. **18:05** (Helsinki is 5 hours ahead of Buenos Aires)
6. **14:32** (Helsinki is 7 hours ahead of Miami, so the time should be 14:54. 14:54 − 22 min = 14:32)
7. **84** (7 × 12 = 84)
8. **100** (1000 ÷ 10 = 100)
9. **29** (1992 is divisible by 4, so it is a leap year)
10. **50**

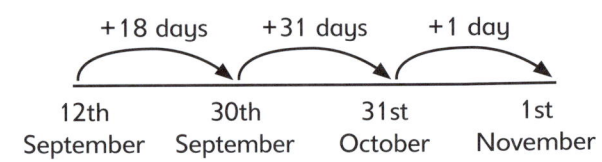

    12th September +18 days→ 30th September +31 days→ 31st October +1 day→ 1st November

Answers

11. **Stevie** (2007 comes before 2008 and August comes before September)

12. **88**

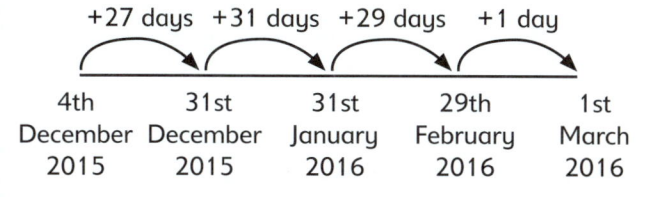

    +27 days +31 days +29 days +1 day

    4th   31st   31st   29th   1st
    December December January   February March
    2015   2015   2016   2016   2016

Measurement practice page 5 (page 104)

1. **49 miles** (travels 42 miles in 2 hr; 20 min to travel 7 miles, so 42 + 7 = 49)
2. **60mph** (330 miles in 5.5 hr = 60 miles in 1 hr, so 60mph)
3. **1.00 p.m.** (freight train – 40 miles at 11.00 a.m., 80 miles at 12 noon, 120 miles at 1.00 p.m.; passenger train – 60 miles at 12 noon, 120 miles at 1.00 p.m.)
4. **£67** (£298 + £134 = £432, £499 − £432 = £67)
5. **£3735** (£15 075 − £11 340 = £3735)
6. **540R** (18 × 30 = 540)
7. **£200** (260 ÷ 1.3 = 200)
8. **2700R** (the South African rand is 1.5 × bigger than the Swedish krona, so 1800 × 1.5 = 2700)
9. **15.5°C** (28°C − 12.5°C = 15.5°C)
10. **43°C** (add 24°C to −24°C to get to 0°C. Add another 19°C to get to 19°C. 24°C + 19°C = 43°C)
11. **22°C** (add 7°C to −7°C to get to 0°C. Add another 15°C to get to 15°C. 7°C + 15°C = 22°C)
12. **15.2°C** (12°C + 3.2°C = 15.2°C)
13. **53.6°F** (12 × 1.8 = 21.6, 21.6 + 32 = 53.6°F)

Measurement practice page 6 (page 105)

1. P = **50cm** (19 + 6 = 25, 25 × 2 = 50)

   A = **114cm²** (19 × 6 = 114)
2. P = **58mm** (11 + 18 = 29, 29 × 2 = 58)

   A = **198mm²** (11 × 18 = 198)
3. **84cm²** (half the perimeter is 19cm, so if the length is 12cm, then the width must be 7cm. 12cm × 7cm = 84cm²)
4. **56mm** (the square root of 196 is 14, so the square has sides of 14mm, therefore the perimeter is 14 × 4 = 56mm)
5. **20cm** (8 + 8 + 4 = 20cm)
6. **143m²** (22 × 13 = 286, 286 ÷ 2 = 143m²)
7. P = **62cm**, A = **138cm²**

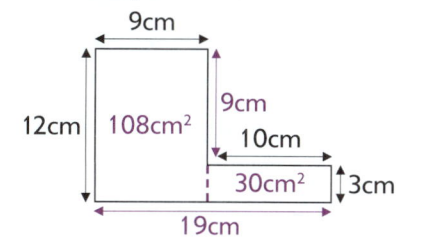

8. P = **108cm**, A = **476cm²**

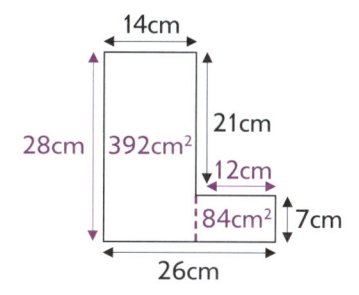

9. P = **50m**, A = **111m²**

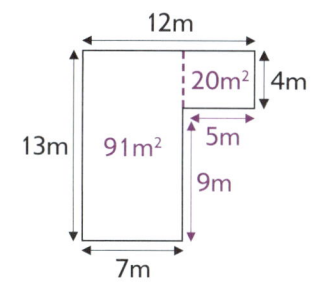

10. V = **2280cm³** (19 × 12 × 10 = 2280cm³)

    SA = **1076cm²** (19 × 12 = 228, 228 × 2 = 456, 12 × 10 = 120, 120 × 2 = 240, 19 × 10 = 190, 190 × 2 = 380, so 456 + 240 + 380 = 1076cm²)
11. V = **930cm³** (31 × 6 = 186, 186 × 5 = 930cm³)

    SA = **742cm²** (31 × 6 = 186, 186 × 2 = 372, 6 × 5 = 30, 30 × 2 = 60, 31 × 5 = 155, 155 × 2 = 310, so 372 + 60 + 310 = 742cm²)

Geometry

Parallel and perpendicular lines (page 106)

1. **perpendicular** (they are at right angles to each other)
2. **neither** (they cross but are not at right angles)
3. **parallel** (the lines stay the same distance apart)

4.

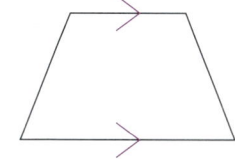

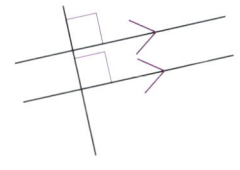

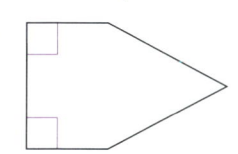

5.

6.

11+ Maths Study and Practice Book

Answers

Angles (pages 108–109)

1. acute
2. obtuse
3. reflex
4. 165°
5. 305°
6. C (100° is just bigger than a right angle. C is the only one that is just bigger than a right angle)
7. 270° (the largest angle is the clockwise angle, which covers 6 angles between SE and NE. 45° × 6 = 270°)
8. a = **39°** (triangles have a total of 180°. Two of the angles are 90° (the right angle) and 51°; 90° + 51° = 141°, 180° − 141° = 39°)
9. b = **129°** (if one angle of the parallelogram is 51°, then so is the opposite angle. The sum of these two angles is 102°. Quadrilaterals have a total of 360°: 360° − 102° = 258°, 258° ÷ 2 = 129°)

    c = **129°** (b and c are opposite angles, so c is 129° as well)
10. d = **49°** (the corner of a rectangle is 90°; 90° − 41° = 49°)
11. e = **77°** (quadrilaterals have a total of 360°. The two right angles total 180°, then 180° + 103° = 283°, 360° − 283° = 77°)
12. f = **83°** (a straight line is 180°; 46° + 51° = 97°, 180° − 97° = 83°)

    g = **46°** (the top left triangle has angles 46° + 90° = 136°. 180° − 136° = 44°, so the bottom angle is 44°; this angle and g make a right angle, so g = 90° − 44° = 46°)
13. h = **132°** (h is equal to the measured angle of 132°)

    i = **48°** (a straight line is 180°; 180° − 132° = 48°)

Directions of turn (page 110)

1. 90° clockwise
2. 135° clockwise
3. 45° anticlockwise
4. 90° anticlockwise
5. 45° anticlockwise
6. 90° clockwise

Properties of 2D shapes (page 112)

1. isosceles triangle
2. trapezium
3. hexagon
4. octagon
5. 5 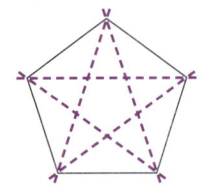
6. equilateral triangle

Regular shapes (page 113)

1. 8 (a regular octagon has 8 sides, so 8 lines of symmetry)
2. 120° (there are 6 exterior angles; 360° ÷ 6 = 60°. Together the exterior and interior angle total 180°, so the internal angle must be 120° (180 − 60 = 120))
3. 5 (a regular pentagon has 5 sides, so it has rotational symmetry of order 5)
4. 18cm (6cm × 3 = 18cm)
5. 7 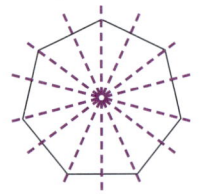
6. 1440° (there are 10 exterior angles; 360° ÷ 10 = 36°. Together the exterior and interior angle total 180°, so the internal angle must be 144° (180 − 36 = 144). All 10 would total 1440° (144 × 10 = 1440))

Circles (page 114)

1. 13.5cm (27 ÷ 2 = 13.5cm)
2. 28.5cm (14.25 × 2 = 28.5cm)
3. 31.4cm (3.14 × 5 = 15.7cm, 15.7 × 2 = 31.4cm)
4. 18.84cm (3 × 2 = 6, 3.14 × 6 = 18.84cm)
5. 2.5cm (the diameter of each circle must be 5cm, so the radius must be 2.5cm)
6. 12.56cm² (4 ÷ 2 = 2, 3.14 × 2² = 3.14 × 4 = 12.56cm²)

Symmetry (page 115)

1. 3 lines of symmetry 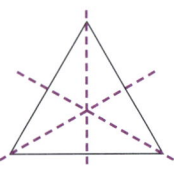
2. 1 line of symmetry 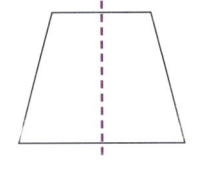
3. 0 lines of symmetry 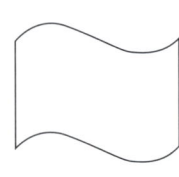
4. 2 lines of symmetry 
5. 5 lines of symmetry 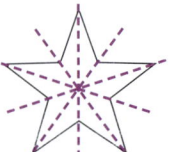
6. pentagon

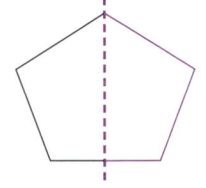

Schofield & Sims

Answers

Rotational symmetry (page 116)

1. **4** (it is a regular quadrilateral)
2. **1** 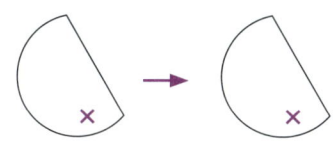
3. **2** 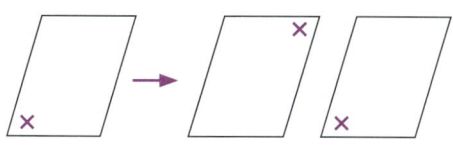
4. **8** (it is a regular octagon)
5. 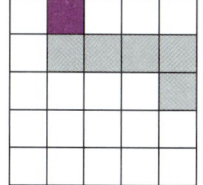
6.

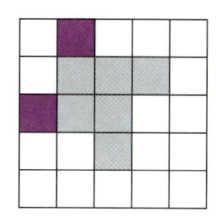

Properties of 3D shapes (page 119)

Shape	Name of shape	Number of faces	Number of edges	Number of vertices
1.	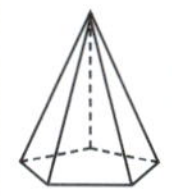 pentagonal pyramid	6	10	6
2.	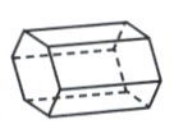 hexagonal prism	8	18	12
3.	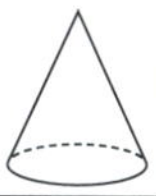 cone	2	1	1
4.	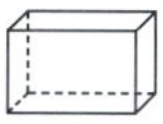 cuboid	6	12	8
5.	 hemisphere	2	1	0
6.	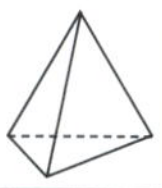 tetrahedron	4	6	4

Nets of 3D shapes (page 120)

1. **C**
2. (net diagram) or (net diagram)
3. **cylinder**
4. **pentagonal pyramid**

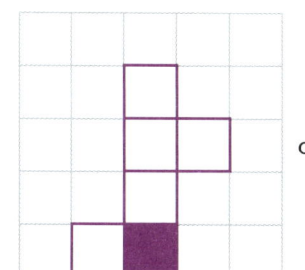

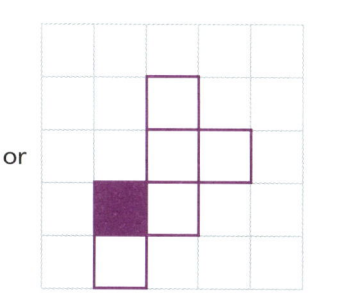

Rotations of 3D shapes (page 121)

1. **B** (it can't be A or D as the single blocks are not at opposite ends of the T-shape. It can't be C as the single block on the left is connected to the wrong side of the T-shape block)
2. **A** (it can't be B, C or D as the 2-cube block is pointing away from the wrong side of the C-shape block)
3. **B** (it can't be A as one of the 2-cube blocks is connected to the wrong side of the 3-cube block. It can't be C or D as the 2-cube block at the front is connected to the wrong side of the 3-cube block)

Coordinates (page 123)

1. $(-3, 2)$ 2. $(2, 2)$ 3. $(2, -3)$ 4. $(-3, -3)$
5. $(15, 9)$ (this point shares the x-coordinate with $(15, 4)$ and the y-coordinate with $(2, 9)$)
6. $(2, 4)$ (this point shares the x-coordinate with $(2, 9)$ and the y-coordinate with $(15, 4)$)

Reflections (page 125)

1. 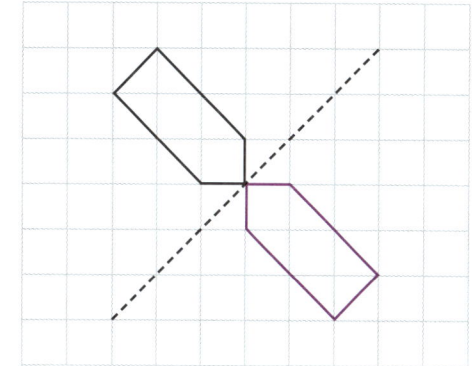
2. 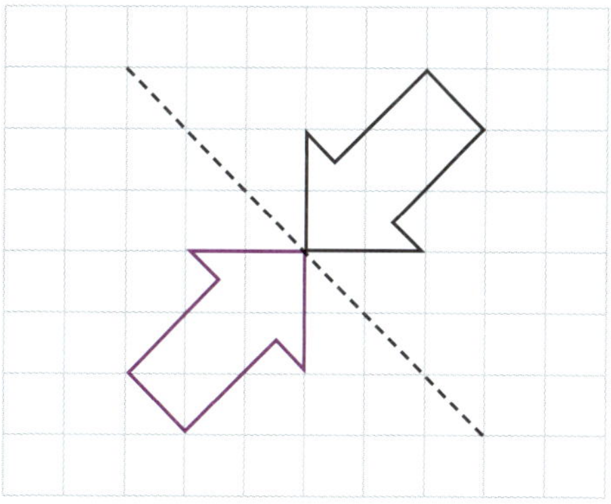
3.

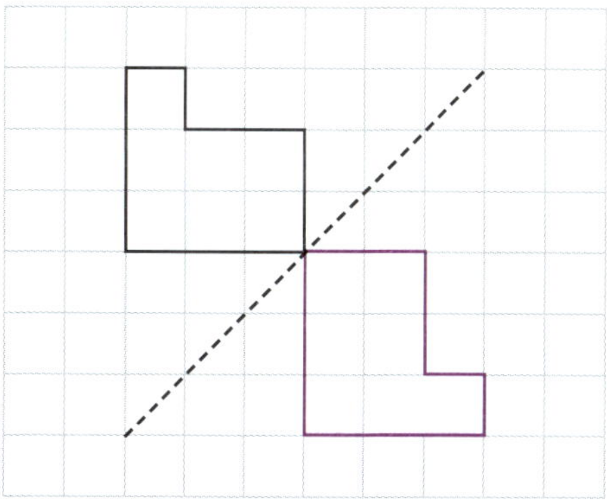

11+ Maths Study and Practice Book

Answers

Reflections (page 125) continued

4.

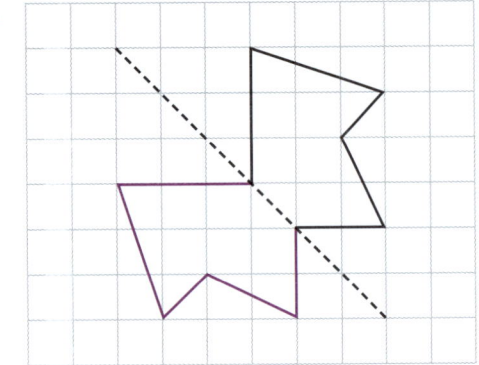

5.

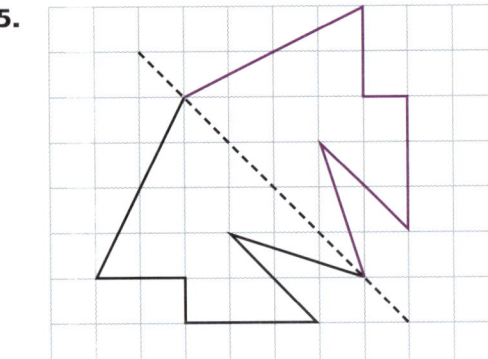

6.

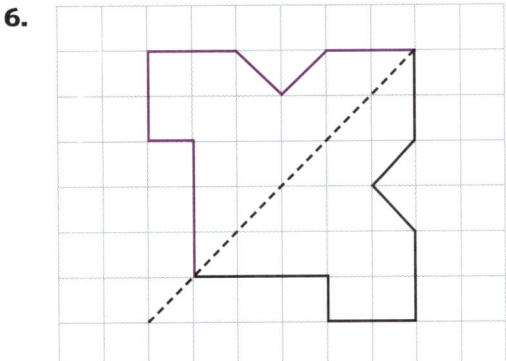

Translations (page 126)

1. and 3.

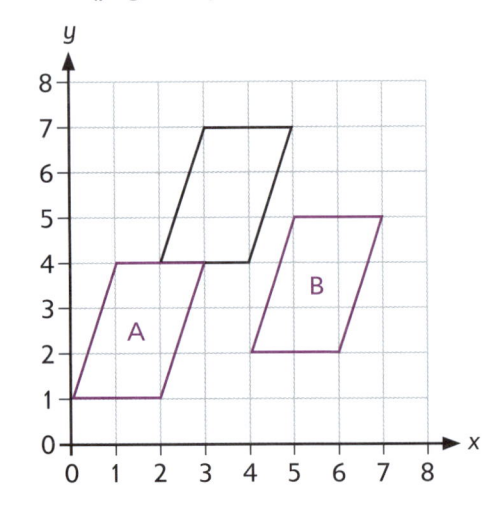

2. (0, 1), (2, 1), (3, 4), (1, 4) (in any order)

4. (4, 2), (6, 2), (7, 5), (5, 5) (in any order)

5. **Right 4, Up 3** 6. **Left 2, Down 2**

Geometry practice page 1 (page 127)

1. **false** (not at right angles)
2. **true** (are at right angles)
3. **true** (stay the same distance apart)
4. **false** (do not stay the same distance apart)
5. 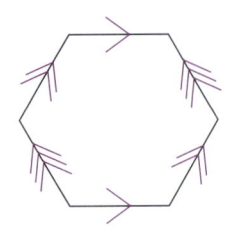
6. 
7. **C** (A has 5 right angles and 1 reflex angle, B has 2 acute angles, 2 obtuse angles, 1 right angle and 1 reflex angle)
8. **90°**
9. **NE**
10. **55°**
11. **310°**
12. $a =$ **70°** (51° + 59° = 110°, 180° − 110° = 70°)
13. $j =$ **59°** (the left-hand angle of the top triangle is 180° − 137° = 43°. The bottom angle is 78° as opposite angles are equal. 43° + 78° = 121°. 180° − 121° = 59°)

    $k =$ **43°** (it is the same angle as the left angle of the top triangle)

Geometry practice page 2 (page 128)

1. **90° anticlockwise**
2. **180°**
3. **45° clockwise**
4. **west** (N then 90° clockwise would be E, then 180° anticlockwise would be W)
5. **rhombus**
6. **scalene triangle**
7. **kite**
8. **hexagon** (all 6-sided shapes are called hexagons)
9. **octagon**
10. **720°**
11.

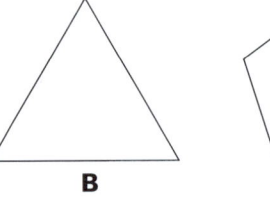

    B 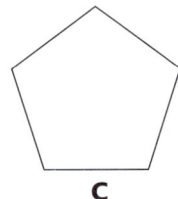   C

12. **6** (regular shapes have the same number of lines of symmetry as number of sides)
13. **8** (regular shapes have the same order of rotational symmetry as number of sides)
14. **80cm** (regular shapes have the same length sides. 10 × 8cm = 80cm)

Answers

Geometry practice page 3 (page 129)

1. **8cm** (16 ÷ 2 = 8cm)
2. **22.5mm** (45 ÷ 2 = 22.5mm)
3. **24cm** (12 × 2 = 24cm)
4. **10m** (5 × 2 = 10m)
5. **43.96cm** (3.14 × 2 = 6.28, 6.28 × 7 = 43.96cm)
6. **314cm^2** (if diameter = 20cm, then radius = 10cm. 10^2 = 100, 3.14 × 100 = 314cm^2)
7. **2 lines of symmetry**
8. **2 lines of symmetry**
9. **0 lines of symmetry** 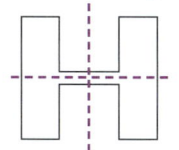
10. **1 line of symmetry**
11.
12. 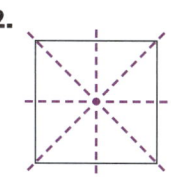
13. **4** (this is a square and regular shapes have the same order of rotation as number of sides)
14. **1**
15. **2**
16. **4**
17. **3** (this is an equilateral triangle and regular shapes have the same order of rotation as number of sides)
18.

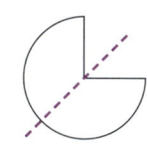

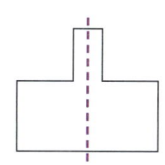

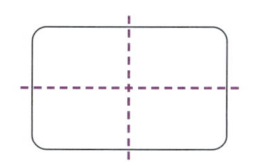

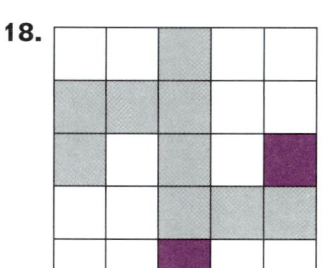

Geometry practice page 4 (page 130)

	Shape	Name of shape	Number of faces	Number of edges	Number of vertices
1.	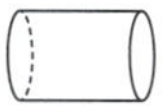	cylinder	3	2	0
2.		octagonal pyramid	9	16	9

3. **hexagonal prism**
4. **tetrahedron**
5. **triangular prism**
6. **cone**
7. **D**
8. **D** (it can't be A as there is only one single block. It can't be B or C as the wrong side of the short L-shaped block is connected to the 3-cube block)
9. **D** (it can't be A, B or C as there is no short L-shaped block)

Geometry practice page 5 (page 131)

1. **(−2, 4)**
2. **(3, 4)**
3. **(4, 1)**
4. **(3, −2)**
5. **(−2, −2)**
6. **(−3, 1)**
7. 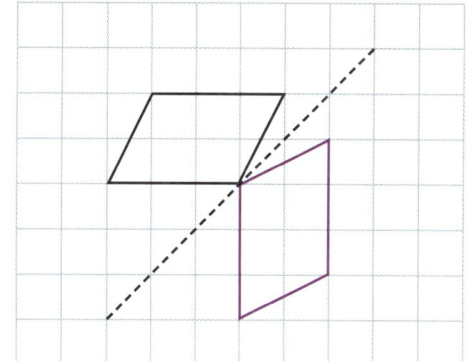
8. 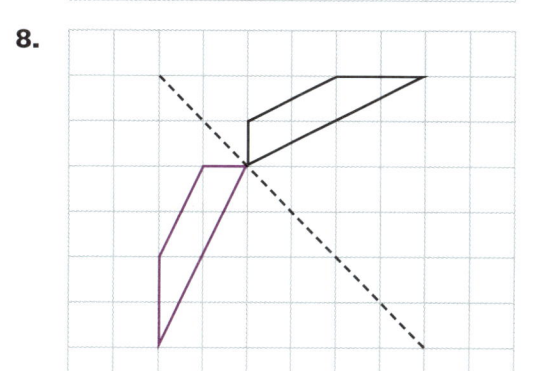
9.

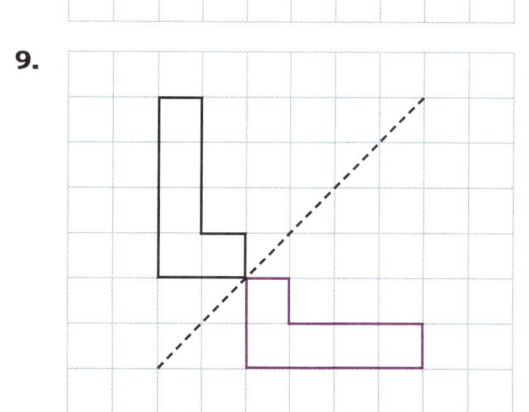

Answers

Geometry practice page 5 (page 131)
continued

10.

11.

12.

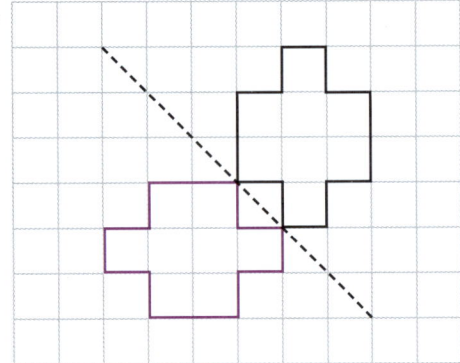

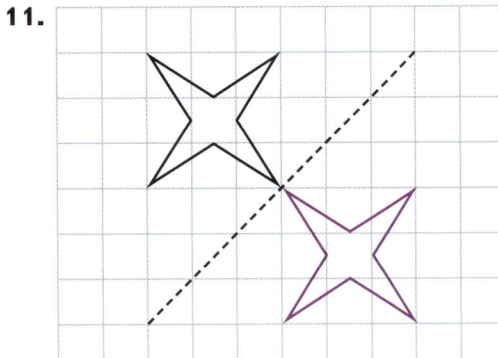

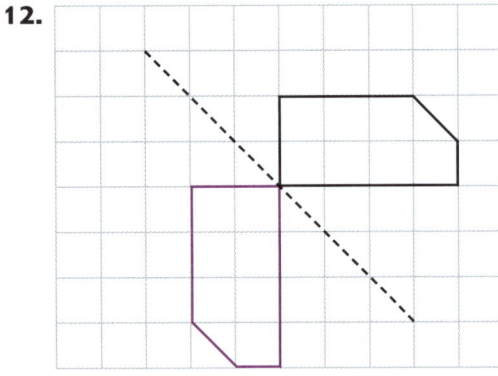

Geometry practice page 6 (page 132)

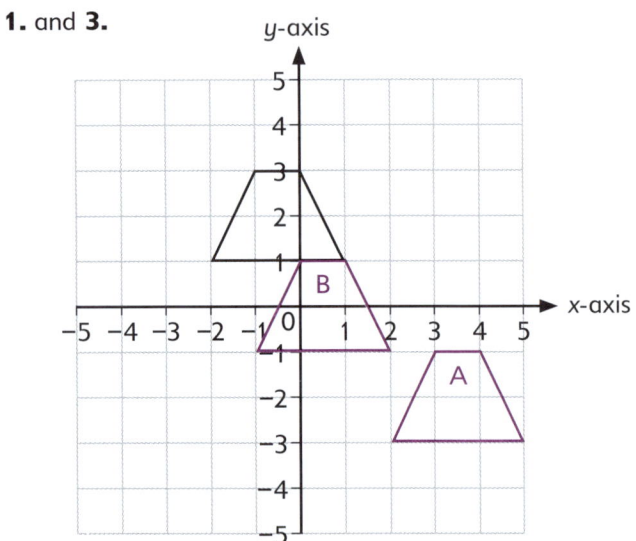

1. and 3.

2. (3, −1), (4, −1), (5, −3), (2, −3) (in any order)

4. (0, 1), (1, 1), (2, −1), (−1, −1) (in any order)

5. and 7.

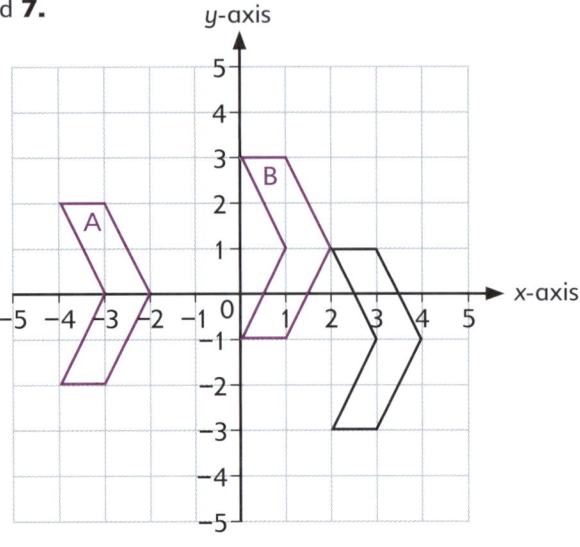

6. (−4, 2), (−3, 2), (−2, 0), (−3, −2), (−4, −2), (−3, 0) (in any order)

8. (0, 3), (1, 3), (2, 1), (1, −1), (0, −1), (1, 1) (in any order)

Statistics

Tables (page 133)

1.

Year group	Girls	Boys	Total
3	42	**46**	88
4	**41**	39	80
5	46	43	**89**
6	**38**	50	88
Total	167	**178**	345

Pictograms (page 134)

1. **9** (there are $4\frac{1}{2}$ hearts, so 9 birds)

2. **5** (there are 3 hearts for the magpies, so he spotted 6 magpies, and $\frac{1}{2}$ a heart for the blue tits, so he only spotted 1 blue tit. 6 − 1 = 5)

3. **19** (there are $9\frac{1}{2}$ hearts, so 19 birds)

4. **29** (there are 5 whole pentagons, which represent 25 monkeys, and then $\frac{4}{5}$ of a pentagon, which represent 4 monkeys, so 29 in total)

5. **3** (there are $4\frac{4}{5}$ pentagons, which represent 24 lions, and $4\frac{1}{5}$ pentagons, which represent 21 hippos. 24 − 21 = 3)

6. **107** (there are 19 whole pentagons. The fractions are $\frac{4}{5}$, $\frac{3}{5}$, $\frac{4}{5}$ and $\frac{1}{5}$, which total $\frac{12}{5} = 2\frac{2}{5}$, so in total $21\frac{2}{5}$ pentagon. 21 × 5 = 105, 105 + 2 = 107)

Schofield & Sims

Answers

Tally charts and frequency tables (page 135)

1.

Fruit	Tally	Frequency
Orange	|||| |||| ||||	14
Apple	|||| |||| |||| ||	17
Pear	|||| |||| |||	13
Banana	|||| ||||		11
Nectarine	|||| |||| ||	12
Kiwi	|||| |||| |||| ||	17

2. **84** (14 + 17 + 13 + 11 + 12 + 17)
3. **6** (17 − 11)

Bar charts (page 136)

1. **science** (48 marks)
2. **English and art** (37 marks in each)
3. **13 marks** (45 − 32 = 13)

Line graphs (page 137)

1. **10 miles**   2. **50 miles**
3. **Daniel stopped.** (he stayed at 30 miles for 10 min)

Pie charts (page 139)

1. **32** ($\frac{1}{2}$ preferred salt and vinegar, $\frac{1}{2}$ of 64 = 32)
2. **4** ($\frac{1}{16}$ preferred roast chicken, $\frac{1}{16}$ of 64 = 4)
3. **4** ($\frac{1}{8}$ preferred cheese and onion, $\frac{1}{8}$ of 64 = 8. $\frac{1}{16}$ preferred pickled onion, $\frac{1}{16}$ of 64 = 4. 8 − 4 = 4)
4. **16** (the section measures 96°: $\frac{96}{360} = \frac{4}{15}$, $\frac{4}{15}$ of 60 families = 16)
5. **8** (the Spain section measures 84°: $\frac{84}{360} = \frac{7}{30}$, $\frac{7}{30}$ of 60 = 14; the England section measures 36°: $\frac{36}{360} = \frac{1}{10}$, $\frac{1}{10}$ of 60 = 6. 14 − 6 = 8)
6. **12** (the Wales section measures 12°: $\frac{12}{360} = \frac{1}{30}$, $\frac{1}{30}$ of 60 = 2; the Italy section measures 60°: $\frac{60}{360} = \frac{1}{6}$, $\frac{1}{6}$ of 60 = 10. 2 + 10 = 12)

Venn diagrams (page 140)

1. **17**   2. **5**   3. **18**
4. **54** (17 + 5 + 14 + 18 = 54)
5. **4** (3 + 1 = 4)   6. **1**   7. **8**
8. **54** (16 + 7 + 9 + 4 + 1 + 3 + 6 + 8 = 54)

Mean, mode, median and range (page 142)

1. mean = **16** (17 + 13 + 19 + 13 + 18 = 80. 80 ÷ 5 = 16)
   mode = **13**
   median = **17** (13, 13, ⑰, 18, 19)
   range = **6** (19 − 13 = 6)
2. **27°C** (26 + 27 + 29 + 29 + 28 + 24 + 26 = 189. 189 ÷ 7 = 27)
3. **£14** (8 × 5 = 40, so £40 sent by relatives. 9 × 6 = 54 (the total after her sister's gift). 54 − 40 = 14)

Probability (page 143)

1. **impossible**   2. **certain**
3. **unlikely** (you might do, but you probably won't)
4. $\frac{1}{2}$ (it can either be heads or tails)
5. $\frac{1}{13}$ (there are 13 different cards in each suit and 1 of those is an ace)
6. $\frac{1}{12}$ (there are 12 months, so a 1 in 12 chance of their birthday being May)

Statistics practice page 1 (page 144)

1.

Day	Dog	Cat	Rabbit	Hamster	Total
Monday	54	37	12	19	**122**
Tuesday	46	**39**	7	12	104
Wednesday	**46**	26	11	6	89
Thursday	61	**19**	9	11	100
Total	**207**	121	39	**48**	**415**

2. **11** (5 whole balloons = 10 votes, 1 half balloon = 1 vote)
3. **19** (football and swimming are sports, so in total 9 whole balloons = 18 votes and 1 half balloon = 1 vote)
4. **5** (10 voted cinema and 5 voted sleepover. 10 − 5 = 5)
5. **45** (football = 13, swimming = 6, crafts party = 11, cinema = 10, sleepover = 5. 13 + 6 + 11 + 10 + 5 = 45)
6. **22** (5 whole doughnuts = 20 sold, half doughnut = 2 sold)
7. **18** (Friday = 32, Thursday = 14. 32 − 14 = 18)
8. **43** (Saturday = 25, Sunday = 18. 25 + 18 = 43)
9. **156** (Monday = 29, Tuesday = 22, Wednesday = 16, Thursday = 14, Friday = 32, Saturday = 25, Sunday = 18. 29 + 22 + 16 + 14 + 32 + 25 + 18 = 156)

Answers

Statistics practice page 2 (page 145)

1.

Number	Tally	Frequency
0	卌 I	6
1	卌 III	8
2	卌 IIII	9
3	IIII	4
4	II	2
5	II	2
6	I	1

2. **6** (only 1 child has 6 siblings)
3. **9** (4 + 2 + 2 + 1 = 9)
4.

Colour	Tally	Frequency
Red	卌 卌 III	13
Yellow	卌 卌 III	13
Blue	卌 卌 IIII	14
Green	卌 卌 III	13
Purple	卌 卌 II	12
Orange	卌 卌 I	11

5. **blue**
6. **76** (13 + 13 + 14 + 13 + 12 + 11 = 76)

Statistics practice page 3 (page 146)

1. **13**
2. **7** (12 − 5 = 7)
3. **wildlife programmes**
4. **51** (13 + 5 + 7 + 14 + 12 = 51)
5. **Monday**
6. **Wednesday and Sunday**
7. **160p** (245p − 85p = 160p)
8. **1135p** or **£11.35** (245p + 135p + 160p + 155p + 85p + 195p + 160p = 1135p = £11.35)

Statistics practice page 4 (page 147)

1. **23**
2. **2** (44 − 23 = 21, so he completed 21 in the 2nd minute, which is 2 less than the 23 he completed in the 1st minute)
3. **74**
4. **92**
5. **8.00 a.m. to 9.00 a.m.** (the steepest part of the line)
6. **2 hours** (the line is flat between 1.00 p.m. and 3.00 p.m.)
7. **15mm** (140mm − 125mm = 15mm)
8. **85mm**

Statistics practice page 5 (page 148)

1. **12** ($\frac{1}{2}$ the pie chart is car, so $\frac{1}{2}$ of 24 = 12)
2. $\frac{1}{8}$
3. **310g** (the total circle = 360°, so 360° = 720g and 1° = 2g. The size of the flour wedge is 155°, 155 × 2 = 310g)
4. **230g** (115° = 230g)
5. **37** (16 + 9 + 4 + 8 = 37)
6. **9** (5 + 4 = 9)
7. **15** (the number outside all of the rings)
8. **4** (the number where all 3 rings cross over)

Statistics practice page 6 (page 149)

1. **82** (83 + 92 + 74 + 83 + 81 + 79 = 492, 492 ÷ 6 = 82)
2. **83** (the most common score is 83)
3. **82** (74, 79, 81, 83, 83, 92; the midway numbers are 81 and 83, so the middle of those is 82)
4. **18** (92 − 74 = 18)
5. **82.5** (the new total will go up to 495, so 495 ÷ 6 = 82.5)
6. **74.4** (372 ÷ 5 = 74.4)
7. **75.5** (the new total will be 372 + 81 = 453, 453 ÷ 6 = 75.5)
8. **18** (if the average is 9 goals between 8 competitors, then the total goals are 9 × 8 = 72. If the average is 10 when a 9th competitor joins in, then the total number of goals must be 9 × 10 = 90. 90 − 72 = 18, so Rosie must have scored 18 goals)
9. **impossible**
10. **unlikely** (it is not a very common colour, but it is not impossible)
11. **even chance** (it will either be heads or tails)
12. $\frac{2}{5}$ (6 out of 15 beads are blue = $\frac{6}{15} = \frac{2}{5}$)
13. $\frac{5}{16}$ (there will now be 5 red beads and 16 beads in total, so $\frac{5}{16}$)
14. $\frac{1}{18}$ (20 out of the 360 tickets will win a prize = $\frac{20}{360} = \frac{1}{18}$)

Answers

15. $\frac{3}{10}$ (3, 6 and 9 are the multiples of 3 between 1 and 10, therefore 3 out of the 10 numbers are multiples of 3 = $\frac{3}{10}$)

16. $\frac{1}{5}$ (there are 90 2-digit numbers. 10, 15, 20, 25, 30, 35, 40, 45, 50, 55, 60, 65, 70, 75, 80, 85, 90 and 95 are the multiples of 5 that are also 2 digits. $\frac{18}{90} = \frac{1}{5}$)

Practice test (pages 151–157)

All questions are worth 1 mark for a correct answer except where marking guidance alongside answers indicates how multiple marks can be earnt. Answers must be fully correct to earn credit on a 1 mark question.

Number and place value

1. **three million, four hundred and eight thousand, two hundred and sixty-four**
2. **9 000 012**
3. **7 122 245   7 123 835   7 123 935   7 124 635   7 132 823**
4. **94 000** (5 rounds up)
5. **−50**
6. **1, 2, 4, 8, 16, 32**
7. **2 and 23**
8. **2 × 2 × 2 × 2 × 2 × 3** (Award 1 mark for a correct factor tree. Award 2 marks for the answer written in the correct form. Maximum 2 marks.)

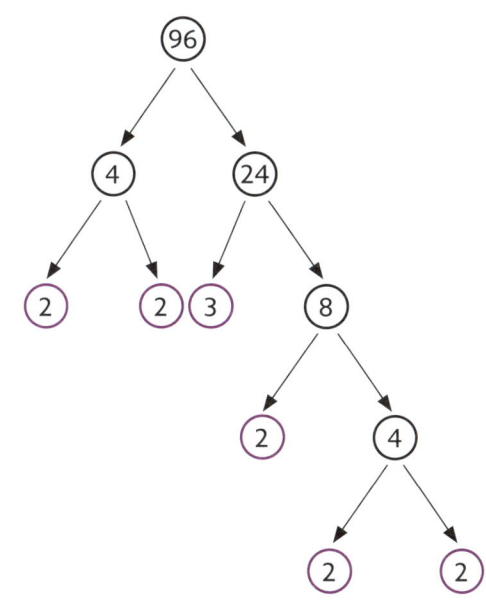

```
        96
       /  \
      4    24
     / \   / \
    2   2 3   8
             / \
            2   4
               / \
              2   2
```

9. **324, 936, 684** (Award 1 mark for each correct answer circled. Maximum 3 marks.)
10. **867** (DCCC = 800, LX = 60, VII = 7)
11. **3674** (MMM = 3000, DC = 600, LXX = 70, IV = 4)

Calculations, algebra and number sequences

12. **65 171** (vertical addition)
13. **2422** (vertical subtraction)
14. **6.7** (mental calculation)
15. **166 842** (long multiplication) (Award 1 mark for correct multiplication by 40 and by 6. Award 2 marks for the correct answer. Maximum 2 marks.)
16. **125** ('bus stop method') (Award 1 mark for part of the division calculation correct. Award 2 marks for the correct answer. Maximum 2 marks.)
17. i) **29** (236 ÷ 8 = 29r.4; each plate needs to be filled, so she will fill 29 plates) (Award 1 mark for the correct answer to the division calculation. Award 2 marks for rounding correctly. Maximum 2 marks.)

    ii) **4**

18. **195** (3 + 6 (2 × 4²) so 3 + 6 (32) = 195) [with 16 above 4² and 192 above 6(32)]
19. **53, 54, 55** (162 ÷ 3 = 54, therefore the middle number is 54 and the other two are 53 and 55) (Award 1 mark for evidence of a logical method (for example, divide by three, x − 1, x, x + 1 = 3x). Award 2 marks for the correct answer. Maximum 2 marks.)
20. **3** and **53** (Award 1 mark for one prime factor of 159. Award 2 marks for two prime factors of 159. Maximum 2 marks.)
21. **112** (17 × 5 = 85, 85 + 27 = 112)

    187 (32 × 5 = 160, 160 + 27 = 187) (Award 1 mark for either 17 or 32 processed correctly. Award 2 marks for both 17 and 32 processed correctly. Maximum 2 marks.)
22. **45, 46, 47, 48** (think of < and > like = in an equation and add or subtract numbers to get c on its own. c + 6 > 50, so c > 44. c − 9 < 40, so c < 49. 44 < c < 49, so c can be 45, 46, 47 or 48) (Award 1 mark for two correct answers. Award 2 marks for all four correct answers. Maximum 2 marks.)
23. i) **−21, −30**   **subtract 9** (Award 1 mark for either both correct terms or the correct rule. Award 2 marks for both correct terms and the correct rule. Maximum 2 marks.)

    ii) **11.1, 12.3**   **add 1.2** (Award 1 mark for either both correct terms or the correct rule. Award 2 marks for both correct terms and the correct rule. Maximum 2 marks.)

11+ Maths Study and Practice Book

Answers

Fractions, decimals and percentages

24. **291** ($\frac{2}{3}$ were adults, so $\frac{1}{3}$ were children. If $\frac{1}{3}$ = 97, then 3 × 97 = 291) *(Award 1 mark for $\frac{2}{3}$ = 194 (adults). Award 2 marks for the correct answer. Maximum 2 marks.)*

25. $\frac{8}{12}$ $\frac{6}{9}$

26. $\frac{49}{8}$

27. $\frac{38}{5}$

28. $4\frac{3}{5}$

29. $4\frac{2}{9}$

30. $\frac{31}{40}$ (common denominator = 40)

31. $\frac{1}{9}$ ($\frac{2}{3} \times \frac{1}{6} = \frac{2}{18} = \frac{1}{9}$)

32. **60** (55% + 10% = 65%, if the rest are about vehicles, then 35% are about vehicles. If 35% = 21, then 5% = 3, so 100% = 60) *(Award 1 mark for 35% = 21 (non-fiction) books. Award 2 marks for either 10% = 6 books or 55% = 33 books. Award 3 marks for the correct answer. Maximum 3 marks.)*

33. **14** (20% of 30 = 6, $\frac{1}{3}$ of 30 = 10. 6 + 10 = 16. 30 − 16 = 14) *(Award 1 mark for working out that 16 are not red. Award 2 marks for the correct answer. Maximum 2 marks.)*

34. Alice = **54** years old   A : F : G
    Frank = **27** years old   6 : 3 : 1 = 10 ⎫
    George = **9** years old   54 : 27 : 9 = 90 ⎭ ×9

    (Award 1 mark for the ratio 6 : 3 : 1. Award 2 marks for multiplying the ratio by 9. Award 3 marks for the correct answer. Maximum 3 marks.)

Measurement

35. **Naomi** (1kg of Laila's oranges = 20p × 2.2 = 44p. Naomi's oranges are 42p per kilogram) *(Award 1 mark for attempting to convert Laila's oranges to kilograms. Award 2 marks for 20 × 2.2 = 44p. Award 3 marks for the correct answer. Maximum 3 marks.)*

36. **18km** (1cm = 400 000cm, so 1cm = 4000m, so 1cm = 4km. If 1cm = 4km, then 4cm = 16km and 0.5cm = 2km, so 4.5cm = 18km) *(Award 1 mark for 1cm = 400 000cm. Award 2 marks for 1cm = 4km. Award 3 marks for the correct answer. Answers must be in km. Maximum 3 marks.)*

37. **12:20** (15 + 90 + 10 + 5 = 120 min. 120 min = 2 hr. 14:20 − 2 hr = 12:20) *(Award 1 mark for 15 + 90 + 10 + 5 = 120. Award 2 marks for 120 = 2 hr. Award 3 marks for the correct answer. Maximum 3 marks.)*

38. **24 miles** (24mph ÷ 2 = 12 miles in 30 min, 18mph ÷ 6 = 3 miles in 10 min, so 12 miles in 40 min. 12 + 12 = 24 miles) *(Award 1 mark for 12 miles in 30 min. Award 2 marks for 12 miles in 30 min and 12 miles in 40 min. Award 3 marks for the correct answer. Maximum 3 marks.)*

39. **20°C** (add 8°C to −8°C to get to 0°C. Add another 12°C to get to 12°C. 8°C + 12°C = 20°C)

40. **Edinburgh and Brisbane** (25°C − 4°C = 21°C)

41. **5** (12 × 5 = 60, 7 × 2 = 14, 60 − 14 = 46m², so 5 bags) *(Award 1 mark for 12 × 5 = 60 and 7 × 2 = 14. Award 2 marks for 60 − 14 = 46m². Award 3 marks for the correct answer. Maximum 3 marks.)*

42. **6cm** and **2cm**

    4cm and **4cm**

    (Award 1 mark for one pair. Award 2 marks for both pairs. Answers must be in cm. Maximum 2 marks.)

Geometry

43.

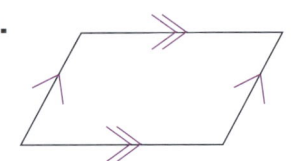

(Award 1 mark for one pair of arrows correctly drawn. Award 2 marks for two pairs of arrows correctly drawn. Maximum 2 marks.)

44. **north** (SE then 90° anticlockwise would be NE, then 135° clockwise would be S, then 180° anticlockwise would be N)

45. **20.25cm** (the circles overlap each other's centre points giving a length of 9 radiuses. The diameter is 4.5cm, so the radius is 2.25cm. 9 × 2.25 = 20.25cm) *(Award 1 mark for either radius = 2.25 or 4.5 × 4.5 with an incorrect answer. Award 2 marks for the correct answer. Maximum 2 marks.)*

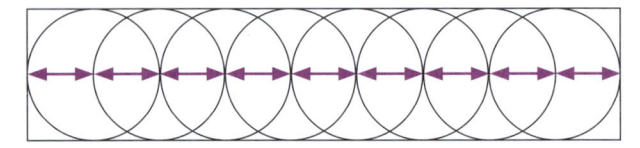

46. **2**

47.

(Award 1 mark for one square correctly shaded. Award 2 marks for two squares correctly shaded. Maximum 2 marks.)

Answers

48. **5** (one at each of the four corners of the square base, one at the point where the four triangular faces meet)

49. **(2, 4)** *(Award 1 mark for either the correct x-coordinate or the correct y-coordinate. Award 2 marks for both the correct x-coordinate and the correct y-coordinate. Maximum 2 marks.)*

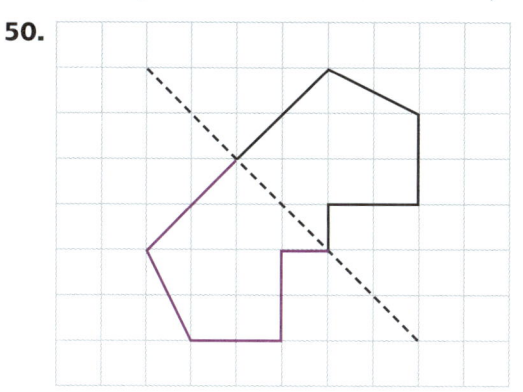

50.

(Award 1 mark for three points correctly placed and connected. Award 2 marks for all six points correctly placed and connected. Maximum 2 marks.)

Statistics

51.

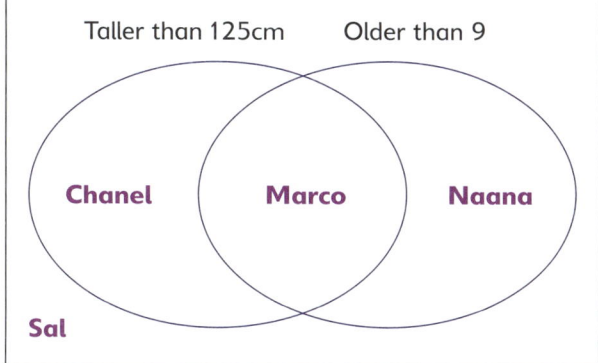

(Award 1 mark for two names correctly placed. Award 2 marks for three names correctly placed. Award 3 marks for all four names correctly placed. Maximum 3 marks.)

52. **12** (the roast dinner section measures 72°, $\frac{72}{360} = \frac{1}{5}$. $\frac{1}{5}$ of 60 = 12) *(Award 1 mark for the correct measurement of the angle. Award 2 marks for the measurement of the angle converted into a fraction with 360 as the denominator and simplified. Award 3 marks for the correct answer. Maximum 3 marks.)*

53. **10** (the jacket potato section measures 60°, $\frac{60}{360} = \frac{1}{6}$. $\frac{1}{6}$ of 60 = 10) *(Award 1 mark for the correct measurement of the angle. Award 2 marks for the measurement of the angle converted into a fraction with 360 as the denominator and simplified. Award 3 marks for the correct answer. Maximum 3 marks.)*

54. **86** (if the average after 5 matches was 68, then 68 × 5 = 340, so the total runs was 340. If the average after 6 matches is now 71 then 71 × 6 = 426, so the total runs must be 426. The difference between the two totals is 426 − 340 = 86) *(Award 1 mark for either 68 × 5 = 340 or 71 × 6 = 426. Award 2 marks for both 68 × 5 = 340 and 71 × 6 = 426. Award 3 marks for the correct answer. Maximum 3 marks.)*

55. $\frac{1}{4}$ (there are 12 counters in total and 3 of these are blue, $\frac{3}{12} = \frac{1}{4}$) *(Award 1 mark for $\frac{3}{12}$. Award 2 marks for $\frac{1}{4}$. Maximum 2 marks.)*

Index and Glossary

acute angle 107	an angle that is less than 90°
algebra 40, 42, 44–47	a type of maths that uses letters and symbols instead of numbers
approximate(ly) 9, 64, 79	close to the actual answer without being exact
area 82, 94–99, 105, 114	the amount of space within a 2D shape
average 141, 142	the result of adding together a set of numbers and dividing the total by the number of values (see also **mean**)
circumference 114	the length of the distance round a circle (see also **perimeter**)
common denominator 54–57, 59, 68	the common **multiple** of all the **denominators**
composite number 17, 18	a number larger than 1 that can be divided exactly by one or more numbers other than 1 and itself
compound shape 97	a shape made up of two or more 2D shapes
congruent 109, 124	shapes and/or angles that have exactly the same shape and size
coordinates 122, 123, 126, 131	the numbers that give the position of points on a map or graph
cube number 19, 24, 41	a number that has been multiplied by itself twice ('cubed')
cube root 19, 36	the number that has been multiplied by itself twice to create a **cube number**
decimal fraction 30, 60, 61, 73	digits located to the right of the decimal point
decimal place 9, 61, 62, 68	the value position of a number after the decimal point
denominator 35, 48, 49, 51–54, 56, 58–60, 68	the bottom number in a fraction
diameter 114	the widest distance across a circle through its centre
dividend 33–35	a number divided by another number
divisible 15–17, 54, 58, 87, 88	able to be divided
divisor 33–35	a number that is divided into another number
edge(s) 117–120	the lines where the **faces** of a 3D shape meet
equation 40	a group of numbers and/or letters in which an equals sign shows that two amounts are the same
equivalent fraction 51, 53, 55, 56, 69, 70, 72	fractions that have the same value even though each has a different **numerator** and **denominator**
face(s) 99, 117–121	one of the flat or curved surfaces of a 3D shape
factor 12, 13, 15, 17, 18, 22, 53, 64	a whole number that divides exactly into another number without a **remainder**
highest common factor (HCF) 13, 53	the largest shared **factor** in a pair or group of numbers
image 124, 126	the new shape made when a shape (or **object**) is reflected or **translated**

Index and Glossary

improper fraction 52, 56–58, 63, 72	a fraction in which the **numerator** is larger than the **denominator**
index 19	the small number used to indicate how many times to multiply a number by itself (see also **power**, **order**)
inverse 12, 38, 39	the opposite of something. For example, multiplication is the **inverse** of division
lowest common multiple (LCM) 14	the lowest number that is a **multiple** of 2 or more given numbers
mean 141, 142, 149	the result of adding together a set of numbers and dividing the total by the number of values (see also **average**)
median 141, 142, 149	the middle value (or number) in a whole set of values that are arranged in order
mirror line 115, 124	a line of **symmetry**
mixed number 52, 55–58, 63, 72	a number that is made up of a whole number and a fraction
mode 141, 142, 149	the number that appears the most times in a list of numbers
multiple 14, 15, 17, 23, 25, 31, 54, 140	a number that is in the multiplication table
net 120, 130	a 2D outline of an unfolded 3D shape
nth term 42, 43, 47	a formula to help find any number within a sequence. *n* is the position of that number, such as the 4th, 12th or 99th
number bonds 25, 26, 28, 63	pairs of numbers that add together to make a specific number, such as **number bonds** of 10
numerator 35, 48, 49, 51–54, 56, 58	the top number in a fraction
object 124, 126	the original shape when looking at reflections and translations
obtuse angle 107	an angle that is greater than 90° but less than 180°
order 36, 113, 116	**1.** the number of times a rotated shape fits its outline through 360° **2.** a mathematical operation that involves multiplying a number by itself. For example, 6^2, 2^3 (see also **power**, **index**)
parallel 106, 109, 112, 127	straight or curved lines that are the same distance apart along their whole length and which never meet
partition 26, 28, 32	divide into parts
percentage 66–69, 72–75, 138	a fraction with a **denominator** of 100, but written in a different way, using the sign %
perimeter 94–98, 105, 114	the distance all the way around the sides of a 2D shape
perpendicular 106, 124, 127	at **right angles**
polygon 111, 113, 114	a 2D shape with three or more straight sides
polyhedron 118	a 3D shape with flat **faces**

Index and Glossary

power 18, 19, 36, 37, 60, 68	the small number used to indicate how many times to multiply a number by itself (see also **index, order**)
prime factors 17, 18, 24	**factors** of a number that are also **prime numbers**
prime number 17, 18, 24, 41, 53	a number that can only be divided by itself and 1. 2 is the smallest and the only even **prime number**
probability 143, 149	how likely it is for something to happen
product 18	the number found by multiplying two or more numbers
proportion 70, 71, 75, 138	the relationship between part of something and the whole thing: it compares 'part with whole'
quotient 33, 35	the answer achieved by dividing one number by another number
radius 114	the distance from the centre to the edge of a circle
range 141, 142, 149	the difference between the largest and the smallest number in a group
ratio 70, 71, 75, 82	the relationship between two or more numbers or quantities: it compares 'part with part'
reflex angle 107	an angle that is greater than 180° but less than 360°
remainder 12, 14, 16, 33–35, 45, 52, 56	the amount left if a number cannot be divided exactly to leave a whole number
right angle 106, 107, 111, 112	an angle that is exactly 90°
rotational symmetry 113, 116, 129	when a shape looks the same after some rotation
scale factor 82	how much a shape has been enlarged
square number 13, 19, 41	a number that has been made by multiplying a number by itself once ('squared')
square root 13, 19, 36	the number that has been multiplied by itself to give a **square number**
symmetry 113, 115, 129	when two parts or halves of a shape are exactly equal to each other
translate 126	move or slide without turning
triangular number 41	part of a sequence of numbers that add an extra 1 each time: 1, then 2, then 3, and so on
unit fraction 48–50	a fraction where the **numerator** is 1
vertex (pl. **vertices**) 117–119	a corner of a 3D shape where the **edges** meet at a point
volume 99, 105	the amount of space within a 3D shape